Pathways, Bridges and Havens:
Psychosocial Determinants of Women's Health

Edited by Joanne Gallivan and Suzanne Cooper

Pathways, Bridges and Havens:
Psychosocial Determinants of Women's Health

Edited by Joanne Gallivan and Suzanne Cooper

Cape Breton University Press
Sydney, Nova Scotia, Canada

Cape Breton University Press recognizes the support of the Canada Council for the Arts, Block Grant program, and the Province of Nova Scotia, through the Department of Tourism, Culture and Heritage, for our publishing program. We are pleased to work in partnership with these bodies to develop and promote our cultural resources.

Canada Council   Conseil des Arts
for the Arts   du Canada

NOVA SCOTIA
Tourism, Culture and Heritage

Cover: Cathy MacLean Design, Pleasant Bay, NS
Cover image: *Safe Havens*, by Carol Kennedy, North River, NS
Content printed on 100% recycled postconsumer fibre, certified EcoLogo and processed chlorine free, manufactured using biogas energy.

Library and Archives Canada Cataloguing in Publication

Pathways, bridges and havens : the psychosocial determinants of women's health / edited by Joanne Gallivan and Suzanne Cooper.

Selected papers from the 2008 SWAP (Section on Women and Psychology) pre-convention institute held in conjunction with the annual meeting of the Canadian Psychological Association, Halifax, N.S., Jun. 11, 2008.

ISBN 978-1-897009-34-5

1. Women--Health and hygiene--Psychological aspects.
2. Women--Psychology. 3. Women--Mental health.
I. Gallivan, Joanne, 1953- II. Cooper, Suzanne M.
(Suzanne Marie), 1973-

RA564.85.P38 2009   613'.04244019   C2009-902742-9

Cape Breton University Press
P.O. Box 5300
Sydney, Nova Scotia B1P 6L2
Canada

Contents

Preface

In recent years, the determinants of health framework has inspired new efforts to explore the impact of psychosocial factors on health. This collection of recent research addresses a variety of psychological and social factors in women's health: critical pathways to wellness and healing; important mediating variables (or bridges) for physical health determinants; coping mechanisms that provide havens for people dealing with the negative consequences of poor health.

The articles in this book showcase diverse topics, methodologies and theoretical perspectives; they are a sampler of the contributions that scholars in psychology and related fields are making to understanding women's health. These papers are based on presentations made at an institute June, 2008, in Halifax, Nova Scotia sponsored by the Section on Women and Psychology (SWAP) of the Canadian Psychological Association, and coordinated by Suzanne Cooper. Institute attendees responded enthusiastically to the day's presentations and it is gratifying to be able to provide a more permanent record of the work and to share it more broadly.

The symposium and the book required the collaboration of many. We appreciate the support of the SWAP executive and the assistance in both initiatives of numerous SWAP members. We are grateful also to Mike Hunter, Editor-in-Chief of Cape Breton University Press who enthusiastically supported the book project from its inception. Most important, we thank the authors who agreed to share their work in this format worked diligently to transform their oral presentations into book chapters and have provided these new insights into women's health.

J.G., S.C.

Paula C. Barata

The Dawning of a New Age in Cervical-Cancer Prevention: The Psychosocial Issues Involved in Implementing HPV Technologies

At the turn of twenty-first century, the scientific community declared human papilloma virus (HPV) a necessary precursor to cervical cancer (Walboomers et al., 1999). This conclusion came after two decades of research on the relationship between HPV and cervical cancer (Bosch, Lorincz, Munoz, Meijer, & Shah, 2002). The public's understanding of the relationship between HPV and cervical cancer has been more akin to the proverbial"ton of bricks." HPV technologies (e.g., HPV testing and HPV vaccines), which have been steadily developing backstage in laboratories and academic circles, are now beginning to make their debut onto the public arena. With their introduction, women are being presented with a novel and somewhat frightening assertion: a sexually transmitted virus can cause cervical cancer. This is a dramatic shift in how most people currently understand cancer and it can be expected to influence women's acceptance of HPV technologies, and even their perspectives on cervical cancer and cervical cancer prevention. Understanding women's desire for knowledge about, attitudes toward, and experiences with HPV technologies will be essential in developing best-practice guidelines in the HPV age of cervical cancer prevention.

Cervical-Cancer Prevention Before HPV Technologies: The Pap Test

Before delving too deeply into the new HPV technologies, it is important to look at women's current understanding and practice regarding cervical-cancer prevention and the insight that has been gained about the psycho-social issues involved in Pap testing. The Pap test (named for the physician George Papanicolaou) involves scraping cells from the cervix and examining them to detect precancerous and cancerous lesions. This is truly a preventive test because it can identify problems before they develop into cancer, and, consequently, it has been nothing short of extraordinary in reducing cervical cancer rates. Specifically, the Pap is credited with the large drop in cervical-cancer rates in countries that have developed screening programs (Cervical Cancer Screening Program, 2005; National Cancer Institute of Canada, 2006; Peto, Gilham, Fletcher, & Mathews, 2004). In Canada, cervical-cancer rates have decreased from 15.4 per 100,000 in 1977 to 7.5 per 100,000 in 2006 (National Cancer Institute of Canada, 2006). Nevertheless, it is the eleventh-most-common cancer diagnosis in Canada and the thirteenth-most-common cancer-related death, killing approximately 500 women per year. One of the main reasons that women continue to die from cervical cancer is that they are inadequately screened or not screened at all. Findings from the National Population Health Survey using self-report found that 87% of women over the age of 18 in Canada had ever been screened, and only 72% had been screened within the past three years (Maxwell, Bancej, Snider, & Vik, 2001). Self-report, however, may overestimate screening rates. One-year screening rates in an Ontario study using a Pap-test registry were more dismal, varying from 11.6% to 73.9% across public-health units, and averaging at 41% (Fehringer et al., 2006).

For many women, the extent of their knowledge on cervical cancer has been limited to an understanding that it is important to have a regular (Pap) test, but the reasons for this can be vague. In a sample of female university students waiting for their yearly gynecological exam, 90% knew that the Pap was a test for precancerous and cancerous lesions of the cervix, but over half incorrectly believed that the Pap also tested for other cancers or sexually transmitted infections (STIs) (Hasenyager, 1999). Studies with low-socioeconomic-status women show particularly poor knowledge about the purpose of the Pap test (Breitkopf, Pearson, & Breitkopf, 2005; Mays et al., 2000). Nevertheless, a review of the literature suggests that most women generally understand that it is a gynecological exam that screens for cancer and believe it to be an important test (Reid, 2001). Yet, as we have seen, not all women obtain a Pap on a regular basis, and the psychosocial research in this area has been quite active in attempting to understand the predictors of inadequate screening and the barriers that exist for obtaining a Pap.

A number of factors have been identified that are associated with inadequate screening in Canada, such as birthplace outside of Canada, single marital status, first language other than English, lower education, not having a recent blood-pressure check or regular physician, age, and infrequent physical activity (Maxwell et al., 2001; Woloshin, Schwartz, Katz, & Welch, 1997). The finding that new immigrants and visible-minority women are especially likely to be under screened (McDonald & Kennedy, 2007) has prompted a significant amount of research in particular ethnic communities. Acculturation has been found to predict both low knowledge about the Pap test and reduced screening (Byrd, Peterson, Chavez, & Hechert, 2004; Gupta, Kumar, & Stewart, 2002; Hislop et al., 2003). However, whether this is largely a result of logistical problems, such as familiarity with the health-care system and proficiency in the dominant language, or more specific cultural barriers is less clear, and probably varies by ethnic group. In a series of studies conducted in Vancouver with Chinese-Canadian women, potentially important traditional health beliefs were identified through focus groups (e.g., karma, an imbalance of yin and yang, or poor qi as causes of cancer and faith; doing qigong, taking herbs, etc., as preventive mechanisms), but these beliefs were not found to be related to Pap testing in a subsequent large-scale survey study (Hislop et al., 2003). However, in a review of the research with Hispanic women, Austin, Ahmad, McNally, & Stewart (2002) reported that cultural beliefs such as fear, fatalism, and divine punishment were important barriers to Pap testing.

Besides culture, a number of other psychosocial barriers have been identified in numerous studies, such as embarrassment (Ahmad, Stewart, Camerson, & Hyman, 2001; Austin et al., 2002; Lee, 2000; Lovell, Kearns, & Friesen, 2007), social anxiety (Kowalski & Brown, 1994), experience with sexual assault (Van Til, MacQuarrie, & Herbert, 2003), fear of the test results (Agurto, Bishop, Sanxhez, Betancourt, & Robles, 2004), and relationship with physician (Van Til, et al., 2003). These are sometimes compounded by structural barriers such as accessibility (Agurto et al., 2004), time constraints (Egbert & Parrot, 2001), and cost (Agurto et al., 2004; Egbert & Parrot, 2001).

There has also been an active body of psychological research using models of preventive health behaviour to understand cervical-screening behaviour. The Health Belief Model has successfully predicted women's intentions to have a Pap test (Henning & Knowles, 1990; Hill, Gardner, & Rassaby, 1985) and their actual Pap-test history (Burak & Meyer, 1997). In addition, elements of the model, especially barriers, have been extensively used to understand women's uptake of Pap testing (Austin et al., 2002; Gillman, 1991; Murray & McMillan, 1993) and their compliance with recommendations after an abnormal Pap (Funke & Nicholson, 1993). A number of other models have been successful in predicting intentions to attend cervical-cancer screening, such as the theory of planned behaviour (Bish, Sutton, & Golombok, 2000), the theory of reasoned action (Henning & Knowles, 1990; Hill et al., 1985), and the Subjective Probability Model (Hill et al., 1985). Additionally, the Implementation Intentions Model has been successful in predicting women's attendance for future cervical-cancer screening (Sheeran & Orbell, 2000). Given how much psychosocial research has contributed to our understanding of women's beliefs, experiences, and behaviours regarding Pap testing, it is natural that we now turn our attention to the role that psychosocial research can bring to cervical-cancer prevention in the new HPV era.

Introducing the HPV Technologies

In this chapter, we will consider three HPV technologies: HPV testing, self-sampling for HPV testing, and prophylactic HPV vaccines. These technologies have generated a lot of excitement because they have the potential to close the gap on the morbidity and mortality we still witness as a result of cervical cancer. They are currently being incorporated into prevention programs that include Pap testing. It is unlikely that the Pap test will disappear any time soon, although some are already predicting that the need for Pap testing may be reduced as the use of HPV technologies increases (Davis, Bogdanovic-Guillion, Grce, & Sancho-Garnier, 2007; Wright, 2007). That is both an exciting and a frightening notion. It is exciting because some of the barriers we have reviewed related to Pap testing may become less important, and it is frightening because the Pap has served us well and we do not yet fully understand the barriers for these technologies, or how women will receive them. Of primary concern is the lack of understanding that women have about HPV and its relationship to cervical cancer. This is not surprising as it is not entirely straightforward.

There are over 100 HPV types, of which 40 are sexually transmitted and infect the genital track (de Villiers, Fauquet, Broker, Bernard, & zur Hausen, 2004). Some HPV types can lead to genital warts and some can lead to cervical cancer. It is important to understand that genital warts do not progress to cancer because they are a result of different types of HPV. Those that are known to progress to cancer are referred to as having high oncogenic risk, and there are approximately 13–18 known types (Trottier & Franco, 2006). HPV is generally considered to be the most common sexually transmitted infection, and most sexually active individuals are likely to be exposed at some point in their lives (Trottier & Franco, 2006). In fact, many women are infected during their first sexual relationship (Collins et al., 2002). Fortunately, most cases of infection result in no symptoms and clear spontaneously within four to twenty months (Trottier & Franco,

2006). Consequently, HPV infection has its highest prevalence in women under the age of 25 years (Franceschi et al., 2006), presumably because older women have already cleared previous infections and are less likely to be engaged in new sexual relationships. For example, in an Ontario study the highest prevalence for high-oncogenic-risk HPV was 24% and found in women aged 20–24, with prevalence rates dropping with increased age (Sellors et al., 2000b). Persistence of high-oncogenic-risk HPV is particularly concerning because it is associated with high-grade squamous intraepithelial lesions that can lead to invasive cervical cancer. HPV is transmitted through skin-to-skin contact (Schiffman & Castle, 2003), and although penetrative sexual activity is much more likely to result in a cervical HPV infection, non-penetrative sexual activity can transmit the virus (Trottier & Franco, 2006). As such, condom use provides incomplete protection against HPV transmission because the virus can be transmitted through skin that is not covered by the condom (Winer et al., 2006). Similarly, a review of the literature on women who have sex with women concludes that HPV transmission does occur between women (Marrazzo, Stine, & Koutsky, 2000). This brief explanation should make it clear that the relationship between HPV and cervical cancer is *not* as simple as sex → STI → cancer, especially because many women are infected with HPV and never develop cervical cancer; however, that is how it can be how understood when this information is first conveyed.

Studies on knowledge about HPV suggest that most people have not made the sex → STI → cancer connection yet, much less understood the intricacies of that connection. A review of current knowledge found that there is a large gap between professional and general knowledge about HPV, and this gap has been found in various populations (Tristram, 2006). A representative telephone survey of British residents found that less than 1% said that cervical cancer was caused by HPV when asked about causes, and only 13.5% mentioned any kind of sexually transmitted infection (Waller, McCaffery, & Wardle, 2004). Predictably, women know more about HPV than do men (Holcomb, Bailey, Crawford, & Ruffin, 2004; Yacobi, Tennant, Ferrante, Pal, & Roetzheim, 1999), but overall knowledge was low in both groups. Adolescents appear to be particularly lacking in information about HPV (Dell, Chen, Ahmad, & Stewart, 2000; Mays et al., 2000; Mosavel & El-Shaarawi, 2007). In a Toronto study of high-school students, 87% had never heard of HPV despite fairly good identification of other STIs (Dell et al., 2000). Of particular interest is understanding how much women who currently obtain a Pap know about HPV, and in this population knowledge about HPV is also low (Benning & Lund, 2006; Le et al., 2004; Waller, et al., 2003). Generally, women know less about HPV than they do about Pap testing even, when Pap-test knowledge is already quite low (Mays et al., 2000; Dell et al., 2000). Even women attending colposcopy due to an abnormal Pap know little about the link between HPV and cervical cancer (Le et al., 2004; Pruitt et al., 2005).

In qualitative research, shock, fear, and disbelief are often described as reactions to learning about the link between HPV and cervical cancer within the context of learning about one of the HPV technologies (e.g., Barata, Stewart, Howlett, Gagliardi, & Mai, in press; Friedman & Shepeard, 2007; McCaffery, et al., 2003). In a focus-group study on self-sampling for HPV testing, my colleagues and I specifically incorporated an educational component into the focus groups before assessing participants impressions of the technology. We found that this in itself resulted in a major theme, a "need (and desire) for information about cervical cancer and HPV" (Barata, et al., in press). This is not entirely surprising given the literature concerning public knowledge about HPV and cervical cancer. What was somewhat surprising, however, was the hunger that participants seemed to have for this information. Learning a little about HPV prompted many more follow-up questions. Also of interest is that women's repeat follow-up questions and general disbelief demonstrated that this information is not readily accepted when it is first introduced, suggesting that women will need time to digest information about HPV before making an informed decision about whether to participate in HPV technologies of any kind.

Given low levels of knowledge about HPV, then, it is understandable that women express shock when they learn about the connection between HPV and cervical cancer. However, it is important that this information be conveyed before participants' opinions about a particular HPV technology can be assessed, or their opinions would not be informed. Understanding their reaction to this basic information is important because it is probable that it will influence their opinions of the particular technology. This needs to be considered both in the interpretation of research results and in the production of educational materials for public use. Although there is some controversy about whether women should even be given basic information about HPV (see, e.g., Braun & Gavey, 1999a; Braun & Gavey, 1999b), most authors are now calling for the creation of educational materials, even suggesting what should be incorporated (Anhang, Goodman, & Goldie, 2004a; Crum & Berkowitz, 2002; Harper, 2004; McFadden & Schumann, 2001; Monk & Wiley, 2004). This is probably because the evidence that women want this information is overwhelming. Women have expressed a desire for information about transmission, prevention, treatment and/or management, level of cervical-carcinoma risk, different types of HPV, implications for sexual partners, latency and regression, implications for pregnancy, and how to be tested (Anhang, Wright, Smock, & Goldie 2004b; Gilbert, Alexander, Grosshans, & Jolley, 2003; McCaffery & Irwing, 2005).

An obvious role for social scientists is to assist in the development of educational materials that can improve knowledge about HPV and cervical cancer without inducing unnecessary fear. These efforts have just begun. Lambert (2001) found that a brief HPV-focused educational intervention improved knowledge in both physicians' assistants and in psychology students; however, an educational campaign designed for Vietnamese-American women was not successful in changing women's understanding of the link between HPV and cervical cancer (Lam et al., 2003). We know less about the impact that information has on participants thinking about cancer and participation in screening programs. There is much speculation that general perceptions of cervical cancer will change as HPV knowledge increases and that this might have a negative impact on cervical-screening rates (see, e.g., Harper, 2004; Waller, McCaffery, Forrest, & Wardle, 2004), but the empirical evidence examining the impact on participation rates is lacking. There is, however, emerging evidence that beliefs about cervical cancer change for some women as they incorporate this information into their model of cervical cancer (Waller, McCaffery, Nazroo, & Wardle, 2005). What is clear is that the public's understanding of HPV is an important consideration for all of the HPV technologies (see table 1). We will now turn to the HPV technologies and consider the unique psychosocial issues involved with each.

HPV Testing

Detecting HPV DNA in cellular specimens rather than waiting to detect cell changes that can result from HPV (i.e., the Pap) is now possible. In fact, this innovation is what prompted the last 25 years of research on HPV technologies, which began in the early 1980s (Bosch et al., 2002). Research on HPV DNA testing suggests that it has the potential to improve cervical-cancer-prevention programs by being incorporated into cytology screening (Franco, 2004; McFadden & Schumann, 2001), or even by superseding cytology as a primary preventive tool (Crum & Berkowitz, 2002; Cuzick et al., 2006). Incorporating HPV testing into regular screening may reduce the number of women that have to undergo a colposcopy. The idea is that women who have a particular kind of abnormal Pap known as ASCUS (atypical squamous cells of undetermined origin) could be followed up with an HPV test. If that test were negative, she would be considered at very low risk for cervical cancer and could wait to have a colposcopy or avoid one altogether. One way of implementing this is to do a "reflex" HPV test. A reflex test is possible because of recent advances in liquid-based cytology and is seamless for the patient because a sample for HPV testing is automatically taken during the gynecological exam for the Pap. The sample could be tested for HPV if the Pap were abnormal, thus providing the physician with an important piece of added information. A recent Ontario guideline review advocates HPV testing in cases of ASCUS for women 30 years or older (McLachlin, Mai, Murphy, & Fung Kee Fung, 2005). The recommendation is that women who test positive for HPV would have a colposcopy and women who test negative would have a repeat Pap in 12 months. If an HPV test is unavailable, the recommendation is a repeat Pap in six months. The medical evidence for these recommendations is beyond the scope of this chapter, but the procedures reviewed here have psychosocial implications.

Table 1. Psychosocial Issues For Each of the HPV Technologies

	HPV testing	HPV self-sampling	HPV vaccines
Knowledge	• Impact of learning the connection between HPV and cervical cancer • Impact of educational materials on attitudes and behaviour		
Understanding	• Interpreting a "+" or "–" result	• Knowing how to obtain a sample	• Making an informed decision
Attitudes and Acceptability	• Acceptance of HPV testing to reduce colposcopy • Acceptance given STI implications	• Acceptance of self-sampling compared with Pap testing	• Acceptance of vaccine by parents, young women, and physicians
Psychological Impact	• Affective response (e.g., guilt, shame, relief, etc.) • Impact on anxiety and distress (↑↓)	• Anxiety related to doing the test correctly • Avoiding embarrassment of gynecological exam • Empowerment: taking control of one's own health	• Potential to reduce negative affect by reducing disease and abnormal test results, but this has not been explored through research
Psychosexual Impact	• Learning one has an STI • Communicating unwanted messages through screening (e.g., infidelity, sexual activity, etc.) • Impact on intimate relationships	• Comfort touching one's genitals	• Beliefs about the impact on promiscuity or unsafe sex
Behavioral Impact	• Especially on follow-up screening after HPV test	• Especially for under-screened women	• Impact on future sexual behaviour

Table 1 lists the psychosocial issues that are most relevant for each of the three HPV technologies covered here. For HPV testing, understanding the test results is of paramount importance. If a woman tests negative, this has the potential to reduce a significant amount of anxiety and distress. If a woman truly understands the implication of a negative result, she should realize that she is at very low risk for cervical cancer and should thus experience some relief. In addition, she would be spared a colposcopy exam and the anxiety that is often felt around that procedure. However, if she does not really understand what a negative result means, she might feel continued or perhaps elevated anxiety because she would not be followed up for additional testing. The recommendation would be to repeat the Pap in 12 months, which might feel like a very long time to a woman who continues to be concerned about cervical cancer. At least one study has examined this question empirically. Maissi et al. (2004) compared four groups of women (i.e., normal Pap, abnormal Pap, abnormal Pap and HPV negative, abnormal Pap and HPV positive) on state anxiety, distress, and concern about the test results four weeks after receiving their results. As predicted, the women with a normal Pap had the most positive emotional response on all measures, and the women with an abnormal Pap and an HPV-positive test had the most negative response on all measures. Contrary to the authors' prediction, however, women with an HPV-negative test did not have a more positive emotional reaction on any of the measures compared with women with an abnormal Pap who were not tested for HPV. In other words, testing negative for HPV did not protect women from the distress of having an abnormal Pap, and testing positive caused more distress than an abnormal Pap alone. The authors concluded that this was largely a result of women not understanding the test results because they found that misunderstanding the results positively predicted state anxiety and distress in the women (Maissi et al., 2004). These results disappeared at the six-month follow-up, where there were no differences between groups (Maissi et al., 2005).

Certainly there has been some concern in the literature about the impact of doubly burdening women with a positive HPV test after an abnormal Pap (Anhang et al., 2004a; Crum & Berkowitz, 2002; Franco, 2004; Harper, 2004). We already know that women who have an abnormal Pap result can have significant distress (Lamont, 1994; Miller, Mischel, O'Leary, & Mills, 1996; Wardle, Pernet, & Stephens, 1995) and the concern is that this distress might be increased with an HPV-positive result. Distress resulting from an HPV-positive result can come from two sources. First, distress may come from believing that an HPV-positive result puts them at increased risk for cervical cancer (a reasonable conclusion, although overestimates about risk may be problematic), and second, women may be distressed because HPV is a sexually transmitted infection. For instance, women with an HPV-positive result compared with women with an HPV-

negative one have reported feeling worse about past and future sexual relationships, (McCaffery et al., 2004) and feeling embarrassment, stigmatized,
shameful and/or guilty (McCaffery, Waller, Nazroo, & Wardle, 2006). In
addition, women have reported anticipating these consequences as a result
of testing positive for HPV (Anhang et al., 2004b; McCaffery et al., 2003).
Women have also reported that simply participating in HPV screening may
communicate unwanted messages such as distrust, infidelity, and promis-
cuity to the women's partners, family, and community (McCaffery et al.,
2003). Additionally, women have expressed anticipated and real fear and
anxiety around disclosure of a positive test result to partners, family, and
friends (Kahn et al., 2005a; McCaffery et al., 2006). The reaction to HPV
testing is not all bad, however; Kahn et al. (2005a) found that some of her
participants felt empowerment by being tested for HPV and confident in
their ability to prevent future disease, and MaCaffery et al. (2003) found
that some women welcomed the introduction of HPV testing.

I am currently involved in an ongoing study of women who were tested
for HPV during a colposcopy exam due to abnormal cytology. We have only
reviewed six interviews in depth, but I am already struck by the diversity of
reactions women have to an HPV-negative test result (all of these women
are white/Caucasian and heterosexual; other basic demographics follow
their quoted remarks, below). Of the four women who tested HPV positive,
these were their initial responses to the first interview question:

> I didn't really know how to feel because I didn't really know much
> about it. [P001; age 18–25; no religious affiliation; some college/uni-
> versity; casually dating]

> Well, I was upset. I just started a new relationship, and how do you
> tell someone that you just started dating? And I was angry because
> who gave this to me? [P003; age 26–35; Catholic; college/university
> degree; no current sexual relationship]

> Disappointed I suppose, because it was 'oh darn, now I have to go
> and do something else'. [P008; age 46–55; Protestant; college/univer-
> sity degree; married]

> Considering what I already have, it was okay. Because I'm HIV posi-
> tive, I took that news way worse. [P009; age 36–45; Catholic; some
> college/university; no current sexual relationship]

The two women who tested negative responded this way:

> I am glad the results were okay, but I am still a little you know un-
> sure. [P002; age 46–55; Catholic; some high school; married]

> I was surprised and relieved ... I was surprised because I thought
> pretty much everybody has HPV. [P006; age 26–35; Jewish; college/
> university degree; no current sexual relationship]

Although it is too early to develop complex themes, a few ideas emerge. Some women clearly find the results very confusing. For instance, one woman talks about her initial mix-up with HIV (human immunodeficiency virus) (P001), and another asks the interviewer if she knows whether she has genital warts (P003). With this confusion comes a clear desire for more information and many questions at the end of the formal interview, when participants were told they could ask about whatever they wanted. This "final" section has often been taking longer than the rest of the interview and will clearly be important in the final analysis. Fear of cancer remains important for both some HPV-positive and some HPV-negative women. That HPV is an STI is clearly important for some women and insignificant for others, as these quotes from HPV-positive women illustrate:

> I'm scared to date anybody, I don't, I feel dirty, I don't want to tell
> them I have HPV, that is a sexually transmitted disease, I mean, how
> do you tell somebody ... I'm very concerned about how it will affect
> my sex life. (P003)

> I think if you have an abnormal Pap and the doctor says 'chances of
> cancer' to you ... it doesn't matter where the heck you got it. (P008)

Overall, the interviews are already proving to contain a variety of experiences and reaction to HPV testing and should be useful in better understanding the potential benefits and concerns that HPV testing brings. Research on women's experiences with HPV testing is essential for developing educational materials that not only provide the information they seek, but also normalize the range of emotions that women experience as a result of being tested.

Another approach to accessing women's perspective on HPV testing is to access their willingness to undergo the test. There has been a limited amount of research directly measuring women's preferences for HPV testing. In one study, 64% of women with an abnormal Pap chose to use HPV testing to determine whether a colposcopy was necessary (Le et al., 2004). The only factors associated with choosing the HPV test were college education and previous treatment for abnormal Pap tests (Le et al., 2004). However, in another study that provided a repeat Pap as an option after an ASCUS result, 58.4% of women choose a repeat Pap, compared with only 7.3% who chose an HPV test (Ferris, Kriegel, Cote, Litaker, & Woodward, 1997). An important next step is to develop and evaluate the effectiveness of educational brochures on women's decisions about HPV testing and their experiences of being tested. We know that educational brochures can increase compliance with Pap testing (Stewart, Buchegger, Lickrish, & Sierra, 1994). Some authors have begun to provide direction in this regard as certain aspects of knowledge around HPV are expected to minimize the potential negative impact of a positive test, such as emphasizing the high prevalence of HPV, the lack of symptoms (e.g., genital warts) with oncogenic HPV, the frequent occurrence of spontaneous clearance, and the possibility of dormancy (meaning they may have been infected a number of years ago) (McCaffery & Irwig, 2005; McCaffery et al., 2006; Waller et al., 2005). For HPV testing to be effective, it must not reduce women's willingness to be screened or to be followed up after an abnormal result. This concern has been voiced a number of times, but the actual behavioural impact on screening attendance has not been measured. A small and limited study suggests that testing positive for HPV does not effect follow-up after an abnormal Pap, compared with women who did not recall being told about an HPV test (Funke & Nicholson, 1993). Kahn et al. (2005a) report their participants' behavioural *intentions*, which included continuing or changing to safe sexual behaviour, returning for screening, and reducing or quitting smoking. In the future it will be important to continue to explore actual behavioural changes that may result from HPV testing.

Self-Sampling

Self-sampling for HPV testing is a procedure that allows women to collect their own sample for standard HPV testing, as reviewed above. Therefore, the only difference between this technology and standard HPV testing is that this procedure allows women to bypass the gynecological exam administered by a health-care worker. Consequently, all of the psychosocial issues reviewed above are also important here. There are, however, new issues that arise directly from the self-sampling technology.

Pap testing involves collecting cells that are sufficient for cytological evaluation, and doing this oneself has been explored but the logistics of actually scrapping cells from one's own cervix make it difficult. HPV testing, on the hand, requires that a sample be obtained that can simply be tested for the presence or absence of HPV, and thus an adequate sample is easier to obtain. A number of procedures have been developed, including methods using a tampon, a Dacron swab, a cytobrush, or a lavage, all of which are inserted into the vagina for a relatively short amount of time. This has lead some to conclude that self-sampling for Pap testing is not an effective substitute for conventional cytology screening, but self-sampling for HPV testing is a promising alternative (Bidus et al., 2005). The research on HPV self-sampling has been quite varied, involving different self-sampling techniques and yielding different outcomes, and the details are beyond the scope of this chapter. Essentially, some have found similar levels of sensitivity (upon biopsy) for patient- and clinician-collected samples (Hillemanns, Kimming, Huttemann, Dannecker, & Thaler, 1999; Morrison, Goldberg, Hagan, Kadish, & Burk, 1992; Nobbenhuis et al., 2002), and a meta-analysis suggests that the sensitivity of self-sampling for HPV is good enough to recommend its use in a low-resource setting or when patients refuse the gynecological exam (Ogilvie et al., 2005). A recent systematic review of this literature concluded that there currently is insufficient evidence to make conclusions for or against self-sampling for HPV DNA testing, but that it is a promising development for cervical-cancer screening (Stewart et al., 2007). Clearly, no one is in a hurry to completely replace the Pap test with self-sampling, because some have found that clinician samples have better sensitivity (Garcia et al., 2003; Lorenzato et al., 2002) and because there are problems with doing an HPV test without cytology. In particular, there would be a large number of false-positive test results because of the high incidence of HPV. Nevertheless, we know that many women do not participate in Pap testing, and self-sampling for HPV testing could provide an alternative for these under-screened women.

The gap in the psychosocial literature on self-sampling for HPV DNA testing is particularly wide in two areas. First, with few exceptions (Bais et al., 2006; Chang et al., 2002; Ogilvie et al., 2007; Wright, Denny, Kuhn, Pollack, & Lorinez, 2000), most studies have not sought to recruit under-screened women. Second, a number of studies have shown that women find self-sampling acceptable (Dannecker et al., 2004; Dzuba et al., 2002; Forrest et al., 2004; Harper, Noll, Belloni, & Cole, 2002b; Hillemanns et al., 1999; Sellors et al., 2000a), but fewer have explored what might influence acceptability. This is compounded by that only two studies (Barata et al., in press; Forrest et al., 2004) have surveyed women who have not performed self-sampling, so the barriers for self-sampling have not been well documented with women who are not willing to do the test. Many women have expressed concern about doing the test properly (Barata et al., in press; Dzuba et al., 2002; Forrest et al., 2004; Harper et al., 2002a; Nobbenhuis et al., 2002), which may prove to be the biggest barrier to implementing self-sampling as a screening method. Other potential barriers such as not knowing why HPV DNA testing is important, not wanting to do the test if one is not ill, the cost of the test, not believing in medical sciences, pain, and fear have all been identified in a study on the acceptance of self-sampling in rural China (Tisci et al., 2003). Pain was reported in another study by 49.3% of women surveyed, although more women found the Pap painful (66.5%) (Dzuba et al., 2002), but it is not entirely clear why pain was reported as neither test should be painful. Women have also cited a lack of confidence in the procedure (Dzuba et al., 2002) and a concern about loosing their annual visit with a physician (Harper et al., 2002b). My colleagues and I conducted three focus groups with women in different Ontario cities: Thunder Bay, Toronto, and Windsor (Barata et al., in press). The three groups were similar in age (mean = 39, range = 19–64) and education (20% had less than a high-school education, 23% had college or a technical diploma, and 57% had a university degree or more). However, the Toronto and Windsor groups were ethnically diverse, speaking 11 different languages regularly at home, while all but one of the Thunder Bay participants spoke English at home. Additionally, fewer women in the Toronto group had had a Pap in the last 24 months (36%), compared with 70% in both Thunder Bay and Windsor. We directly explored their perspectives on self-sampling for HPV testing compared with Pap testing and interpreted the results within the health-belief model, which examines peoples readiness to perform a health action (Rosenstock, 1974; Rosenstock, Strecher & Becker, 1988). The women in our study also reported many of the barriers described above, but a few new issues were also brought up. Our participants were concerned that women might be lost to follow-up, might forget to do self-sampling on a regular basis, and might be blamed by doctors if they were to develop cervical cancer (Barata et al., in press). Consistent with the previous literature, the biggest concern was that women might not do the test properly, and that the test seemed unreliable and even "primitive." This concern is particularly troubling because it might cause adverse psychological affects, such as anxiety. As a woman in the Windsor group said, "But I am always going to have that in my mind, I did it right? It has been three years I have been doing it on my own. How do I know that I did it right?" (Barata et al., in press). Our research, however, included both women who had and had not had a Pap test in the past. Given that the largest potential gains are for women who have not undergone screening, this group of women should be the focus of future research on self-sampling.

Despite potential problems with self-sampling, women report a willingness to do self-sampling as part of routine screening (Harper et al., 2002b; Forrest et al., 2004). And all studies that have directly examined preference find that more women prefer self-sampling to physician-collected samples (Dannecker et al., 2004; Dzuba et al., 2002; Hillemanns et al., 1999; Nobbenhuis et al., 2002; Sellors et al., 2000a). Additionally, a substantial minority of previously screened women have indicated that self-sampling at home would increase their likelihood of participating in cervical screening (Anhang, Nelson, Telerant, Chiasson & Wright, 2005). Given the general acceptance of the procedure, it is possible that women who have not taken part in Pap testing because of barriers related to the gynecological exam itself might take part in self-sampling for HPV testing. For instance, Dzuba et al. (2002) found that women report feeling more comfortable and less embarrassed as reasons for preferring self-sampling to clinician-collected sampling. In our own focus-group study, the benefit of avoiding embarrassment and discomfort by doing away with the gynecological exam was a dominant area of discussion (Barata et al., in press). However, some other interesting benefits were mentioned, such as the relief of knowing the virus is not there or gone, being able to take one's time and thus perhaps increase the accuracy of the screen (physicians are often perceived as rushed), and taking control of one's own body and own health. For instance, a Windsor woman said, "I think, for me and for many women, it would give them more control of their own bodies ("umm hmms" from another participant). More of a sense of knowing that they take their own health under control" (Barata et al., in press).

Of note is that unlike the other two HPV technologies reviewed here, psychosexual issues have not been explored in much depth with respect to self-sampling (although those reviewed with respect to HPV testing alone would also be relevant). An exception is a study with rural women in China, where the authors found that the vast majority of women (99.6%) did *not* think husbands would forbid their wives from taking part, and most women (97.6%) were comfortable touching their genital area for the procedure (Tisci et al., 2003). Similarly, a majority (96.6%) of culturally diverse British residents reported that they did not believe self-sampling was contrary to religious or cultural belief (Forrest et al., 2004).

A study in the Netherlands has assessed the uptake of self-sampling in a group of under-screened women (Bais et al., 2006). The authors compared a control group of women who were simply invited for conventional cytology with women mailed a self-sampling device. They found that more women (34.2%) responded to self-sampling than to an invitation for conventional screening (17.6%). A follow-up cost analysis revealed that cost per lesion detected through self-sampling was similar to those costs for conventional screening, leading the authors to conclude that this was an alternative for cervical-cancer screening with under-screened women. This is certainly an exciting finding and needs further analysis in Canada, especially given the high rates of under screening in certain domestic populations. One group of researchers has started this process by doing a feasibility study of self-sampling with under-screened women from Vancouver's Downtown Eastside neighbourhood (a location known for prostitution and drug use) (Ogilvie et al., 2007). They found that approximately 50% of the women who agreed to participate, which is similar to other studies in the area, 28.5% tested positive for high-risk oncogenic HPV, and 81.45% of these were located again and referred for further testing. Certainly there are other groups of Canadian women that might benefit from self-sampling, such as new immigrants, institutionalized women, and women living in northern communities with limited access to health care.

It will be especially important to provide women with options around self-sampling. In our own study, an overriding theme was the need for options (Barata et al., in press). Some women clearly wanted to continue with physician-collected samples for Pap testing, whereas others would only participate in screening if they could do it themselves. Additionally, a particularly popular suggestion was self-sampling at a physician's office, which should be assessed for feasibility. It does follow that the more options women have available to them for cervical screening, the more that will participate, but this assertion needs to be assessed empirically. There is some potential for harm in providing options if the options are not all equal in terms of outcome. For instance, self-sampling for HPV testing is almost certainly better than no screening, but for women who are currently screened regularly, self-sampling may be appealing to them but medically inferior to their current standard of care. These issues need careful consideration as we begin to implement self-sampling into screening guidelines.

Prophylactic HPV Vaccines

Finally, we will consider prophylactic HPV vaccines. Two vaccines have been developed. Merck Frosst has developed Gardasil, which was approved for use in Canada in July 2006. GlaxoSmithKline has developed Cervarix, which is currently undergoing regulatory review by Health Canada. Both vaccines contain HPV-like particles (not the live virus), but there are structural differences between the two that are beyond our scope here. There are some details, however, that are relevant to understanding the psychosocial issues involved. Gardasil contains antigens for HPV types 16 and 18, which account for approximately 70% of cervical cancers worldwide, and for types 6 and 11, which are estimated to account for 90% of genital warts. Cervarix contains only types 16 and 18. Research outcomes from both vaccines have been reported for phase I to III trials, and follow-up data now exceeds five years. Women between the ages of 15 and 26 have participated in the trials (see Dawar, Deeks, & Dobson [2007] for an overview of the different vaccines). Rambout, Hopkins, Hutton, and Fergusson (2007) have conducted a systematic review of the literature, which included six available randomized clinical trials (nine individual reports). The results of both sets of trials have been impressive, and HPV vaccines are considered highly efficacious in preventing vaccine-type-specific HPV infection and precancerous cervical lesions in girls and women who have not been previously exposed to the HPV types included in the vaccine (Rambout et al., 2007). The HPV vaccines have not performed well with women who were previously infected with HPV (Hildesheim et al., 2007). As such, the vaccines are most efficacious for girls and women before they become sexually active. Both vaccines require three doses within six months, and Gardasil costs between $400 and $500 for all three shots. The majority of adverse events reported have been relatively minor (i.e., reaction at the topical injection site, headache, fatigue, myalgia, inching, gastrointestinal complaints, fever) and the incidence of serious adverse events has been balanced between vaccine and control groups (Rambout et al., 2007). The vaccines do not protect against HPV types that are not included in the vaccine (although there is some evidence that limited cross-protection for types 31 and 52 occurs with Cervarix, but this is a contentious issue). It is, therefore, important to remember that a number of other HPV types are associated with cervical cancer. In particular, types 45, 31, and 52 are estimated to account for 12% of cervical cancers, and a number of other types account for the remaining 18%. Thus, cervical screening must continue in women that are vaccinated.

The psychosocial literature on HPV vaccines has largely focused on the acceptability of the vaccine and the factors that effect acceptability in three important target groups: parents, health-care providers, and young women. The research on parental attitudes in Mexico, the United Kingdom, and the United States is largely positive as the majority of parents report acceptance of the vaccine (Brabin, Robersts, Farzaneh, & Kitchener, 2006; Constantine & Jerman, 2007; Hopenhayn, Christian, & Christian, 2007; Lazcano-Ponce et al., 2001; Olshen, Woods, Austin, Luskin, & Bauchner, 2005; Slomovitz et al., 2006). However, Washam (2005) found some parental resistance toward immunizing adolescents with the HPV vaccine. Specific concerns, voiced by a minority of parents, have also been noted, such as believing that vaccination may lead to early initiation into sexual activity (Brabin et al., 2006; Davis, Dickman, Ferris, & Dias, 2004), believing that it will be difficult to explain the need for the vaccine to their children (Zimet et al., 2005), denying the need for the vaccine (Constantine & Jerman, 2007), and worrying about vaccine safety (Slomovitz et al., 2006).

The research on health-care providers' attitudes has shown that the vaccine is largely supported by family physicians (Riedesel et al., 2005), gynecologists (Raley, Followwill, Zimet, & Ault, 2004), pediatricians (Kahn et al, 2005b), and nurse-practitioners (Mays & Zimet, 2004). Pediatricians (Kahn et al, 2005b) and family doctors (Riedesel et al., 2005) are more inclined to vaccinate girls versus boys and older versus younger adolescents. In addition, recommendation to vaccinate by professional organizations has shown to be particularly important in shaping physicians intentions to vaccinate (Daley, Liddon, & Crane, 2006; Kahn et al, 2005b; Mays & Zimet, 2004; Raley et al., 2004; Riedesel et al., 2005).

Young women have reported their own acceptance of the HPV vaccine (Kahn, Rosenthal, Hamann, & Bernstein, 2003; Zimet et al., 2000). Women who have recently begun to engage in sexual activity or have had an abnormal Pap test may be more likely to request vaccination (Crosby, Schoenberg, & Hopenhayn, 2007). Adolescents have generally been found to have favourable attitudes toward the HPV vaccine (Zimet et al., 2000), especially when they are knowledgeable about HPV and the vaccine (Woodhall et al., 2007). Having the approval of significant others, such as partners, parents, and doctors, appears to increase the likelihood that young adults would accept a vaccine against a sexually transmitted disease (Boehner, Howe, Bernstein, & Rosenthal, 2003). Potential recipients are also more likely to accept the vaccine if they believe it to be safe (Gerend, Lee, & Shepherd, 2007). When a sample of people with generally limited awareness of HPV and the vaccine were provided with information, their concerns about the vaccine centered on its safety, possible side effects, and level of protection provided (Friedman & Shepeard, 2007).

Although a fair amount of concern has been expressed about the unacceptability of the vaccine because of the sexually transmitted nature of HPV (Zimet, 2005). This has generally not been a dominant finding in the research literature to date. Only a minority of parents (11.3%) have indicated that their decision to vaccinate would be influenced by concerns that the vaccine would encourage sexual behaviour in their children (Brabin et al., 2006). However, those apposed to the vaccine do cite the perceived promotion of sexual intercourse (Davis et al., 2004) or unsafe sex (Olshen et al., 2005) in teens as reasons to oppose the vaccine. Young women themselves have reported that receiving the vaccine would not make them more likely to reduce condom use, have more sexual partners, or increase smoking (Kahn et al., 2003).

There is mixed evidence regarding the role that knowledge about the HPV vaccine and educational materials play in influencing attitudes toward the vaccine. Some authors have found that increased knowledge about HPV predicts intentions to receive the vaccine (Kahn et al., 2003), but others have found that baseline knowledge about HPV does not predict parental acceptability of the vaccine for their children (Davis et al., 2004). Similarly, providing parents with written educational materials about the vaccine both has (Chan, Cheung, Lo, & Chung, 2007; Davis et al., 2004) and has not (Dempsey, Zimet, Davis, & Kautsky, 2006) predicted acceptability of the vaccine for their children.

Certainly, understanding the acceptability of the HPV vaccine is important, but it is probably time to move past this focus. Research has revealed positive attitudes toward the vaccine; however, the uptake of the vaccine in some Canadian immunization programs has been lower than expected in terms of the numbers of girls vaccinated (Dyer, 2007). Future research will need to explore the disconnection between the reviewed literature and the actual behaviour of parents and their children. We also need to consider the most appropriate outcome variables in determining the success of HPV vaccination programs. The rates of vaccine uptake provide only one piece of the story. The rates of parents and young women who believe they have made an informed decision is also likely to be an important outcome variable. If the focus changes to informed decision making, the research questions shift to include the type of information that parents and young girls want, how they made their decision, how they feel about their decision, and the likelihood of obtaining a vaccination in the future. It will be particularly important to understand whether lower-than-expected HPV vaccination rates were a result of informed decision making or a result of avoiding a decision altogether. The latter of which is particularly problematic if it resulted from fear that simply paralyzed parents and girls from making a decision.

There has been a fair amount of media attention and commentary on the vaccine, and the issues involved can be quite complex and certainly move beyond initial concerns that vaccination might be perceived as also promoting sexual activity in young girls. The way these issues (e.g., universality of HPV vaccination programs, target groups for vaccination, safety and efficacy, impact on cervical-cancer screening, cost, cost effectiveness, information needs, politics) are understood and used in decision making need to be considered. To that end, I am currently recruiting participants for a Q-methodology study that will explore current perspectives on HPV vaccines and consider how these various issues come together in creating cohesive perspectives.

In order to do this, my colleagues and I have developed a list 62 statements that reflect the issues that have garnered media and academic attention regarding HPV vaccines. A group of diverse participants will sort these statements according to their individual perspectives. In this study, a number of different population are of interest: people who have publicly declared an opinion about the HPV vaccine (through media or academic writings); parents of 9- to 17-year-olds; young woman (aged 18–26); physicians (e.g., family, gynecologist, pediatrician, pathologist); researchers and people affiliated with different types of organizations, including: religious groups, women's health organizations, cancer organizations, vaccine manufacturers, and adolescent centres. Each participant's perspective will be reflected in how she or he sorts the statements and will be compared with other participants' perspectives through factor analysis. However, Q methodology is fundamentally different from how factor analysis is normally applied because it is the individuals (or more accurately, their perspective as indicated by how they have sorted the statements) that are intercorrelated and factored in the usual way (Brown, 1980). The result is a number of factors, which each identify people with similar perspectives. Participants with similar perspectives are grouped together in each factor, and the way they have sorted their statements gives that factor meaning. The factors that result from this Q-methodology study will help illuminate the different perspectives that exist about HPV vaccines. We believe the results will be important in helping to illuminate the gray space between the outright rejection or acceptance of HPV vaccines, lead to a more nuanced debate about the merits of these vaccines, and lead to a greater understanding of how people form their opinions about HPV vaccines.

Conclusion

The psychosocial research to date has added to our understanding of women's knowledge, attitudes, and experiences regarding specific HPV technologies, and it will be useful as these technologies are incorporated into cervical-cancer-prevention programs. The next step is to think more broadly. Some have already begun thinking about how combinations of HPV technologies will impact upon cervical-cancer prevention in order to develop prevention programs that work with all the HPV technologies (Davies et al, 2007). It is likely that all the technologies will have an impact on women's decision making around cervical-cancer prevention. A paradigm shift is likely as women begin to understand the causes of cervical cancer and the various options available to prevent it. Women need to make informed decisions about cervical cancer prevention, and these can only be made when one considers these technologies together and in conjunction with Pap testing. We need to think in more complex ways. It is no longer enough to simply understand whether a woman intends to be vaccinated; we should also explore how that decision is made within the context of the other technologies. For instance, a young woman's decision to be vaccinated may depend on her understanding of a recent HPV-negative test result or her knowledge about cervical screening options.

We also need to do a better job of creating ways to assess behaviour, not only intentions and acceptability. This will be essential if we are to understand whether the new technologies will improve participation in cervical cancer programs. Many have expressed concern that some women will opt out of cervical screening in the new HPV era, but we must determine whether that is a legitimate concern. If it is, then we must develop new strategies. The preventive health models that psychology is known for have not yet been used to predict and improve upon the use of HPV technologies. There is still much room for psychology in the new HPV era as we begin to understand the complex decisions that lead to participation in cervical cancer programs. Psychosocial research has been very important in the Pap era in identifying barriers, strategizing solutions, and implementing programs, and there is now much to do in the new HPV era. Certainly we are well equipped for the challenge, and now we must prepare for the work ahead.

References

Agurto, I., Bishop, A., Sanchez, G., Betancourt, Z., & Robles, S. (2004). Perceived barriers and benefits to cervical cancer screening in Latin America. *Preventive Medicine, 39,* 91–98.

Ahmad, F., Stewart, D. E., Cameron, J., & Hyman, I. (2001). Rural physicians' perspecitives on cervical and breast cancer screening: A gender-based analysis. *Journal of Women's Health and Gender-Based Medicine, 10,* 201–208.

Anhang, R., Nelson, J., Telerant, R., Chiasson, M., & Wright, T. C., Jr. (2005). Acceptability of self-collection of specimens for HPV DNA testing in an urban population. *Journal of Women's Health, 14,* 721–728.

Anhang, R., Goodman, A., & Goldie, S. J. (2004a). HPV communication: Review of existing research and recommendations for patient education. *CA: A Cancer Journal for Clinicians, 54,* 248–259.

Anhang, R., Wright, T. C., Smock, L., & Goldie, S. J. (2004b). Women's desired information about human papillomavirus. *Cancer, 100,* 315–320.

Austin, L. T., Ahmad, F., McNally, M. J., & Stewart, D. E. (2002). Breast and cervical cancer screening in Hispanic women: A literature review using the health belief model. *Women's Health Issues, 12,* 122–128.

Bais, A. G., van Kemenade, F. J., Berkhof, J., Verheijen, R. H. M., Snijders, P. J. F., Voorhorst, F., et al. (2006). Human papillomavirus testing on self-sampled cervico-vaginal brushes: An effective alternative to protect nonresponders in cervical screening programs. *International Journal of Cancer, 120,* 1505–1510.

Barata, P. C., Stewart, D. E., Howlett, R., Gagliardi, A., & Mai, V. (in press). Discussions about self-obtained samples for HPV testing as an alternative for cervical cancer prevention. *Journal of Psychosomatic Obstetrics and Gynecology.*

Benning, B. R., & Lund, M. R. (2006). Patient knowledge about human papillomavirus and relationship to history of abnormal Papanicolaou test results. *Journal of Lower Genital Tract Disease, 11,* 29–34.

Bidus, M. A., Zahn, C. M., Maxwell, G. L., Rodriguez, M., Elkas, J., & Rose, S. G. (2005). The role of self-collection devices for cytology and human papillomavirus DNA testing in cervical cancer screening. *Clinical Obstetrics and Gynecolgoy, 48,* 127–132.

Bish, A., Sutton, S., & Golombok, S. (2000). Predicting uptake of a routine cervical smear test: A comparison of the health belief model and the theory of planned behaviour. *Psychology and Health, 15,* 35–50.

Boehner, C. W., Howe, S. R., Bernstein, D. I., & Rosenthal, S. L. (2003). Viral sexually transmitted disease vaccine acceptability among college students. *Sexually Transmitted Diseases, 30,* 774–778.

Bosch, F. X., Lorincz, A., Munoz, N., Meijer, C. J. L. M., & Shah, K. (2002). The causal relation between human papillomavirus and cervical cancer. *Journal of Clinical Pathology, 55,* 244–265.

Brabin, L., Robersts, S. A., Farzaneh, F., & Kitchener, H. C. (2006). Future acceptance of adolescent human papillomavirus vaccination: A survey of parental attitudes. *Vaccine, 24,* 3087–3094.

Braun, V., & Gavey, N. (1999a). "Bad girls" and "good girls"? Sexuality and cervical cancer. *Women's studies international forum, 22,* 203–213.

Braun, V., & Gavey, N. (1999b). 'With the best of reasons': cervical cancer prevention policy and the suppression of sexual risk factor information. *Social Science and Medicine, 48,* 1463–1474.

Breitkopf, C. R., Pearson, H. C., & Breitkopf, D. M. (2005). Poor knowledge regarding the Pap test among low-income women undergoing routine screening. *Perspectives on Sexual and Reproductive Health, 37,* 78–84.

Brown, S. R. (1980). *Political subjectivity applications of Q methodology in political sciences.* New Haven, CT: Yale University Press.

Burak, L. J., & Meyer, M. (1997). Using the health belief model to examine and predict college women's cervical cancer screening beliefs and behavior. *Health Care for Women International, 18,* 251–262.

Byrd, T. L., Peterson, S. K., Chavez, R., & Hechert, A. (2004). Cervical cancer screening beliefs among young Hispanic women. *Preventive Medicine, 38,* 192–197.

Cervical Cancer Screening Program (2005). *Annual Report.* Vancouver: BC Cancer Agency.

Chan, S. S. C., Cheung, T. H., Lo, W. K., & Chung, T. K. H. (2007). Women's attitudes on human papillomavirus vaccination to their daughters. *Journal of Adolescent Health, 41,* 204–207.

Chang, C.-C., Tseng, C.-J., Liu, W.-W., Jain, S., Horng, S.-G., Soong, Y.-K., et al. (2002). Clinical evaluation of a new model of self-obtained method for the assessment of genital human papilloma virus infection in an underserved population. *Chang Gung Medical Journal, 25,* 664–671.

Collins, S., Mazloomzadeh, S., Winter, H., Blomfield, P., Bailey, A., Young, L., et al. (2002). High incidence of cervical human papillomavirus infection in women during their first sexual relationship. *British Journal of Obstetrics and Gynaecology, 109,* 96–98.

Constantine, N., & Jerman, P. (2007). Acceptance of human papillomavirus vaccination among California parents of daughters: A representative statewide analysis. *Journal of Adolescent Health, 40,* 108–115.

Crosby, R., Schoenberg, N., & Hopenhayn, C. (2007). Correlates of intent to be vaccinated against HPV: An exploratory study of college aged women. *Journal of Adolescent Health, 40,* S47.

Crum, C. P., & Berkowitz, R. S. (2002). Human papillomaviruses. Applications, caveats and prevention. *The Journal of Reproductive Medicine, 47,* 519–528.

Cuzick, J., Clavel, C., Petry, K.-U., Meijer, C. J. L. M., Hoyer, H., Ratnam, S., et al. (2006). Overview of the European and North American studies on HPV testing in primary cervical cancer screening. *International Journal of Cancer, 119,* 1095–1101.

Daley, M., Liddon, N., & Crane, L. (2006). A national survey of pediatrician knowledge and attitudes regarding human papillomavirus vaccination. *Pediatrics, 118,* 2280–2289.

Dannecker, C., Siebert, U., Thaler, C., Kiermeir, D., Hepp, H., & Hillemanns, P. (2004). Primary cervical cancer screening by self-sampling of human papillomavirus DNA in internal medicine outpatients clinics. *Annals of Oncology, 15,* 863–869.

Davies, P., Bogdanovic-Guillion, A., Grce, M., & Sancho-Garnier, H. (2007). The future of cervical cancer prevention in Europe. *Collegium Antropologicum, 31,* 11–16.

Davis, K., Dickman, E. D., Ferris, D., & Dias, J. K. (2004). Human papillomavirus vaccine acceptability among parents of 10- to 15-year-old adolescents. *Journal of Lower Genital Tract Disease, 8,* 188–194.

Dawar, M., Deeks, S., & Dobson, S. (2007). Human papillomavirus vaccines launch a new era in cervical cancer prevention. *Canadian Medical Association Journal, 177,* 456–461.

de Villiers, E., Fauquet, C., Broker, T., Bernard, H., & zur Hausen, H. (2004). Classification of papillomaviruses. *Virology, 324,* 17–27.

Dell, D., Chen, H., Ahmad, F., & Stewart, D. (2000). Knowledge about human papillomavirus among adolescents. *Obstetrics and gynecology, 96,* 653–656.

Dempsey, A. F., Zimet, G. D., Davis, R. L., & Kautsky, L. (2006). Factors that are associated with parental acceptance of human papillomavirus vaccines: A randomized intervention study of written information about HPV. *Pediatrics, 117,* 1493.

Dyer, Owen (2007, December 15). HPV vaccine campaign struggles. National Review of Medicine. 4, 20, n.p.

Dzuba, I. G., Diaz, E. Y., Allen, B., Leonard, Y. F., Ponce, E. C. L., Shah, K. V., et al. (2002). The acceptability of self-collected samples for HPV testing vs. the Pap test as alternatives in cervical cancer screening. *Journal of Women's Health and Gender-Based Medicine, 11,* 265–275.

Egbert, N., & Parrott, R. (2001). Self-efficacy and rural women's perfomance of breast and cervical cancer detection practices. *Journal of Health Communication, 6,* 219–233.

Fehringer, G., Howlett, R., Cotterchio, M., Klar, N., Majpruz-Moat, V., & Mai, V. (2006). Comparison of Papanicolaou (Pap) test results across Ontario and factors associated with cervical screening. *Canadian Journal of Public Health, 96,* 140–144.

Ferris, D., Kriegel, D., Cote, L., Litaker, M., & Woodward, L. (1997). Women's triage and management preferences for cervical cytologic reports demonstrating atypical squamous cells of undetermined significance and low-grade squamous intraepithelial lesions. *Archives of Family Medicine, 6,* 348–353.

Forrest, S., McCaffery, K., Waller, J., Desai, M., Swarewski, A., Cadman, L., et al. (2004). Attitudes to self-sampling for HPV among Indian, Pakistani, African-Caribbean and white British women in Manchester, UK. *Journal of Medical Screening, 11,* 85–88.

Franceschi, S., Herrero, R., Clifford, G., Snijders, P., Arslan, A., Anh, P., et al. (2006). Variations in the age-specificy curves of human papillomavirus prevalence in women worldwide. *International Journal of Cancer, 119,* 2677–2684.

Franco, E. (2004). Randomized controlled trials of HPV testing and pap cytology: toward evidence-based cervical cancer prevention. *International Journal of Cancer.Journal International du Cancer, 110,* 1–2.

Friedman, A. L., & Shepeard, H. (2007). Exploring the knowledge, attitudes, beliefs and communication preferences of the general public regarding HPV: Findings from the CDC Focus groups research and implications practice. *Health Education and Behaviour, 34,* 471–485.

Funke, B. L., & Nicholson, M. E. (1993). Factors affecting patient compliance among women with abnormal pap smears. *Patient Education and Couseling, 20,* 5–15.

Garcia, F., Barker, B., Santos, C., Brown, E. M., Nuno, T., Giuliano, A., et al. (2003). Cross-sectional study of patient- and physician- collected cervical cytology and human papillomavirus. *Obstetrics and gynecology, 102,* 266–272.

Gerend, M., Lee, S., & Shepherd, J. (2007). Predictors of human papillomavirus vaccination acceptability among underserved women. *Sexually Transmitted Diseases, 34,* 468–471.

Gilbert, L. K., Alexander, L., Grosshans, J. F., & Jolley, L. (2003). Answering frequently asked questions about HPV. *Sexually Transmitted Diseases, 30,* 193–194.

Gupta, A., Kumar, A., & Stewart, D. (2002). Cervical cancer screening among South Asian women in Canada: The role of education and acculturation. *Health Care for Women International, 23,* 123–134.

Harper, D. M. (2004). Why am I scared of HPV? *CA: A Cancer Journal for Clinicians, 54,* 245–247.

Harper, D. M., Raymond, M., Noll, W. W., Belloni, D. R., Duncan, L. T., & Cole, B. F. (2002a). Tampon sampling with longer cervicovaginal cell exposures are equivalent to two consecutive swabs for the detection of high-risk human papillomavirus. *Sexually Transmitted Diseases, 29,* 628–636.

Harper, D. M., Noll, W. W., Belloni, D. R., & Cole, B. F. (2002b). Randomized clinical trial of PCR-determined human papillomavirus detection methods: self-sampling versus clinician-directed -biological concordance and women's preferences. *American Journal of Obstetrics and gynecology, 186,* 365–373.

Hasenyager, C. (1999). Knowledge of cervical cancer screening among women attending a university health centre. *Journal of American College Health, 47,* 221–224.

Henning, P., & Knowles, A. (1990). Factors influencing women over 40 years to take precautions against cervical cancer. *Journal of Applied Social Psychology, 20,* 1612–1621.

Hildesheim, A., Herreco, R., Wacholder, S., Rodriguez, A. C., Solomon, D., Bratti, M. C., et al. (2007). Effect of human papillomavirus 16/18 L1 virus-like particle vaccine among young women with preexisting infection. *Journal of the American Medical Association, 298,* 743–753.

Hill, D., Gardner, G., & Rassaby, J. (1985). Factors predisposing women to take precautions against breast and cervix cancer. *Journal of Applied Social Psychology, 15,* 59–79.

Hillemanns, P., Kimmig, R., Huttemann, U., Dannecker, C., & Thaler, C. J. (1999). Screening for cervical neoplasia by self-assessment for human papillomavirus DNA. *The Lancet, 354,* 1970.

Hislop, T. G., Jackson, C., Schwartz, S. M., Deschamps, M., Tu, S.-P., Kuniyuki, A., et al. (2003). Facilitators and barriers to cervical screening among Chinese Canadian women. *Canadian Journal of Public Health, 94,* 68–73.

Holcomb, B., Bailey, J. M., Crawford, K., & Ruffin, M. T. (2004). Adults' knowledge and behaviors related to human papillomavirus infection. *Journal of the American Board of Family Practice, 17,* 26–31.

Hopenhayn, C., Christian, A., & Christian, W. (2007). Human papillomavirus vaccine: knowledge and attitudes in two Appalachian Kentucky counties. *Cancer Causes Control, 18,* 627–634.

Kahn, J. A., Rosenthal, S. L., Hamann, T., & Bernstein, D. I. (2003). Attitudes about human papillomavirus vaccine in young women. *International Journal of STD and AIDS, 14,* 300–306.

Kahn, J. A., Slap, G. B., Bernstein, D. I., Kollar, L., Tissot, A. M., Hillard, P. A., et al. (2005a). Psychological, behavioral, and interpersonal impact of human papillomavirus and pap test results. *Journal of Women's Health, 14,* 650–659.

Kahn, J. A., Zimet, G. D., Bernstein, D. I., Riedesel, J. M., Lan, D., Huang, B., et al. (2005b). Pediatricians' intention to administer human papillomavirus vaccine: the role of practice characteristics, knowledge, and attitudes. *Journal of Adolescent Health, 37,* 502–510.

Kowalski, R. M., & Brown, K. J. (1994). Psychosocial barriers to cervical cancer screening: Concerns with self-presentation and social evaluation. *Journal of Applied Social Psychology, 24,* 941–958.

Lam, T. K., McPhee, S. J., Mock, J., Wong, C., Doan, H. T., Nguyen, T., et al. (2003). Encouraging Vietnamese-American women to obtain pap tests through lay health worker outreach and media education. *Journal of General Internal Medicine: Official Journal of the Society for Research and Education in Primary Care Internal Medicine, 18,* 516–524.

Lambert, E. C. (2001). College students' knowledge of human papillomavirus and effectiveness of a brief educational intervention. *The Journal of the American Board of Family Practice/American Board of Family Practice, 14,* 178–183.

Lamont, J. (1994). Psychosexual reactions of women to the diagnosis of conditions associated with pre-invasive cervical cancer. *The Canadian Journal of Human Sexuality, 3,* 181–183.

Lazcano-Ponce, E., Rivera, L., Arillo-Santillan, E., Salmeron, J., Hernandez-Avila, M., & Munoz, N. (2001). Acceptability of human papillomavirus (HPV) trial vaccine among mothers of adolescents in Cuernavaca, Mexico. *Archives of Medical Research, 32,* 243–247.

Le, T., Hicks, W., Menard, C., Boyd, D., Hewson, T., Hopkins, L., et al. (2004). Human palilloma virus testing knowledge and attitudes among women attending colposcopy clinic with ASCUS/LGSIL Pap smears. *Journal of Obstetrics and Gynaecology Canada, 26,* 788–792.

Lee, M. C. (2000). Knowledge, barriers, and motivators related to cervical cancer screening among Korean-American women: A focus group approach. *Cancer Nursing, 23,* 168–175.

Lorenzato, F. R., Singer, A., Ho, L., Santos, L. C., Batista, R. d. L., Lubambo, T. M., et al. (2002). Human papillomavirus detection for cervical cancer prevention with polymerase chain reaction in self-collected samples. *American Journal of Obstetrics and gynecology, 186,* 962–968.

Lovell, S., Kearns, R. A., & Friesen, W. (2007). Sociocultural barriers to cervical screening in South Auckland, New Zealand. *Social Science and Medicine, 65,* 138–150.

Maissi, E., Marteau, T. M., Hankins, M., Moss, S., Legodd, R., & Gray, A. (2004). Psychological impact of human papillomavirus testing in women with borderline or mildly dyskaryotic cervical smear test results: cross sectional questionnaire study. *British Medical Journal, 328*, 1293–1298.

Maissi, E., Marteau, T. M., Hankins, M., Moss, S., Legodd, R., & Gray, A. (2005). The psychological impact of human papillomavirus testing in women with borderline or mildly dyskaryotic cervical smear test results: 6-month follow-up. *British Journal of Cancer, 92*, 990–994.

Marrazzo, J. M., Stine, K., & Koutsky, L. A. (2000). Genital human papillomavirus in women who have sex with women: a review. *American Journal of Obstetrics and gynecology, 183*, 770–774.

Maxwell, C. J., Bancej, C. M., Snider, J., & Vik, S. A. (2001). Factors important in promoting cervical cancer screening among Canadian women: Findings from the 1996–97 national population health survey (NPHS). *Canadian Journal of Public Health, 92*, 127–133.

Mays, R. M., & Zimet, G. D. (2004). Recommending STI vaccination to parents of adolescents: The attitudes of nurse practitioners. *Sexually Transmitted Diseases, 31*, 428–432.

Mays, R. M., Zimet, G. D., Winston, Y., Kee, R., Dickes, J., & Su, L. (2000). Human papillomavirus, genital warts, pap smears, and cervical cancer: Knowledge and beliefs of adolescent and adult women. *Health Care for Women International, 21*, 361–374.

McCaffery, K., Forrest, S., Waller, J., Desai, M., Szarewski, A., & Wardle, J. (2003). Attitudes towards HPV testing: a qualitative study of beliefs among Indian, Pakistani, African-Caribbean and white British women in the UK. *British Journal of Cancer, 88*, 42–46.

McCaffery, K., Waller, J., Nazroo, J., & Wardle, J. (2006). Social and psychological impact of HPV testing in cervical screening: a qualitative study. *Sexually Transmitted Infections, 82*, 169–174.

McCaffery, K., & Irwig, L. (2005). Australian women's needs and preferences for information about human papillomavirus in cervical screening. *Journal of Medical Screening, 12*, 134–141.

McCaffery, K., Waller, J., Forrest, S., Cadman, L., Szarewski, A., & Wardle, J. (2004). Testing positive for human papillomavirus in routine cervical screening: examination of psychosocial impact. *British Journal of Obstetrics and Gynaecology, 111*, 1437–1443.

McDonald, J. T., & Kennedy, S. (2007). Cervical cancer screening by immigrant and minority women in Canada. *Journal of Immigrant Minority Health, 9*, 323–334.

McFadden, S. E., & Schumann, L. (2001). The role of human papillomavirus in screening for cervical cancer. *Journal of the American Academy of Nurse Practitioners, 13*, 116–128.

McLachlin, C., Mai, V., Murphy, J., & Fung Kee Fung, M. (2005). *Cervical screening: A clinical practice guideline.* Toronto: Cancer Care Ontario.

Miller, S. M., Mischel, W., O'Leary, A., & Mills, M. (1996). From human papilloma virus (HPV) to cervical cancer: psychological processes in infection, detection, and control. *The Society of Behavioral Medicine, 18*, 219–228.

Monk, B. J., & Wiley, D. J. (2004). Human papillomavirus infections: Truth or consequences. *Cancer, 100,* 225–227.

Morrison, E. A. B., Goldberg, G. L., Hagan, R. J., Kadish, A. S., & Burk, R. D. (1992). Self-administered home cervicovaginal lavage: A novel tool for the clinical-epidemiologic investigation of genital human papillomavirus infections. *American Journal of Obstetrics and gynecology, 167,* 104–107.

Mosavel, M., & El-Shaarawi, N. (2007). "I have never heard that one": Young girls' knowledge and perception of cervical cancer. *Journal of Health and Communication, 12,* 707–719.

Murray, M., & McMillan, C. (1993). Health beliefs, locus of control, emotional control and women's cancer screening behaviour. *British Journal of Clinical Psychology, 32,* 87–100.

National Cancer Institute of Canada. (2006). *Progress in Cancer Control: Screening.*

Nobbenhuis, M., Helmerhorst, T., van den Brule, A., Rozendaal, L., Jaspars, L., Voorhorst, F., et al. (2002). Primary screening for high risk HPV by home obtained cervicovaginal lavage is an alternative screening tool for unscreened women. *Journal of Clinical Pathology, 55,* 435–439.

Ogilvie, G., Krajden, M., Maginley, J., Isaac-Renton, J., Hislop, G., Elwood-Martin, R., et al. (2007). Feasibility of self-collection of specimens for human papillomavirus testing in hard-to-reach women. *Canadian Medical Association Journal, 177,* 480–483.

Ogilvie, G., Patrick, D., Schulzer, M., Sellors, J., Petric, M., Chambers, K., et al. (2005). Diagnostic accuracy of self collected vaginal specimens for human papillomavirus compared to clinician collected human papillomavirus specimens: a meta-analysis. *Sexually Transmitted Infections, 81,* 207–212.

Olshen, E., Woods, E. R., Austin, S. B., Luskin, M., & Bauchner, H. (2005). Parental acceptance of the human papillomavirus vaccine. *Journal of Adolescent Health, 37,* 248–251.

Peto, J., Gilham, C., Fletcher, O., & Matthews, F. E. (2004). The cervical cancer epidemic that screening has prevented in the UK. *The Lancet, 364,* 249–256.

Pruitt, S. L., Parker, P. A., Peterson, S. K., Le, T., Follen, M., & Basen-Engquist, K. (2005). Knowledge of cervical dysplasia and human papillomavirus among women seen in a colposcopy clinic. *Gynecologic Oncology, 99,* S236–S244.

Raley, J. C., Followwill, K. A., Zimet, G. D., & Ault, K. A. (2004). Gynecologists' attitudes regarding human papilloma virus vaccination: a survey of Fellows of the American College of Obstetricians and Gynecologists. *Infectious Diseases in Obstetrics and Gynecology, 12,* 127–133.

Rambout, L., Hopkins, L., Hutton, B., & Fergusson, D. (2007). Prophylactic vaccinations against human papillomavirus infection and disease in women: a systematic review of randomized controlled trials. *Canadian Medical Association Journal, 177,* 469–479.

Reid, J. (2001). Women's Knowledge of pap smears, risk factors for cervical cancer, and cervical cancer. *Journal of obstetric, gynecologic, and neonatal nursing: JOGNN/NAACOG, 30,* 299–305.

Riedesel, J. M., Rosenthal, S. L., Zimet, G. D., Bernstein, D. I., Huang, B., Lan, D., et al. (2005). Attitudes about human papillomavirus vaccine among family physicians. *Journal of Pediatric and Adolescent Gynecology, 18*, 391–398.

Rosenstock, I. M. (1974). Historical origins of the health belief model. *Health Education Monographs, 2*, 328–335.

Rosenstock, I. M., Strecher, V. J., & Becker, M. H. (1988). Social learning theory and the health belief model. *Health Education Quarterly, 15*, 175–183.

Schiffman, M., & Castle, P. E. (2003). Human Papillomavirus: Epidemiology and Public Health. *Archives of Pathology and Laboratory Medicine*, 127, 930–934.

Sellors, J. W., Lorincz, A. T., Mahony, J. B., Mielzynska, I., Lytwyn, A., Roth, P., et al. (2000a). Comparison of self-collected vaginal, vulvar and urine samples with physician-collected cervical samples for human papillomavirus testing to detect high-grade squamous interaepithelial lesions. *Canadian Medical Association Journal, 163*, 513–518.

Sellors, J. W., Mahony, J. B., Kaczorowski, J., Lytwyn, A., Bangura, H., Chong, S., et al. (2000b). Prevalence and predictors of human papillomavirus infection in women in Ontario, Canada. *Canadian Medical Association Journal, 163*, 503–508.

Sheeran, P., & Orbell, S. (2000). Using implementation intentions to increase attendance for cervical cancer screening. *Health Psychology, 19*, 283–289.

Slomovitz, B. M., Sun, C. C., Frumovitz, M., Soliman, P. T., Schmeler, K. M., Pearson, H. C., et al. (2006). Are women ready for the HPV vaccine? *Gynecologic Oncology, 103*, 151–154.

Stewart, D. E., Gagliardi, A., Johnston, M., Howlett, R., Barata, P. C., Lewis, N., et al. (2007). Self-collected samples for testing of oncogenic human papillomavirus: A systematic review. *Journal of Obstetrics and Gynaecology Canada, 29*, 817–828.

Stewart, D. E., Buchegger, P. M., Lickrish, G. M., & Sierra, S. (1994). The effect of educational brochures on follow-up compliance in women with abnormal papanicolau smears. *Obstetrics and gynecology, 83*, 583–585.

Tisci, S., Shen, Y. H., Fife, D., Huang, J., Goycoolea, J., Ma, C. P., et al. (2003). Patient acceptance of self-sampling for human papillomavirus in rural China. *Journal of Lower Genital Tract Disease, 7*, 107–116.

Tristram, A. (2006). HPV information needs. *Best Practice and Research Clinical Obstetrics and Gynaecology, 20*, 267–277.

Trottier, H., & Franco, E. (2006). The epidemiology of genital human papillomavirus infection. Vaccine, 24, (Suppl. 1) S4-15.

Van Til, L., MacQuarrie, C., & Herbert, R. (2003). Understanding the barriers to cervical cancer screening among older women. *Qualitative Health Research, 13*, 1116–1131.

Walboomers, J. M., Jacobs, M. V., Manos, M. M., Bosch, F. X., Kummer, J. A., Shah, K. V., et al. (1999). Human papillomavirus is a necessary cause of invasive cervical cancer worldwide. *Journal of Pathology, 189*, 12–19.

Waller, J., McCaffery, K., Nazroo, J., & Wardle, J. (2005). Making sense of information about HPV in cervical screening: a qualitative study. *British Journal of Cancer, 92*, 265–270.

Waller, J., McCaffery, K., Forrest, S., Szarewski, A., Cadman, L., & Wardle, J. (2003). Awareness of human papillomavirus among women attending a well woman clinic. *Sexually Transmitted Infections, 79,* 320–322.

Waller, J., McCaffery, K. J., Forrest, S., & Wardle, J. (2004). Human papillomavirus and cervical cancer: Issues for biobehavioral and psychosocial research. *Annals of Behavioral Medicine, 27,* 68–79.

Waller, J., McCaffery, K., & Wardle, J. (2004). Beliefs about the risk factors for cervical cancer in a British population sample. *Preventive Medicine, 38,* 745–753.

Wardle, J., Pernet, A., & Stephens, D. (1995). Psychological consequences of positive results in cervical cancer screening. *Psychology and Health, 10,* 185–194.

Washam, C. (2005). Targeting teens and adolescents for HPV vaccine could draw fire. *Journal of the National Cancer Institute, 97,* 1030–1031.

Winer, R. L., Hughes, J. P., Feng, Q., O'Reilly, S., Kiviat, N. B., Holmes, K. K., et al. (2006). Condom use and the risk of genital human papillomavirus infection in young women. *New England Journal of Medicine, 354,* 2645–2654.

Woloshin, S., Schwartz, L. M., Katz, S. J., & Welch, H. G. (1997). Is language a barrier to the use of preventive services? *Journal of General Internal Medicine, 12,* 472–477.

Woodhall, S., Lehtinen, M., Verho, T., Huhtala, H., Hokkanen, M., & Kosunen, E. (2007). Anticipated acceptance of HPV vaccination at baseline of implementation: A survey of parental and adolescent knowledge and attitudes in Finland. *Journal of Adolescent Health, 40,* 469.

Wright, T. C. Jr. (2007). Cervical cancer screening in the 21st century: Is it time to retire the Pap smear? *Clinical Obstetrics and Gynecolgoy, 50,* 313–323.

Wright, T. C., Denny, L., Kuhn, L., Pollack, A., & Lorinez, A. (2000). HPV DNA testing of self-collected vaginal samples compared with cytologic screening to detect cervical cancer. *Journal of the American Medical Association, 283,* 81–85.

Yacobi, E., Tennant, C., Ferrante, J., Pal, N., & Roetzheim, R. (1999). University students' knowledge and awareness of HPV. *Preventive Medicine, 28,* 535–541.

Zimet, G. D. (2005). Improving adolescent health: Focus on HPV vaccine acceptance. *Journal of Adolescent Health, 37,* S17–S23.

Zimet, G. D., Mays, R. M., Sturm, L. A., Ravert, A. A., Perkins, S. M., & Juliar, B. E. (2005). Parental attitudes about sexually transmitted infection vaccination for their adolescent children. *Archives of Pediatric and Adolescent Medicine, 159,* 132–137.

Zimet, G. D., Mays, R. M., Winston, Y., Kee, R., Dickes, J., & Su, L. (2000). Acceptability of human papillomavirus immunization. *Journal of Women's Health and Gender-Based Medicine, 9,* 47–50.

Cyndi Brannen and Laura Hambleton

The Health-Care System: At the Intersection of Caregiving, Health, Stress, and Gender

Caregiving is a central activity of life—we provide care for our children, partners, parents, and other loved ones. Gender and caregiving are intertwined constructs; women are much more likely to provide the normative care for healthy children and also for sick children, partners, and others. But for many women (and some men), non-professional caregiving becomes burdensome in time (for a review, see Hunt, 2003) and often leads to the development of significant health problems, including depression (e.g., Hawranik & Strain, 2000) and increased risk of mortality (e.g., Schulz & Beach, 1999). The chronic physiological stress that can accompany caregiving contributes to health problems, which may be compounded by the enduring nature of most caregiving situations. At the intersection of gender, caregiving, stress, and health lies the underlying assumptions of the health-care system, which can present a four-way stop for many. The first road leading to the intersection is gender: many women are raised to believe their role is that of caregiver, the second road at the intersection. The third avenue is stress, and an individual's ability to cope with the stress of caregiving greatly influences the degree to which the fourth road, health, is influenced by caregiving. Gender contributes to an individual's perception of stress and health as women are more likely to have chronic health problems. Thus, the four roads intersect at a potential four-way stop when a caregiver is confronted with a fundamental assumption of the health-care system: that women are willing and able to provide complex care with little impact on their own wellness.

In the first part of this chapter we summarize the pathways from caregiving through stress to poor health outcomes, focusing on Canadian research and, in particular, drawing from studies within the Healthy Balance Research Program in Halifax, Nova Scotia, while the middle section focuses on caregiving education and support programs, and the assumptions of the health-care system. The rest of the chapter is devoted to a discussion of future directions for caregiving research, policy, and practice within the Canadian health-care system.

Caregiving and Stress

The stress of providing care for a sick child or family member can be considerable. Folkman and Lazarus (1980) view stress as resulting from one's inability to effectively cope with the demands of an environment. This comprises both the subjective feeling of being stressed and the physiological stress process. Most caregiving and stress research has focused on perceived stress and health in caregivers for adults (e.g., Brannen & Keefe, 2006; Brannen & Petite, 2008; Brannen, Keefe, Woodman, & Hawkins, in press; Keating, Fast, Fredrick, Cranswick, & Perrier, 1999; Roeher Institute, 2000) and chronically ill children (e.g., Hastings, 2003; MacDougall & Miller, 2003; Mandleco, Olsen, Dyches, & Marshall, 2003; Melynk et al., 2006; Tsai, Liu, Tsai, & Chou, 2006). MacDonald, Phipps, and Lethbridge (2005), as part of the Healthy Balance Research Program of caregiving, reported that women are more likely to provide care and to experience stress as a result of trying to balance their work and home responsibilities. They found that women, regardless of the amount of hours of paid work performed outside the home, still report more hours of unpaid caregiving in the home compared with their male partners. In addition, MacDonald et al. noted that women in the "sandwich generation"—those providing care for both children and aging family members—may experience more stress than any other group of caregivers. Further, the authors found that for men there is no association between stress and hours of unpaid caregiving, but that for women increased caregiving hours lead to increases in stress.

Physiological stress is clearly linked to health problems via activation of the sympathetic nervous system. Overactivation contributes to illness responses, including suppressed immune system and coronary heart disease. This physiological model fits laboratory experiments and traumatic life events. However, the impacts of chronic moderate stressors such as caregiving are not well established, although chronic worrying is a new avenue of research that may help to explain the impact of chronic stress. Worrying consists of negative affect and high self-perceived stress, and contributes to poor health. While the study of worrying offers a relatively new approach, self-perceived stress—a commonly used indicator in individual studies for over three decades—has been linked to poor health outcomes. Worry can be viewed as chronic perceived stress arising from multiple inputs of stressors.

Caregiving Stressors

An organizing framework for the influence of stress on health for caregivers is presented in figure 1, and is informed by the determinants-of-health model. The figure is adapted from a model of stress for rural Canadians (Brannen, Johnson-Emberly, & McGrath, in press). Stress duration is an important consideration. For example, stress that arises as a result of an acute event (e.g., relationship breakdown) is substantively different from the chronic stress typical for caregivers of sick children and adults, which can contribute to perpetually high levels of stress. Denton and Waters (1999) grouped stress into categories of social-life stress, financial stress, environmental stress, family-health stress, parenting stress, and job stress. Brannen et al. (in press) expanded this model to include additional categories that encompass the diversity of stressors. In the present model of caregiving stressors, a category of individual stressors—including cognitive and emotional factors, age, gender, and health—was added. In addition, a category of relationship stressors incorporating relationship factors involved in caregiving—such as availability of support, family relationships, or caregivers' relationship with the care recipient—was added. Studies have reported that relationship variables are related to stress and health for caregivers (e.g., Sit, Wong, Clinton, & Fong, 2003; Sawatzky & Fowler-Kerry, 2003).

Employment stress includes aspects of work not directly connected to a specific job. For example, caregivers may face considerable employment uncertainty if their responsibilities for the care recipient interfere with the requirements of their paid work, thus contributing to increased stress and negative health outcomes (e.g., Cannuscio et al., 2004; Fast, Eagles, & Keating, 2001). Furthermore, in Canada caregivers—typically women—are often not eligible for employment benefits or tax breaks (Fast et al., 2001; Keefe, Hawkins, & Fancey, 2006). Education may be an additional source of stress given that caregivers may not have access to training due to time constraints, or they may lack the financial resources to participate in formal education. Transportation has been identified as a major stress for caregivers (Keefe et al., 2006; Litt, 2004). In Canada, caregivers often have to drive long distances to access the health-care services required by the care recipient. Community was included as a specific potential stressor because of the

Figure 1. Model of the Pathways from Caregiving Stressors to Health Impacts.

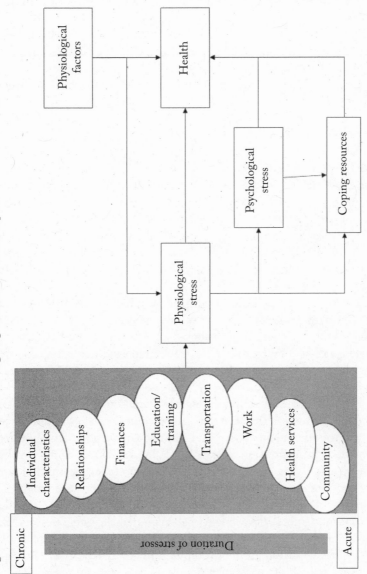

Adapted for caregivers from Brannen, Johnson-Emberly & McGrath (2008)

changing demography of Canada; many caregivers are "assigned" their role given their geographic proximity to a care recipient (Keefe et al., 2006). If this option isn't viable for a family, the caregiver may have to travel long distances to provide care, or arrange for caregiving support within the community. In rural Canada, the out-migration of young adults has depleted available informal support within communities, while contributing to the centralization of health-care services in larger towns and cities (Brannen et al., 2008). Thus, health services are included in our framework. The lack of appropriate and accessible services for care recipients is a major stressor for caregivers (Keefe et al., 2006). Support and education services for caregivers that are appropriate and accessible are scarce, a topic addressed later in this chapter.

Caregiving and Health

Given the considerable sources of stress for Canadian caregivers, it is not surprising that caregiving is stressful and often burdensome, thus contributing directly to considerable health risks. Caregiving responsibilities are often measured using a scale of perceived burden, with low scores indicating that a caregiver is unburdened and high scores the opposite. Schulz and Beach (1999) reported a 63% greater mortality rate between burdened caregivers and controls in a large sample of caregivers for disabled adults in the United States. This effect was not found for unburdened caregivers or for those with a disabled spouse who did not provide care. Countless studies on the negative health impacts of caregiving have been conducted (for a review with a Canadian perspective, see Morris, 2001). For Canadians, a study conducted by Keating et al. (1999) reported that caregiving negatively effected the health of 10.6% of male caregivers and 27.5% of female caregivers.

The mental-health implications of burdensome caregiving have received more attention than the physical outcomes. Several studies concerning caregivers for adults have found a strong connection between caregiving burden and depression (Bokmal & Schwarz, 2000; Chang, Brecht, & Carter, 2001; Cohen & Eisdorfer, 1988). For example, one-third of female caregivers for individuals with multiple sclerosis were distressed to the point they met criteria for diagnosis of a clinical mental disorder (Pakenham, 2005). Other studies have found that many female caregivers of Alzheimer's patients were clinically depressed (e.g., Gallant & Connell, 1997). Feelings of depression are more common than a diagnosis of clinical depression. The majority of women find caregiving stressful regardless of the type of care they provide, although more intense caregiving experiences are associated with greater risk of clinical depression. Qualitative studies have yielded similar results—many of the female focus-group participants from the Healthy Balance Research Program reported that caregiving led to feelings of depression and helplessness (Brannen, 2006a; 2006b). These women also discussed poor eating habits and disrupted and disturbed sleep, a finding echoed in quantitative research (e.g., Carter, 2002; Brummett, Babyak, Vitaliano, Ballard, Gwyther, & Williams, 2006). Chronic psychological distress and poor health behaviour can lead to major health consequences such as obesity and high blood pressure in caregivers (e.g., Atienza, Henderson, Wilcox, & King, 2001) and cardiovascular disease for those chronically stressed (Vitaliano, Scanlan, Zhang, Savage, Hirsch, & Siegler, 2002).

Caregiving, Health, Stress, and Gender

There have been numerous reports that women are more likely than men to suffer the negative health effects of caregiving, especially in regards to mental health (e.g., Feeney, Alexander, Noller, & Hohaus, 2003; Gallicchio, Siddiqi, Langenberg, & Baumgarten, 2002). One explanation for these findings is that caregiving is central to a woman's identity and, therefore, is more likely to lead to distress than in men (Haegedoorn, Sanderman, & Buunk, 2002). A second explanation is the differential-vulnerability hypothesis, which proposes that women, because of their higher risk of negative health outcomes and their lower status on the social gradient, have more stress and thus a greater likelihood of developing chronic health problems (e.g., Denton, Prus, & Walters, 2004; Elliot, 2000). Another possible explanation is that women shoulder the burden for the vast majority of caregiving and are more likely to be responsible for the most stressful tasks. Pinquart and Sörensen (2006) reported in their meta-analysis that women indicated their care recipient had more behavioural problems, that they provided more caregiving hours, helped with more caregiving tasks, and that they assisted with more personal care. Further, women had higher levels of caregiving burden and depression and lower levels of subjective well-being and physical health. However, once these stressors were controlled for, the gender differences in depression and physical health diminished and were similar to rates in non-caregiving samples. The results of this meta-analysis indicate that differential vulnerability and caregiving responsibilities interact for female caregivers.

Caregiving, Health, and Coping Resources

There is a tendency in the literature on caregiving to focus on external conditions, such as care-recipient characteristics, and ignore the role of individual abilities, such as coping resources. Two studies (Brannen & Keefe, 2006; Brannen et al., 2008). found higher levels of stress, poorer health, and lower life satisfaction were associated with increased age, being female, and lower education levels. However, these effects were diminished by personal competence, caregiver appraisal, and perceived available support. In addition, men reported smaller support networks and decreased caregiving satisfaction than did women. Using structural equation modelling, Brannen et al. found no significant moderating role of the coping resources of competence, satisfaction, or support-network size on health outcomes. In addition, there were no significant gender differences in the pathways among these constructs. These findings highlight the importance of effective coping strategies in offsetting the negative impacts of caregiving.

A separate study (Brannen & Petite, 2008) used a qualitative approach to explore themes of problem-focused, emotion-focused, and meaning-focused coping in a sample of 98 women from diverse backgrounds and caregiving situations. A narrative approach situated coping within the context of the caregiving experiences the women discussed. This permits a broader understanding of how coping strategies can help women to navigate caregiving and reduce stress. The framework was adapted from the Folkman & Lazarus (1980) approach to coping, which divides coping skills into problem-focused and emotion-focused. Problem-focused coping refers to strategies designed to reduce stress by working toward solutions, while emotion-focused strategies are those that help manage emotions and thereby reduce stress. Brannen & Petite added a category of meaning-focused strategies, such as benefit-finding, in their analysis. Successful meaning-focused coping leads to a reduction in stress because the individual finds relief in believing that there is meaning or purpose in the situation (see Folkman & Moskowitz, 2004). Religious beliefs, family obligations and values, or feelings of destiny are other types of meaning-focused strategies. In addition, perceived control over a stressor (in this case, caregiving) is a crucial moderator of the ability of a selected strategy to reduce stress and offset negative health impacts (e.g., Guzell, 2001; Park, Folkman, & Bostrom, 2001) A review of research with parents of chronically ill children found that five out of eight studies reported parents' need for control over their child's illness (Fisher, 2001).

Given these findings, Brannen & Petite (2008) postulated that high perceived control matched with problem-focused strategies was linked to lower stress, while emotion-focused strategies (e.g., positive reframing) fit best with lower perceived-control situations. Participants' narratives reflected this "goodness of fit" coping framework; the different strategies were more effective for stress reduction in relation to the amount of perceived control (see Park & Folkman, 1997; Park et al., 2001).

In Brannen & Petit (2008), the participants discussed more problem-focused than emotion-focused coping, and also demonstrated more controllability than had been hypothesized given the predictive bias that caregiving was a stressor over which women had little control. In situations of little control, caregivers tended to focus more on their ability to control their own emotions, while in situations with higher perceived control, participants turned their coping efforts toward managing the problem. This suggests that perceived control may be more important in managing caregiving burden than engaging in a specific coping strategy. When the participants engaged in emotion-focused strategies they were likely to discuss low perceived control and rarely reported a reduction in stress. Higher levels of control were more often found within problem-focused coping. In addition, higher levels of control accompanied participants' reduction in stress more frequently than any one coping strategy. Finally, the study explored whether stress reduction occurred as a result of participants' attempts to cope with caregiving. As predicted, where we could find explicit discussions around how participants felt in relation to their coping, stress reduction occurred when coping best matched their level of perceived control. Certainly, if caregivers can learn to incorporate these kinds of strategies into their experience, it may help to reduce stress.

Caregiving Education and Support Programs

Training in coping strategies is one aspect of caregiving education and support programs. While there are several successful examples of programs that incorporate coping-skills training and stress-management techniques, and provide education on the care recipient's condition and needs (Gitlin, Corcoran, Winter, Boyce, & Hauck, 2001; Hart et al., 2000; Hepburn, Tornatore, Center, & Ostwald, 2001; Lavoie et al., 2005), there has yet to be a structured review of the best practices for programs that support caregivers within specific conditions. Caregiving support and education programs are typically care-recipient condition-specific, whether for adults or children. A brief scan of existing programs for adults indicates that they typically include content that explicitly addresses management of caregiving strain, general stress, and coping techniques (e.g., Lavoie et al., 2005; Lesveque et al., 2003). Support programs for caregivers of children with significant health problems usually only include support and education for the management of the child's condition. In particular, parent-training programs concerning children with mental illness have been demonstrated as very effective, although they rarely include general stress-management techniques and training in coping skills for the primary caregiver (Brannen, van Zanten, Curran, Lawton, Whitney & Hambleton, 2008).

Participants in the focus groups of the Healthy Balance Research Program reported many positive aspects of caregiving; their responsibilities made them feel good about themselves and the skills they had acquired (Brannen, 2006a; 2006b). Women who reported these benefits did not have a "lighter" caregiving load than did depressed and stressed women, but, for a variety of reasons (some unclear), they were better able to manage their load and they did not feel depressed. One strategy to manage the caregiving load was the ability to draw on strong personal and community-support networks and knowledge of programs and services available to care recipients. Women in the focus groups who did not experience caregiving as stressful also believed that they had had a right to support and services. Thus, caregiving education and support programs should also incorporate techniques designed to help participants focus on the benefits of their responsibilities.

Caregiving support programs —with stress-management and coping-skills training—are a promising means for reducing caregiving burden but may also reduce health-system access and improve care recipients' health status if education is also provided in the intervention. However, the assumption that caregivers are willing and able to provide care without support from the health-care system underlies the general lack of such programs and poses a formidable barrier to their widespread development and implementation. A later section in this chapter will focus on this and other assumptions about caregiving within the health-care system, but here we turn to a discussion on additional barriers to education and support programs to set the context for the section on health-care assumptions.

Barriers to Participating in Programs

While caregiving education and support programs are a promising means for reducing caregiving burden and potentially improving the care recipient's health status, there are significant roadblocks at this intersection of caregiving, health, stress, and gender. As previously mentioned, assumptions about caregiving within the health-care system are perhaps the most daunting barrier. Additional challenges include resources, individual factors, family characteristics, and societal aspects. Resources for programs must be considered at both the system and individual level. However, almost all existing caregiving programs require the individual caregiver to physically attend. This practice requires considerable individual resources on the part of the caregiver. First, the programs are typically delivered during normal working hours, when the caregiver may be working herself or engaged in the health system with the care recipient. Second, physical attendance may require arranging care for the care recipient while the caregiver is at the program. Third, there are considerable incidental costs associated with attending such programs, from transportation to meals. Thus, these programs may further deplete the caregiver's financial resources. In addition, in-person settings are not for everyone—privacy is an important consideration for caregivers who may wish to treat their participation with discretion, and caregivers may perceive their attendance in programs as a sign of inability to cope with their responsibilities. This latter concern is squarely connected to the societal stigma surrounding caregiving: that women are natural-born caregivers and can cope with their responsibilities no matter how complex.

Overcoming Caregiving Program Barriers

We are proposing an inclusive model for caregiving education and support programs. At the core of the model is the caregiver; as such, there must be content that addresses her coping and stress-management capabilities. These skills are perhaps the best way to have benefits distributed across the family system. Education about the care recipient's health condition and health-service need is also vital to a successful program. Finally, content designed to facilitate family health ought to be included as family members (e.g., spouses, children) are often at risk of stress and negative health outcomes. These components are based on existing research as regards each part of the model. In addition, there is ample evidence regarding the delivery of such programs in a manner that is appropriate and accessible for the caregiver, care recipient, and the recipient's family. One way to help ensure that the programs are suitable is to include community in the development of research and intervention. Community-based participatory research, such as the model used in the Caregiving, Health, and Work (Brannen, Norris, Petite, & Baldwin, 2007), increase the likelihood that research projects will lead to implemented programs. Another important variable concerns programs that are focused on the caregiver's reality rather than the requirements of the health-care system. Telecommunications technologies, such as telehealth and e-health, can be applied to caregiving education and support programs that can be delivered within the caregiver's home and at her convenience. Smith and Toseland (2006) developed a telephone support program for caregivers of the elderly that demonstrated significant reductions in burden and depression. The REACH for TLC program effectively delivered information using interactive voice-response technology (i.e., similar to telephone banking; Mahoney, Tarlow, & Jones, 2003). As part of the Family Help program, we are currently piloting a similar approach for parent training with parents of young children with disruptive behaviour (Whitney, Varalli, Brannen, McGrath, & Cunningham, 2007). The Family Help model delivers a variety of parent training (Lingley-Pottie, Watters, McGrath, & Janz, 2005) and caregiver support programs (e.g., for postpartum depression; Brannen et al., 2006), a self-directed approach based on cognitive-behavioural techniques, with the support of a telephone coach and manual. Stress-management and mindfulness training are techniques that are also promising for caregiving education and support programs. Such programs are more economical at both the individual and the system level; however, systematic assumptions about caregiving must be overcome before an organized movement to implement these programs is undertaken.

Assumptions in the Health-Care System

There are four overarching assumptions at the intersection of caregiving and the health-care system. First, there is the assumption that caregivers provide the bulk of care, not professional health-care providers. This no-cost provision of services, which are often complex, is at the core of the Canadian balance between the so-called social safety net and individual responsibility for sick family members. This assumption has been reported by others (e.g., Blakley & Jaffe, 1999).

Second, agents in the health-care system, from policy-makers to front-line staff, often hold the assumption that caregivers have the necessary skills required to acquire, interpret, and implement health information. This perceived ability to navigate the system has been discussed by Aronson and Neysmith (2001). Sawatzky and Fowler-Kerry (2003) contend that the movement to the wellness model within the health-care system actually increases the system's reliance on caregivers. Further to this, increasing rates of chronic disease across the lifespan indicate corresponding increases in the requirements of caregivers (e.g., Hawyard & Colman, 2003). Preliminary results from our study on disability and health-care stress among rural Nova Scotians (aged 18 to 49) indicated that 40% of participants either had a chronic illness themselves or were providing care for a family member with one in their household, or both (Brannen, Gallant, Johnson-Emberly, & McGrath, forthcoming). In addition, the aging of the Canadian population indicates that the increase in the prevalence of chronic disease and the associated need for caregivers will amplify in the coming years (e.g., Evans, McGrail, Morgan, Barer, & Hertzman, 2001). All these factors contribute to the necessity of addressing this assumption through systemic change, ranging from policy to caregiving education and support programs (for a review of proposed changes to policy, see Keefe et al., 2006).

Caregiving support and education programs may attempt to provide caregivers with information needed to better manage the care recipient's health (e.g., Silver, Wellman, Galindo-Ciocon, & Johnson, 2004). However, the health literacy of the caregiver is not typically considered. Health literacy—an individual's ability to interpret and apply health information—is an area of concern given the amount of research indicating that many do not adhere to treatments and therefore do not end up accessing services. As a result, health literacy has been identified as a priority by the Canadian Public Health Association (Rootman & Gordon-El-Bihbety, 2008). Caregiving programs need to include health literacy as an embedded feature, with attention to evaluating individual ability to interpret and apply both of the caregiving-focused aspects (e.g., stress management, coping-skills training) and those directed at improving the care recipient's health (e.g., treatment information).

The third assumption is not limited to the health-care system and exists in society overall: that caregivers have the ability to cope with the demands of care provision and that their own health doesn't suffer as a result of their responsibilities. There needs to be a translation of the literature extant to all levels of the health-care system.

The final assumption is that caregivers' lives do not interact with treatment. This is evidenced in many ways. Caregiving programs that are focused on the health-care system and not on the caregiver assume that the caregiver has no time or resource constraints, and, if she does, that these are secondary to the health-care system. In addition, the lack of formal supports for caregivers, such as practical employment support programs, provides further evidence. These four assumptions are at the intersection of caregiving, health, stress, and gender.

Where Do We Go From Here?

In order to overcome the assumptions, all those involved with caregiving—from policy-makers to researchers to caregivers themselves—need to work together to devise an agenda to support caregivers and get them moving out of the intersection through appropriate education and support programs and other mechanisms, such as income programs. Gender-based analyses is an analytical approach that is well-suited to undoing these assumptions (Health Canada, 2000). An underdeveloped area of research is how the assumptions within the health-care system interface with families. In particular, there has been a scarcity of inquiry on how these assumptions effect the delivery of health services—from the individual provider to the policy level. For example, do health-care providers who hold these assumptions treat caregivers differently than those who do not? On the other hand, how do families who believe in the assumptions approach caregiving? In particular, do caregivers within families holding these assumptions feel greater burden? These are a couple of potential avenues for research. There should also be a knowledge exchange between researchers and those within the health-care system regarding the various populations of caregivers, particularly between caregiving for disabled adults and children with chronic illness.

Caregiving For a Child With a Chronic Illness

Caregiving for chronically ill children has not benefited from the same level of inquiry as caregiving for adults has, although there is a considerable literature on parental stress in relation to children with chronic illness (as previously noted). These are two different foci of caregiving for an individual who is ill. In the adult-caregiving literature, there is an assumption that caregiving for another adult could be burdensome because it is an exception from normal adult life. In the latter, there is the assumption that providing care for one's own children—whatever their health status—is natural and, therefore, not burdensome. In the former, caregiver attributes are not seen as pivotal for the health status of the care recipient, while parents' mental health, stress, and socio-demographic variables are viewed as direct correlates of child-health status. Not surprisingly, this is where the bulk of research investigation has focused. As discussed, providing care for a chronically ill child can compound normative parenting stress. In addition, parents may encounter secondary traumatic stress arising from the onset (i.e., an accident) or health care (i.e., high-stakes surgery) required for their child (Brannen & Grandia, 2007). Parent-training programs concerning children with disruptive behaviour disorders offer an entry point for the development of similar programs for caregiving for a chronically ill child. One problem with most parent-training programs, regardless of the child's condition, is that the focus is on the management of the child's health problem. Another feature of these programs is that they focus on the mother, with little opportunity for fathers to be involved. Fathers' changing role as caregivers needs to be addressed in program development in particular, and in caregiving research in general (Health Canada, 2003). There needs to be education and support programs for parents of chronically ill children that incorporate techniques used in successful training programs, but that also include stress-management and coping-skills training.

Development of Caregiving Programs

Researchers, practitioners, policy-makers, and caregivers have to work together from the outset of projects in order to develop caregiving education and support programs that will work in the real world. This collaborative approach helps to ensure implementation of research findings. There are models for developing education and support programs that increase the likelihood that they will be used by caregivers and become integrated within the health-care system. On the latter point, there is also a need to develop expertise in cost-benefit analyses of caregiving programs within the Canadian health-care system. While cost-benefit analyses have been undertaken in other countries, such as the United States, there is a lack of within Canada. Finally, programs need to be implemented within the health-care system in a manner that enables caregivers to participate before their own health is in jeopardy. All of these ambitions require the development of networks prior to studies being undertaken; health-research funding, particularly from the Canadian Institutes of Health Research, should provide funding opportunities that are suitable for the development of collaborations and the ensuing research programs testing interventions.

Conclusions

This chapter has attempted to use the analogy of a four-way intersection to illustrate how gender, stress, health, and caregiving all meet at the access point to the health-care system. Studies on coping resources and skills demonstrate their role in diminishing stress and the negative health impacts often associated with burdensome caregiving, regardless of gender. Thus, coping skills may be one important way to move beyond being at a four-way stop with the health-care system and move toward better caregiver and care-recipient health. Evidence-based education and support programs incorporating training in coping, developed in conjunction with all those surrounding the caregiver—from policy-makers to caregivers and care recipients—have the potential to reduce health-system usage by both the care recipient and the caregiver. However, the underlying assumptions about caregiving within the health-care system block caregiving programs from being widely implemented. In order to remedy this situation, researchers must engage in knowledge exchange with those working within the health-care system, especially decision makers. By developing collaborative teams, researchers can develop and the health-care system can implement education and support programs that work in the real world. Education and support programs are not sufficient to stop the amplifying requirements of informal caregiving, but they offer promise as a solution that empowers caregivers through skills augmentation, while reducing health-care costs. The ultimate outcome of this approach will be the reduction of burden and improved health for caregivers, with added benefits of better care-recipient health and savings within the health-care system.

References

Aronson, J., & Neysmith, S. (2001). Manufacturing social exclusion in the home care market. *Canadian Public Policy/Analyse de politiques, 26*(2), 151–165.

Atienza, A. A., Henderson, P. C., Wilcox, S., & King, A. C. (2001). Gender differences in cardiovascular response to dementia caregiving. *The Gerontologist, 41*(4), 490–498.

Blakley, B., & Jaffe, J. (1999) *Coping as a Rural Caregiver: The Impact of Health Care Reforms on Rural Women Informal Caregivers.* Winnipeg, MB: Prairie Centre of Excellence for Women's Health.

Brannen, C. (2006a). Beliefs, choice and coping: Examining the role of agency in women's caregiving experiences. *Poster presented at the Annual Convention of the Canadian Psychological Association,* Calgary, AB.

Brannen, C. (2006b). Coping with caring: Women's use of coping mechanisms to ease caregiving stress. Presented at Narrative Matters 2006 (international conference on qualitative research), Wolfville, NS.

Brannen, C., McGrath, P. J., Johnston, C., Dozois, D., Elgar, F., & Whitehead, M. (2006). Managing Our Mood

(MOM): Distance treatment for post-partum depression in rural Nova Scotia. Presented at the annual conference of the Canadian Rural Health Research Society, Prince George, BC.

Brannen, C., & Grandia, P. (N.p.). Support and Family Education for Secondary Traumatic Stress (SAFESTS) Proposal Development Project. (2007, March). *Disaster and Trauma Times of Canada. Canadian Psychological Association.*

Brannen, C., & Keefe, J. (2006). Coping with caregiving: The roles of personal competence and perceived support on caregiver well-being. Presented at the 35th Annual Scientific & Educational Meeting of the Canadian Association on Gerontology, Quebec City, QC.

Brannen, C., & Petite, K. (2008). A qualitative exploration of women's coping with caregiving. *Journal of Health Psychology, 13,* 355–365.

Brannen, C., Johnson-Emberly, D., & McGrath, P. J. (in press). A review of sources of stress for rural Canadians. *Health & Place.*

Brannen, C., Gallant, S., Johnson-Emberly, D., & McGrath, P. J. (Forthcoming). Chronic illness and health care stressors in rural Nova Scotians aged 18-49. N.p.

Brannen, C., Keefe, J., Woodman, T., & Hawkins, G. (in press). Exploring the connections between caregiving intensity, coping resources, and the well-being of caregivers. *Journal of Health Psychology* .

Brannen, C., Petite, K., Norris, D., & Baldwin, C. (2007). A collaborative framework exploring the connections between mental health and caregiving of Canadian military members: Reflections on a work-in-process. *Australian Community Psychologist, 19*(1), 74–82.

Brannen, C., van Zanten, S., Curran, J., Lawton, E., Whitney, M., & Hambleton, L. Stress management interventions for caregivers of children with disruptive behaviour disorders. [Protocol]. Cochrane Database of Systematic Reviews. http://www. cochrane.org/index.htm

Brummett, B. H., Babyak, M. A., Vitaliano, P. P., Ballard, E. L., Gwyther, L. P., & Williams, R. B. (2006). Associations among perceptions of social support, negative affect, and quality of sleep in caregivers and noncaregivers. *Health Psychology, 25*(2), 220–225.

Cannuscio, C. C., Colditz, G. A., Rimm, E. B., Berkman, L. F., Jones, C. P., & Kawachi, I. (2004). Employment status, social ties, and caregivers' mental status. *Social Science and Medicine, 58,* 1247–1256.

Carter, P. A. (2002). Caregivers' descriptions of sleep changes and depression. *Oncology Nursing Forum, 29,* 1277–1283.

Chang, B. L., Brecht, M-L., & Carter, P. A. (2001). Predictors of social support and caregiver outcomes. *Women and Health, 33*(1/2), 39–61.

Cohen, D., & Eisdorfer, C. (1988). Depression in family members caring for a relative with Alzheimer's disease. *Journal of the American Geriatrics Society, 36*(10), 885–889.

Denton, M., Prus, S., & Walters, V. (2004). Gender differences in health: A Canadian study of the psychosocial, structural and behavioural determinants of health. *Social Science and Medicine, 58,* 2585–2600.

Denton, M., & Waters, V. (1999). Gender differences in structural and behavioural determinants of health: An analysis of the social production of health. *Social Science and Medicine, 48,* 1221–1235.

Elliot, M. (2000). The stress process in neighborhood context. *Health & Place, 6,* 287–299.

Evans, R. G., McGrail, K. M., Morgan, S. G., Barer, M. L., & Hertzman, C. (2001). Apocalypse now: Population aging and the future of health care systems. *Canadian Journal on Aging,* 20(1), 160–191.

Fast, J., Eales, J., & Keating, N. (2001) *Economic Impact of Health, Income Security and Labour Policies on Informal Caregivers of Frail Seniors.* Ottawa: Status of Women Canada.

Feeney, J., Alexander, R., Noller, P., & Hohaus, L. (2003). Attachment insecurity, depression, and the transition to parenthood. *Personal Relationships, 10*(4), 475–493.

Fisher, H. R., (2001). The needs of parents with chronically sick children: A literature review. *Journal of Advanced Nursing, 36*(4), 600–607.

Folkman, S., & Lazarus R. S. (1980). An analysis of coping in a middle-aged community sample. *Journal of Health and Social Behavior, 21,* 219–239.

Folkman, S., & Moskowitz, J. T. (2004). Coping: Pitfalls and promise. *Annual Review of Psychology, 55,* 745–774.

Gallant, M. P., & Connell, C. M. (1997). Predictors of decreased self-care among spouse caregivers of older adults with dementing illnesses. *Journal of Aging and Health, 9,* 373–395.

Galliccho, L., Siddiqi, N., Langenberg, P., & Baumgarten, M. (2002). Gender differences in burden and depression among informal caregivers of demented elders in the community. *International Journal of Geriatric Psychiatry, 17,* 154–163.

Gitlin, L. N., Corcoran, M., Winter, L., Boyce, A., & Hauck, W. W. (2001). A randomized, controlled trial of a home environmental intervention: Effect on efficacy and upset in caregivers and on daily function of persons with dementia. *Gerontologist, 41*(1), 4–14.

Guzell, J. R. (2001). Perceived control over caregiving: Association with mothers' and fathers' observed interactions with their 12 month old infants. *Dissertation Abstracts International: Section B: The Sciences & Engineering, 61*(8-B), 4447.

Haegedoorn, M., Sanderman, R., & Buunk, B. P. (2002). Failing in spousal caregiving: The 'identity-relevant stress' hypothesis to explain sex differences in caregiver distress. *British Journal of Health Psychology, 7*(4), 481–487.

Hart, G., Meagher-Stewart, D., Stewart, M. J., MacPherson, K., Doble, S., & Makrides, L. (2000). Dyadic peer support for family caregivers. In M. J. Stewart (Ed.), *Chronic Conditions and Caregiving in Canada: Social Support Strategies* (pp. 147–171). Toronto: University of Toronto Press,.

Hastings, R. P. (2003). Child behaviour problems and partner mental health as correlates of stress in mothers and fathers of children with autism. *Journal of Intellectual Disability Research, 47*(4-5), 231–237.

Hawranik, P., & Strain, L. (2000) *Health of informal caregivers: Effects of gender, employment and use of home care services.* Winnipeg, MB: Prairie Women's Health Centre of Excellence.

Hayward, K., & Colman, R. (2003). *The tides of change: Addressing inequity and chronic disease in Atlantic Canada. A Discussion Paper.* Prepared for Population and Public Health Branch, Atlantic Regional Office, Health Canada. Retrieved May 27, 2008, from http://www.gpiatlantic.org/ publications/health.shtml

Health Canada. (2003). Canadian Caregiver Coalition: Roundtable on the Role of Men in Caregiving. Health Canada. Retrieved June 6, 2007, from http://www.hc-sc.gc.ca/hcs-sss/pubs/home-domicile/2003-men-hommes/2003-men-hommes-3-eng.php

Hepburn, K. W., Tornatore, J., Center, B., & Ostwald, S. W. (2001). Dementia family caregiver training: affecting beliefs about caregiving and caregiver outcomes. *Journal American Geriatric Society, 49*(4), 450–457.

Keating, N., Fast, J., Frederick, J., Cranswick, K., & Perrier, C. (1999) *Eldercare in Canada: Context, content and consequences.* Ottawa: Statistics Canada.

Keefe, J., Hawkins, G., & Fancey, P. (2006). *A Portrait of Unpaid Care in Nova Scotia.* Halifax, NS: Atlantic Centre of Excellence for Women's Health.

Lavoie J. P., Ducharme, F., Levesque, L., Hebert, R., Vezina, J., Gendron, C., Preville, M., St-Laurent, C., & Voyer, L. (2005). Understanding the outcomes of a psycho-educational group intervention for caregivers of persons with dementia living at home: A process evaluation. *Aging Mental Health, 9(1)*, 25–34.

Levesque, L., Gendron, C., Vezina, J., Hebert, R., Ducharme, F., Lavoie, J. P., Gendron, M., Lingley-Pottie, P., Watters, C., McGrath, P., & Janz, T. (2005). Providing family help at home. Proceedings of 38th annual Hawaii International Conference on System Sciences [CD-ROM]. New York: Computer Science Press.

Litt, J. (2004). Women's carework in low-income households: The special case of children with Attention Deficit Hyperactivity Disorder. *Gender & Society, 18(5)*, 625–644.

Lingley-Pottie, P., Watters, C., McGrath, P., & Janz, T. (2005). Providing family help at home. Proceedings of the 38th Annual Hawaii International Conference, 03–06 January 2005, 138a–138a. IEEE.

MacDonald, M., Phipps, S., & Lethbridge, L. (2005). Taking its toll: Implications of paid and unpaid work responsibilities for women's well-being. *Feminist Economics, 11*(1), 63–94.

Mahoney, D. F., Tarlow, B. J., & Jones, R. N. (2003). Effects of an automated telephone support system on caregiver burden and anxiety: Findings from the REACH for TLC intervention study. *The Gerontologist, 43*(4), 556–567.

Mandleco, B., Frost Olsen, S., Dyches, T., & Marshall, E. (2003). The relationship between family and sibling functioning in families raising a child with a disability. *Journal of Family Nursing*, 9(4), 365–396.

McDougall, J., & Miller, L. (2003). Measuring chronic health condition and disability as distinct concepts in national surveys of school-aged children in Canada: A comprehensive review with recommendations based on the ICD-10 and ICF. *Disability & Rehabilitation, 25*(16), 922–939.

Morris, M. (2001). Gender sensitive home and community care and caregiving research: A synthesis paper. Health Canada: Ottawa. Retrieved June 2, 2008, from http://www.cewh-cesf.ca/PDF/health_reform/synthesis.pdf

Pakenham, K. I. (2005). Relations between coping and positive and negative outcomes in carers of personal with Multiple Sclerosis (MS). *Journal of Clinical Psychology in Medical Settings, 12*(1), 25–38.

Park, C. L., & Folkman, S. (1997). Meaning in the context of stress and coping. *Review of General Psychology, 1,* 115–144.

Park, C. L., Folkman, S., & Bostrom, A. (2001). Appraisals of controllability and coping in caregivers and HIV + Men: Testing the Goodness-of-Fit Hypothesis. *Journal of Consulting and Clinical Psychology, 69*(3), 481–488.

Pinquart, M., & Sörensen, S. (2006). Gender differences in caregiver stressors, social resources, and health: An updated meta-analysis. *Journal of Gerontology, 61*(1), 33–45.

Roeher Institute. (2000) *Beyond the Limits: Mothers Caring for Children with Disabilities.* North York, ON: L'Institut Roeher Institute.

Rootman, I., & Gordon-El-Bihbety, D. (2008). *A vision for a health literate Canada.* Ottawa: Canadian Public Health Agency.

Sawatzky, J. E., & Fowler-Kerry, S. (2003). Impact of caregiving: Listening to the voice of informal caregivers. *Journal of Psychiatric and Mental Health Nursing, 10,* 277–286.

Schulz, R., & Beach, S. R. (1999). Caregiving as a risk factor for mortality: The caregiver health effects study. *Journal of the American Medical Association, 282*(23), 2215–2219.

Silver, H. J., Wellman, N. S., Galindo-Ciocon, D., & Johnson, P. (2004). Family caregivers of older adults on home enteral nutrition have multiple unmet task-related training needs and low overall preparedness for caregiving. *Journal of the American Dietetic Association, 104,* 43–50.

Sit, J. W. H., Wong, T. K. S., Clinton, M., Li, L. S. W., & Fong, Y. (2003). Stroke care in the home: The impact of social support on the general health of family caregivers. *Journal of Clinical Nursing, 13,* 816–824.

Smith, T. L., & Toseland, R. W. (2006). The effectiveness of a telephone support program for caregivers of frail older adults. *The Gerontologist, 46*(5), 620–629.

Tsai, T. C., Liu, S. I., Tsai, J. D., & Chou, L. H. (2006). Psychosocial effects on caregivers for children on chronic peritoneal dialysis. *Kidney International, 70,* 1983 – 1987.

Vitaliano, P. P., Scanlan, J., Zhang, J., Savage, M. V., Hirsch, I. B., & Siegler, I. C. (2002). A path model of chronic stress, the metabolic syndrome, and coronary heart disease. *Psychosomatic Medicine, 64,* 418–435.

Whitney, M., Varalli, V., Brannen, C., McGrath, P., & Cunningham, C. (2007). *CATHI: An automated telephone intervention for families.* Poster session presented at the IWK Interdisciplinary Research Conference, Halifax, NS.

Toba Bryant

The Canadian Welfare State as a Determinant of Women's Health

Introduction

Public policies and their impact on the health of populations have gained the attention of population-health researchers in recent years (Bambra, 2007; Eikemo & Bambra, 2008). Research has shown that countries with public policies that support populations, such as higher public spending on health and social programs and services, have lower premature mortality, lower infant mortality, and lower child-poverty rates than countries with lower spending in these public-policy areas (Navarro, 2002; Navarro & Shi, 2001). These countries also tend to have higher population-health status in general (Raphael, 2007a). In addition, women in such countries tend to have better health (Bambra, 2004).

This chapter builds upon on an earlier analysis that examined the influence of the welfare state on the health of Canadian women (Raphael & Bryant, 2004). The chapter focuses on the welfare state as a vehicle for progressive social and health policies. It looks at public policy and how it influences the distribution of social and economic resources in a society through the welfare state, thereby influencing population health and the quality of life of women. Comparing data on health and social spending in Canada with four comparison nations, it is argued that public policies that highlight deficit reduction by reducing public spending will accentuate social and economic inequalities and contribute to lower quality of life for the population in general, and for women in particular.

Feminist Political Economy

The analysis of these issues is guided by a feminist political-economy approach that emphasizes the influence of societal structures and economic and political interests on public-policy outcomes. It does so through a gender analysis. The political-economy approach is concerned with how the organization of the production and distribution of social and economic goods such as income, employment, and housing influences the health of a population in general (Coburn, 2006). A feminist political economy considers issues of gender as critical for understanding the impact of these processes on women and men (Armstrong, 2004). Specifically, it considers how gender, social class, and race/ethnicity structure opportunities for access to, and the quality of, various social determinants of health, such as employment, housing, and income.

Quality of Life

Quality of life is an interdisciplinary concept upon which there has been little consensus on a definition, yet has an intuitive importance that makes it an attractive concept for researchers attempting to influence public policy by engaging the public (Michalski, 2001). One contributor to its increased popularity has been the health-promotion movement, (Raphael, Brown, Renwick, & Rootman, 1997; Raphael, Renwick, Brown, & Rootman, 1996). "Quality of life" tends to refer to positive aspects of health, as does health promotion, and attempts to identify "the good life" (Lindstrom, 1992). Hence, the term has application for understanding and evaluating the well-being of women, and specifically how the public policies of the welfare state influence the quality of life and health outcomes for women.

A key aspect of the welfare state is its provision of citizen security through the development of supportive social and health policy (Teeple, 2006). Women's economic vulnerability renders them particularly susceptible to changes in these policies. Women's economic status in advanced political economies such as Canada and the United States makes them more likely to experience adverse effects as a result of public policies that reduce social and health spending by governments (Davies & McMullin,

2001). Women are more likely to be adversely affected by policy changes in unemployment insurance, health and social-service provision, and housing, among others (Pederson & Raphael, 2006). This is particularly the case if they are lone parents.

Importance of Public Policy

Public policies are critical determinants of resource distribution and this distribution influences the health of populations (Raphael, 2004). They influence the distribution of income, power, and material resources in a society. These resources have come to be known as the "social determinants of health." These refer to living conditions such as housing security, income security, food security, and employment security, among others (Raphael, 2004).

Promoting public policies that benefit the health of a population has been identified as a critical pathway for influencing the social determinants of health (Canadian Public Health Association, 1996). As one example, public policies that emphasize deficit reduction and expanding the role of the private sector in health care and other social-policy areas can lead to poorer health within a population (Armstrong, Amaratunga, Bernier, Grant, Pederson, & Wilson, 2002; Coburn, 2004). Such policies can increase inequalities between high- and low-income groups and between women and men, and can increase conflict between groups in a society. Systematic differences in policy approaches to these issues have been identified as being related to variations in the form the welfare state takes in different nations (Esping-Andersen, 1990; 1999).

The Welfare State

The welfare state refers to intervention by government in health and social-policy areas to provide services and programs to support the population (Briggs, 1961). Canada and the United Kingdom both developed their welfare states in the years immediately following the Second World War. In these nations, the welfare state developed in response to demands from unions and the working class, among other groups, for protection from the insecurity many experienced during the Depression of the 1930s (Teeple, 2000). A series of income-support programs, such as social assistance and pensions for seniors, were developed, in addition to public-health-care programs to ensure access to these services. Access came to be seen as an entitlement of citizenship.

The welfare state also represents a means of redistribution from high-income groups to low-income groups in a society (Teeple, 2000). For example, the establishment in Canada of Medicare, the national health-insurance program, is financed by public revenues. High-income groups pay higher income taxes than do low-income groups, yet they make less use of these services than do low-income Canadians.

Numerous typologies of welfare states have been developed to classify the different types of regimes and programs provided (Bambra, 2007). Of these typologies, Esping-Andersen's welfare-state typology is one of the most cited (Esping-Andersen, 1990; 1999). At the time of his initial development of the three distinct welfare-state regimes, in 1990's *The Three Worlds of Welfare Capitalism*, Esping-Andersen recognized that while the societies he included in the welfare-state typology did not comprise a large number of cases, they did distinguish themselves into three distinct groups. The distinguishing feature of these nations was their identification with three specific ideological traditions of political mobilization and political philosophy: conservatism, liberalism, and socialism. He argued that these features were linked to particular aspects of their contemporary social-policy approach, as well as to their broader political and economic features (Arts & Gelissen, 2001). In other words, the form that welfare states assume in different countries is shaped by economic interests and political ideology. The next sections examine and explain the three welfare regimes in Esping-Andersen's typology.

Social-Democratic Welfare State

The social-democratic welfare state provides generous income support and other social programs (Esping-Andersen, 1990). These programs are universal in scope. The social-democratic welfare state has an overall mission to reduce inequalities, eliminate poverty, and promote full employment (Saint-Arnaud & Bernard, 2003). Typical such states include Sweden, Norway, Denmark, and Finland. Sweden began to form its welfare state in the 1930s. It is well ahead of most other advanced political economies in developing programs supportive of the health and well-being of its population (Burstrom, Diderichsen, Ostlin, & Ostergren, 2002). For example, Sweden has integrated a social-determinants-of-health approach into public policies (Agren & Hedin, 2002). It thereby recognizes the impact of income and other living conditions on the health of a population. Sweden's income support and other programs have reduced its poverty rate significantly compared with other member countries of the Organization for Economic Co-operation and Development (OECD; 2007).

Liberal Welfare State

In contrast, the liberal welfare state represents the most undeveloped form of the three types of welfare regimes (Myles, 1998). It provides modest universal transfers and social-insurance plans to its citizens, who must undergo some form of means or income testing to determine eligibility (Esping-Andersen, 1990). As a result, social assistance is the primary form of support provided and is usually targeted to the least well-off. This type of regime provides basic social-safety nets, minimal relief for individuals who are unable to compete successfully in the marketplace, and benefits or programs as a right of citizenship or national residency. It is a residual approach to social welfare based on the belief that if welfare benefits are too generous, recipients will prefer to depend on these benefits rather than seek out employment for earned income (Saint-Arnaud & Bernard, 2003). For Esping-Andersen, the liberal welfare state is exemplified by Australia, Canada, Ireland, New Zealand, the United States, and the United Kingdom.

Conservative/Corporatist Welfare State

The conservative/corporatist (also termed Christian democratic) welfare regime is characterized by either paternalist or sometimes authoritarian approaches that historically have had strong ties with the church (Esping-Andersen, 1990). Examples of such have been found in Germany, France, Netherlands, Belgium, Spain, and Italy. Esping-Andersen considers these nations "corporatist" because of their "statist" and "organicist" traits. In other words, conservative welfare states are structured to maintain and reproduce existing differences in status, income, and wealth among social classes and sectors. There is rather little commitment to creating an egalitarian society. Conservative welfare regimes use a range of separate but state-mandated and state-directed social-insurance programs for members of different sectors of the economy (Esping-Andersen, 1990). These are financed primarily by employers and workers. The benefit levels provided vary by sector, with higher-paid employees receiving more generous benefits. Conservative welfare states stress social insurance as opposed to social assistance or universal measures. They redistribute income over the life cycle of a single individual or family to ensure that support is available in old age, sickness, or during periods of unemployment.

Value of *The Three Worlds of Welfare Capitalism*

Esping-Andersen's typology has received mixed reviews. While some analysts consider that his typology has value, they also argue that it may need to be modified to reflect recent developments and changes in the welfare state and in political economy, such as the impact of economic globalization on the welfare state (Bambra, 2007). Some criticize Esping-Andersen's welfare clusters as promoting ideal types of welfare states, as few can be defined as "pure types" (Arts & Gelissen, 2001). It has been argued that ideal-type welfare states cannot sufficiently capture the differences and unique features of different welfare-state regimes. Some attribute this limitation to the lack of theory in the area.

Treatment of Gender in *The Three Worlds of Welfare Capitalism*

Esping-Andersen has also been criticized for not being sufficiently sensitive to gender issues with respect to the welfare state. Bambra's (2004) analysis showed that Esping-Andersen was neither "gender-blind nor illusory". His later work focused on some of these neglected issues (Esping-Andersen, 1999).

Feminist analysts argue that Esping-Andersen's typology should include the sexual division of paid and unpaid work, particularly care and domestic work done inside the home that women usually chiefly perform (Lewis, 1992; O'Connor, 1993; Sainsbury, 1996). Specifically, feminist authors also note that women continue to experience discrimination with respect to social rights because of their differing labour-market position compared with men. Women's employment is usually related to their gender roles and responsibilities (Armstrong, 2006; Bourgeault, 2006).

Creation of New Welfare Clusters

Some also disagree with the inclusion of Mediterranean countries as underdeveloped welfare states in the corporatist/conservative cluster (Bonoli, 1997; Ferrera, 1996; Leibfried, 1992). These analysts advocate creating a fourth cluster for Mediterranean countries, arguing that they represent an exemplar of their own as opposed to a subgroup within the corporatist cluster (Bambra, 2007; Saint-Arnaud & Bernard, 2003).

Similarly, Castles (1998) argues that Australia and New Zealand differ significantly from other liberal welfare states. He proposes an antipodean cluster to reflect their unique and more inclusive approach to social support than is reflected in Esping-Andersen's liberal cluster.

As the above illustrates, many amendments and additions have been proposed to Esping-Andersen's welfare-state typology; yet it remains one of the most used typologies in spite of the absence of theory in the area and its apparent limitations.

Exclusion of Health and Health Care from the Clusters Typology

Another important limitation of the typology is its exclusive focus on income-support programs and the exclusion of health care. Indeed, all but the United States in the liberal welfare cluster have universal health-care programs.

Drawing on Esping-Andersen's welfare-state typology, Navarro and Shi (2001) added health to compare the impact of political traditions in the developed OECD countries from 1945 to 1980 using social-democratic, Christian-democratic, liberal, and ex-fascist regimes. They examined four specific policy areas: the primary determinants of income inequality, levels of public expenditures and health-care coverage, support programs for families, and infant mortality as a measure of population health. They found that political traditions that favour economic- and social-redistributive policies and full employment tended to be more successful in their efforts to improve the health of their populations. The social-democratic countries of Sweden, Norway, Denmark, Finland, and Austria scored highest for union density; public spending on health, education, and welfare; and women's participation in the paid labour force.

All of these analyses provide insights into the primary characteristics of welfare states, and on the influence of political traditions on the form of welfare states. In virtually all of the welfare-state typologies, Canada and the United States are in the liberal cluster (Bambra, 2007). Although it tends to score higher than the United States on health care and for its public spending on social and health programs, much recent evidence suggests that Canada's welfare state is becoming more similar to that of the United States'. To wit, it provides minimal support to families and less to income-support programs, and has allowed the expansion of the private sector into health care (Raphael, 2008).

Ideological Differences Among Welfare States

Despite the critiques of the three welfare-state clusters, Esping-Andersen demonstrated how ideology influences the form the welfare state takes in different nations. Figure 1 shows the basic forms of the welfare state in developed political economies such as Canada and the United States (Saint-Arnaud & Bernard, 2003). The key elements of the guiding principles and the primary institutions in each type of welfare state are outlined in the figure.

Saint-Arnaud and Bernard (2003) devised this figure to map the differences among the welfare-state clusters identified by Esping-Andersen. Using cluster analysis, they identify the key institutions in each type of welfare state, the guiding principle of each type of regime, the focus, and the key institution for delivering these programs.

The social-democratic welfare states, exemplified by the Scandinavian countries, emphasize equality, which requires a strong role for the state in the delivery of programs and services to a population (Saint-Arnaud & Bernard, 2003). As stated above, these countries are committed to reducing inequality and eliminating poverty. They also are committed to a greater extent than other nations to promoting gender equity (Bambra, 2004).

Figure 1. Ideological Variations in Forms of the Welfare State

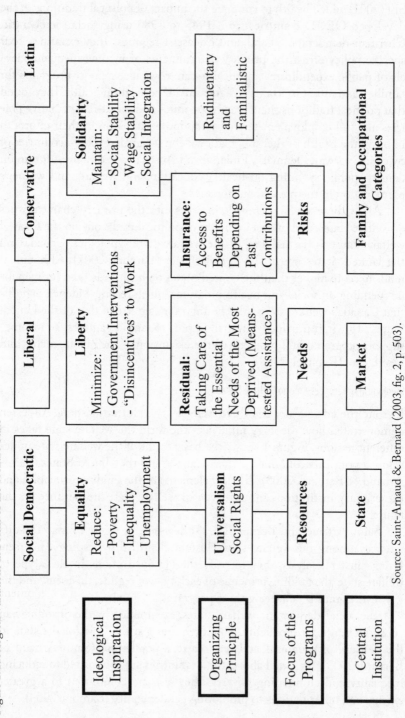

Source: Saint-Arnaud & Bernard (2003, fig. 2, p. 503).

In contrast, liberal welfare states exemplified by the Anglo-Saxon countries of Canada, the United States, and the United Kingdom emphasize minimal government intervention and, usually, means-tested social provision. Such provision is targeted to destitute populations and is only concerned with addressing short-term or immediate need. The principle organization in the liberal welfare state is the market.

Research has shown that countries with universal social programs, such as Sweden and the other social-democratic nations, have lower poverty rates compared with liberal welfare states, such as Canada and the United States (Navarro, 2002). They also tend to have more inclusive programs that reflect the differences in women's and men's employment patterns. It should come as no surprise that the liberal countries have more income inequality and poorer population health.

Methodology and Analysis

The purpose of this chapter is to provide an update on women's quality of life in Canada in specific relation to two exemplars of the divergent forms of the welfare state: liberal (United States and United Kingdom) and social democratic (Sweden and Denmark). It interprets these findings within a gender-based political-economy analysis.

Several Canadian policy organizations have outlined aspects of a quality-of-life analysis. For the present analysis, the quality-of-life themes defined by the Canadian Policy Research Networks (CPRN) will be applied (Michalski, 2001). The CPRN developed quality-of-life themes based on a consultation with Canadian citizens on the priority areas that affect quality of life in Canada.

Among the priority themes identified in the CPRN consultation are: political rights and general values and health including health care, education, and social programs. This chapter examines the extent to which these quality-of-life themes identified by the CPRN are supported by government action in Canada and four comparison nations. The information used to examine these issues is derived from indicators supplied by the OECD and the human-development measures provided in the UN *Human Development Report* (OECD, 2006; OECD, 2007; United Nations Development Programme [UNDP], 2007b).

What Does the International Evidence Show?

Many indicators that measure human development have been devised. These include indicators of health, measures of inequality, and a variety of indicators of social and public policy in support of citizen security.

Life Expectancy

Among the most important of these is life expectancy at birth. Life expectancy at birth is an important indicator of well-being and quality of life in a nation. Compared with men, women in most industrialized countries tend to have longer life expectancies. The United Nations Development Programme (UNDP) provides women's life expectancy for all nations. Figure 2 shows the rates for Canada and the four comparison nations: Sweden, Denmark, the United States, and the United Kingdom.

Canadian women have a high life expectancy of almost 83 years on average, which is close to Sweden's (82.5 years). Between 1960 and 2002, average life expectancy in Canada rose by 8.4 years. Life expectancy for women in the United Kingdom and the United States fall well behind Sweden and Canada, and Denmark is well behind all, an issue that remains an active area of debate.

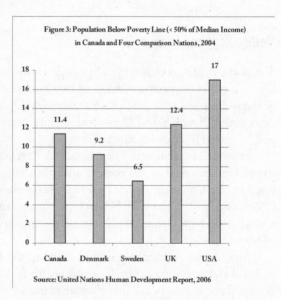

Figure 3: Population Below Poverty Line (< 50% of Median Income) in Canada and Four Comparison Nations, 2004

Source: United Nations Human Development Report, 2006

Poverty as a Measure of Women's Quality of Life

The international definition of living in poverty is an income of less than 50% of the median income—half of the population has income above the median and half below—within a society (Innocenti Research Centre, 2000; 2005). Living in poverty means that one is unable to participate in cultural and other activities and obtain the basic amenities usually expected of citizens living in these nations. Among the five nations in this analysis, Canada ranks third in its ability to maintain vulnerable populations above the poverty line (see fig. 3).

Among the comparison nations examined, the social-democratic nations of Sweden and Denmark have been able to make significant reductions in poverty with their comprehensive social programs. Income transfers serve to lower poverty rates for the most vulnerable populations. In contrast, the United Kingdom and the United States have the highest poverty rates.

Income Inequality

The depth of poverty in a society reflects overall inequality in the distribution of income between high- and low-income groups. An important measure of income inequality is the share of income held by the richest and poorest 10% of a population (see fig. 4).

As figure 4 shows, the richest 10% of the population in Canada hold almost 25% of the income in the country, while the poorest 10% have less than 3% of the income. In Sweden, for example, the richest 10% have 22% of the income. While this may appear to be only a slight statistical difference between the two nations, the disparity is huge in terms of the quality of life of the poorest 10% in Canada compared with the same group in Sweden. Not surprisingly, the United States and United Kingdom perform poorly on this measure, while Denmark is very similar to Sweden.

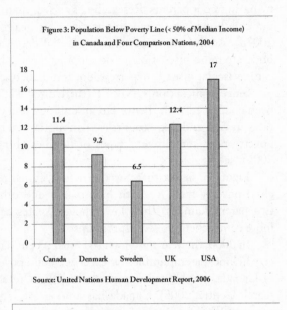

Figure 3: Population Below Poverty Line (< 50% of Median Income) in Canada and Four Comparison Nations, 2004

Source: United Nations Human Development Report, 2006

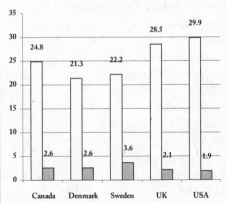

Figure 4: Inequality in Income in Canada and Four Comparison Nations, 2000: Share held by Riches and Poorest 10% of the Population

Source: United Nations Human Development Report, 2006

Child Poverty

Increasing income inequality has led to increasing child-poverty rates. Child poverty is a reflection of family poverty as poor children are defined by having poor parents. Research has shown that material deprivation during childhood has serious implications for health in adulthood (Raphael, 2007d). Adults who experienced material deprivation during their childhood are more susceptible to developing chronic health conditions such as cardiovascular disease, hypertension, and diabetes.

Since its inception, UNICEF (the United Nations Children's Fund) has been concerned with the welfare of children and documents child-poverty rates in rich and poor countries. Among its interests is comparing child-poverty rates for different types of families (Innocenti Research Centre, 2005) (see fig. 5).

Figure 5 shows that Sweden and Denmark have among the lowest child-poverty rates for both lone-parent and other family types, such as two-parent families. Their lower poverty rates can be attributed to their more comprehensive social programs.

In 2000, the year for which the most recent data is available, child poverty in lone-parent families far exceeded child poverty in other family types in Canada, the United Kingdom, and the United States (Innocenti Research Centre, 2005). Canada has among the highest child-poverty rates among OECD countries, particularly for lone-parent families. Canada's 2006 census (the most recent) shows that women lead 83% of lone-parent families. Indeed, unattached women in Canada of all ages are more likely to live in poverty and for longer periods than are unattached men (McCracken & Watson, 2004).

Poverty among families deepens when the lone parent is unemployed (see fig. 6). Lone parents who are unemployed are more likely to be living in poverty than lone parents who are employed (OECD, 2005).

As at 2000, lone-parents who are unemployed in Canada and the United States have higher poverty rates, respectively, than the other three comparison

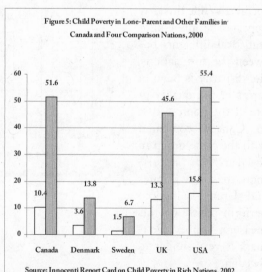

Figure 5: Child Poverty in Lone-Parent and Other Families in Canada and Four Comparison Nations, 2000

Source: Innocenti Report Card on Child Poverty in Rich Nations, 2002

nations. Almost 90% of unemployed lone parents in Canada are living in poverty. Few supports are provided to reduce poverty in this group. Canada has been more successful at reducing poverty in elderly families, but not in non-elderly families with children. Canada's poverty rate far exceeds those of Sweden's, Denmark's, and the United Kingdom's.

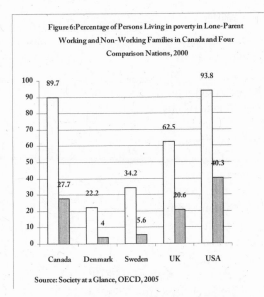

Figure 6: Percentage of Persons Living in poverty in Lone-Parent Working and Non-Working Families in Canada and Four Comparison Nations, 2000

Source: Society at a Glance, OECD, 2005

Public Spending

Spending by governments on education, social programs, and health care has a significant impact on health outcomes and on poverty, particularly for women (Rainwater & Smeeding, 1995; Vleminckx & Smeeding, 2001). The OECD and the UNDP report annually on government spending on health and social programs and on indicators of government activities, such as the provision of supports and services to citizens in a country. Government transfers are a key indicator of social provision (Bryant, 2006). Transfers are fiscal resources generated by the economy that governments use to distribute to the population in the form of services, income supports, or investments in social infrastructure. Such infrastructure includes education, employment training, social assistance and welfare payments, and family supports (i.e., child-care programs), among others. Research has shown that countries with high expenditures in these areas have lower poverty rates and better population health (Navarro & Shi, 2001; Raphael, 2007d).

In 2003, gross public social spending represented 21% of GDP on average across the OECD countries (OECD, 2006). The largest areas of public social spending included pensions (7% of GDP on average), health (6%), and income transfers to the working-age population.

Canada spent more than the OECD average on health, at just under 7% of its GDP, and over 5% on education (see fig. 7). Among the comparison nations, Sweden spent the most on health and education. Denmark spent less on health and more on education, followed by the United Kingdom and the United States.

Social Spending

As noted above, government spending is an important indicator of population health in general and of women's health in particular. Spending in several broad social-policy areas can highlight the extent of government commitment to maintaining the health of a population.

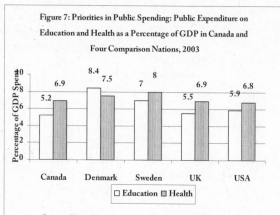

Figure 7: Priorities in Public Spending: Public Expenditure on Education and Health as a Percentage of GDP in Canada and Four Comparison Nations, 2003

Source: United Nations Human Development Report, 2006

Against the other compared nations, Canada's total social spending lags behind Sweden's and Denmark's. Canada again is more consistent with the U.S. approach to cash benefits and services, whose rates are the lowest among the four countries presented here. Social spending in the United States is the lowest among the comparison nations, at less than 8%. Low spending has implications for quality of life and health of women, and for achieving gender equality (fig. 8).

Gender Equality

An important measure of gender equality is labour-force activity by men and women. In terms of economic activity by gender, Canadian women's participation rate is 78% of men's levels and their earnings are 68% of men's earnings. Once again, Sweden ranks higher. The U.S. and U.K. rates are consistent with Canada's.

Participation in Elected Governmental Institutions

Figure 10 shows that in the social-democratic nations, political participation in elected office mirrors the percentage women earn of men's earnings. These findings are consistent with measures of gender empowerment. Again, Denmark and Sweden outrank Canada, the United States, and the United Kingdom on these measures. The Scandinavian countries have implemented measures to improve gender equality, which have also contributed to lower poverty rates for all groups.

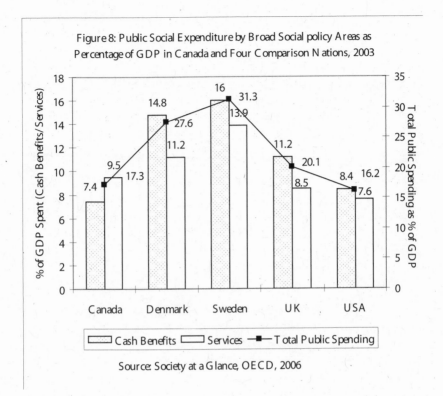

Figure 8: Public Social Expenditure by Broad Social policy Areas as Percentage of GDP in Canada and Four Comparison Nations, 2003

Source: Society at a Glance, OECD, 2006

Discussion

Canada's rank on many of the human-development indicators falls well below the representatives of the social-democratic regimes. Further levels of Canadian achievement on these indicators fall below the average of the OECD nations (Raphael, 2007a). Among this larger sample of developed nations, Canada ranks sixth for life expectancy for women (OECD, 2005), for example.

Public-policy commitments to spending in support of social and health programs are also below the OECD average (OECD, 2007a; OECD, 2007b). Canadian spending trends in recent years suggest that the federal and provincial governments will continue to reduce social spending (Scarth, 2004). Although women's life expectancy at birth in Canada is as high as that for Swedish women, it may very well not keep up with increases made in OECD nations demonstrating such commitments.

The reduction in federal-government spending in health and social services programs has forced provincial governments to spend more on these programs. The reduced federal spending in income support and housing programs, for example, has prompted some provincial governments to download social housing to municipal governments (Shapcott, 2004). The

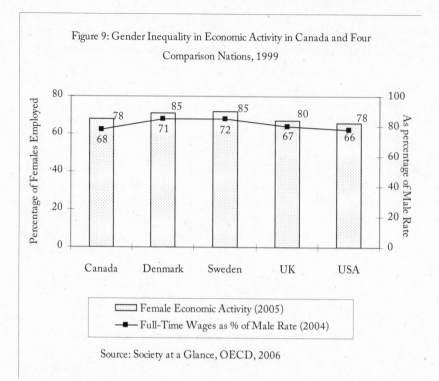

Figure 9: Gender Inequality in Economic Activity in Canada and Four
Comparison Nations, 1999

Source: Society at a Glance, OECD, 2006

withdrawal of senior governments from these areas has contributed to income and housing insecurity, which research shows has adverse implications for the health of a population (Bryant, 2004).

Reduced spending levels also contributes to higher poverty rates among
female lone-parent families (Raphael, 2007b). Female lone parenting does
not have to mean living in poverty, though. In Sweden, for example, female
lone parents are entitled to numerous programs and supports that reduce
their familiar poverty rates to levels low by Canadian standards (Innocenti
Research Centre, 2005).

An examination of employment patterns, as shown in figure 9, illustrates
the differences between Canada as an exemplar of a liberal welfare state and
Sweden as an exemplar social-democratic welfare state. The Swedish state
provides universal daycare and has a strong commitment to active labour
policy (OECD, 2004). Active labour policy refers to policies and programs
such as training and retraining programs for employees who have lost their
jobs through restructuring. Such programs enable the unemployed to re-
enter the labour force. Daycare enables female lone parents to work or to
participate in retraining programs to facilitate their re-entry into the work
force (Freiler, Rothman, & Barata, 2004).

Lone parents in Canada face living in poverty whether they are employed or unemployed, although the poverty rate for unemployed lone par-

ents is higher. While there is still some inequality in Sweden and Denmark, Canada, the United Kingdom, and the United States have extremely high poverty rates among families in general and for lone-parent families in particular. Employment alone does not appear to protect against poverty (Campaign 2000, 2004). Many jobs in Canada are precarious—about 25%, in fact—and Canada has one of the highest rates of women working in low-wage occupations (31%) (Jackson, 2004). That is, they have low job security, few or no benefits, and low remuneration.

Women's Employment Situation

Women's employment situation has contributed to their insecurity. During the early 1980s and early 1990s, Canada endured deep recessions that led to high levels of unemployment (Jackson, 2005). Although the national unemployment rate fell below 7% for the first time since the 1980s, economic growth has produced more jobs with little security and has increased income inequality in Canada. Some argue, in fact, that the contemporary unemployment rate is actually closer to 12% (Swartz, 2003).

Canada has one of the highest employment-participation rates among advanced industrialized economies. Approximately eight in ten (78%) of people aged 15 to 64 years participate in the paid labour force (Jackson, 2005). In 2004, 58% of all women aged 15 years and older were part of the paid labour force. This represents an increase of 42% since 1976 (Statistics Canada, 2006). The proportion of men who were employed fell to 68% from 73%. Women comprised 47% of the paid workforce in 2004. By 2004, 65% of women with children under three-years-old were working.

Women are more likely than men to work part-time (Jackson, 2005; Statistics Canada, 2006). In 2004, women comprised roughly seven in ten of all part-time employees. There is continued occupational and industrial segregation between men and women (Jackson, 2005; Statistics Canada, 2006). Women continue to be concentrated in public and social services as opposed to the business sector. In 2004, 67% of all employed women were in teaching, nursing and related health occupations, clerical or other administrative occupations, and sales and services.

The types of jobs women have tend to be more precarious and insecure compared with those of men (Jackson, 2005). Precarious jobs, also called "non-standard jobs" in Canada, are insecure jobs that have a high risk of unemployment and/or low pay, and offer limited access to benefits, such as pensions and drugs and dental plans. They usually entail limited control of hours and conditions of work. While some women choose part-time employment to accommodate educational pursuits or child-care responsibilities, approximately one in three women who work part-time would work full time if they could (Jackson, 2004). In 2004, 26% of female part-time employees reported that they worked part-time because they were unable to find full-time employment (Statistics Canada, 2006). And since they tend to have low job insecurity women may be more likely to experience frequent periods of unemployment, and they are especially likely to have difficulty accessing unemployment benefits (Townsend & Hayes, 2007; Tremblay, 2004).

Decline of the Canadian Welfare State

The welfare state has helped to improve the quality of women's lives in most countries. However, during the 1980s, most industrialized political economies, including Sweden, reduced social spending. The Canadian welfare state has seen serious erosion to programs that provided support to individuals during periods of unemployment, for example.

Unemployment insurance (UI), long a feature of the Canadian welfare state, was replaced by employment insurance (EI) in 1992. A worker paid into UI benefits, and was entitled to these benefits upon losing a job until their re-entry into the labour force. Under EI, unemployed workers are entitled to receive only 52 weeks of benefits. Upon termination of EI benefits, a worker unable to secure employment within the benefit period must apply for social assistance. Social assistance is provincially administered. Restricting eligibility for EI benefits has caused social-assistance rolls to swell and has contributed to increasing incidence of poverty for female lone-parent families, as shown (Townsend & Hayes, 2007).

In 1996, the Liberal federal government tightened eligibility requirements, making it more difficult for part-timer workers—the majority being women—to collect their EI contributions (Black & Shillington, 2005). Continuing cuts to EI has led to limited eligibility for benefits and to lower amounts paid out. Such change exacerbates insecurity, which research consistently shows has material implications for health and well-being. The Canadian Centre for Policy Alternatives found that (Townsend & Hayes, 2007) about 40% of unemployed men receive EI, compared with 32% of unemployed women. This gap has been attributed to the failure of the program to recognize the different patterns of women's paid employment, and their care responsibilities within their families.

Lack of a National Child-Care Program

Canada has also failed to support women in other areas of service provision. For example, Canada has yet to establish a national child-care program. In 2005, under pressure from the leader of the left-of-centre New Democratic Party, Jack Layton, then-Prime Minister Paul Martin committed to establish a national child-care program, among other programs, to support families and urban centres in the country. In November 2005, Martin's government was defeated in a non-confidence motion. Upon its election in January 2006, the minority Conservative government of Stephen Harper

scrapped the agreement that Martin had reached with Layton. The government replaced the proposed universal program by paying families with
children $100 per child per month for child-care expenses. This amounts to
$1,200 a year, which barely covers child-care expenses.

There is a continuing lack of child-care spaces across Canada, a situation that forces many parents to enrol their children in unlicensed child
care, or, in some cases, women to leave their jobs to care for their children
(Friendly, 2004). Child care increases women's participation in the labour
force, as demonstrated by the proportion of working women in Sweden and
Denmark, discussed earlier.

Implications for the Health of Women

Limited employment opportunities and income insecurity have serious implications for the health of women. Their economic insecurity tends to increase their susceptibility to developing chronic diseases such as cardiovascular disease, hypertension, and diabetes, among others (Raphael, 2007c).

An important report shows that low-income women—primarily those
living on social assistance or working in non-standard employment—have
four times the incidence of type 2 diabetes compared with high-income
women (Hux, Booth, & Laupacis, 2002). Indeed, Statistics Canada found
that women living in low-income neighbourhoods had a much greater incidence of mortality related to diabetes compared with women in high-
income neighbourhoods (Wilkins, Berthelot, & Ng, 2002). Moreover, the
incidence of diabetes in low-income neighbourhoods in Canada has increased dramatically compared with high-income neighbourhoods.

Implications for Gender Equality

Canada's failure to support health and social programs has implications not
only for women's health but also for achieving gender equality. In 1995,
Canada's performance on the UN's human-development index ranked first.
But its ranking in the United National Development Index fell to ninth
when women's equality was factored in. Currently, Canada's ranking has
fallen to eighth (from first) in the most recent UN *Human Development
Report* (UNDP, 2007a), suggesting that little has changed from 1995.

In 1995, the UN noted:

> [I]nequality (for women) is entrenched in every facet of Canadian
> life. Not only has progress been too slow, but in the past few years

the situation for women in Canada has been progressively worse in all areas of social, economic and political life. Every indicator shows that there has been a growth of women's inequality—as a direct result of policies and political choices made by the government of Canada."

Decisions to implement public policies to support population health and the health of women are political decisions. They are driven by the ideological commitments of governments (Raphael, 2007b). Canada's performance on a range of social and health indicators shows that while Canada has the resources to expand and improve social and health programs, it has failed to do so. This is largely a reflection of Canada being identified as a liberal welfare state. Such categorization, however, is not destiny, and concerned political activity can shift this orientation. Continued vigilance by international tribunals such as the UN and by domestic social and health movements is essential to improve women's health and quality of life. Key to this is establishing and implementing public policies in support of gender equity.

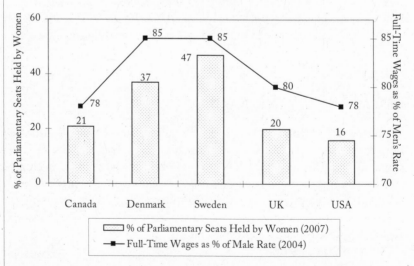

Figure 10: Two Measures of Gender Empowerment: % of Parliamentary Seats Held by Women (2007) and Gender Inequality in Full-Time Wages (2004) in Canada and Four Comparison Nations,

Source: Society at a Glance, OECD, 2006 and United Nations Human Development Report, 2007/2008

References

Agren, G., & Hedin, A. (2002). *The New Swedish Public Health Policy.* Retrieved http://www.fhi.se/pdf/roll_eng.pdf

Armstrong, P. (2004). Health, Social Policy, Social Economies, and the Voluntary Sector. In D. Raphael (Ed.), *Social Determinants of Health: Canadian Perspectives, 331-44.* Toronto: Canadian Scholars' Press.

Armstrong, P. (2006). Gender, Health, and Care. In D. Raphael, T. Bryant & M. Rioux (Eds.), *Staying Alive: Critical Perspectives on Health, Illness and Health Care,* 287-303. Toronto: Canadian Scholars' Press.

Armstrong, P., Amaratunga, C., Bernier, J., Grant, K., Pederson, A., & Wilson, K. (2002). *Exposing Privatization: Women and Health Care Reform in Canada.* Toronto: Garamond.

Arts, W., & Gelissen, J. (2001). Welfare states, solidarity and justice principles: Does the type really matter? *ACTA Sociologica, 44,* 283–299.

Bambra, C. (2004). The worlds of welfare: illusory and gender blind? *Social Policy and Society, 3*(3), 201–211.

Bambra, C. (2007). Going beyond The three worlds of welfare capitalism: regime theory and public health research 10.1136/jech.2007.064295. *J Epidemiol Community Health, 61*(12), 1098–1102.

Black, J., & Shillington, E. R. (2005). *Employment Insurance: Research Summary for the Task Force for Modernizing Income Security for Working Age Adults.* Toronto: Toronto City Summit Alliance.

Bonoli, G. (1997). Classifying Welfare States: A two-dimension approach. *Journal of Social Policy, 26*(3), 351–372.

Bourgeault, I. (2006). The provision of care: Professions, politics, and profit. In D. Raphael, T. Bryant, & M. Rioux (Eds.), *Staying alive: Critical perspectives on health, illness, and health care.* Toronto: Canadian Scholars' Press.

Briggs, A. (1961). The welfare state in historical perspective. *European Journal of Sociology, 2,* 251–259.

Bryant, T. (2004). Housing and health. In D. Raphael (Ed.), Social Determinants of Health: Canadian Perspectives, 217-232. Toronto: Canadian Scholars' Press.

Bryant, T. (2006). Politics, public policy and population health. In D. Raphael, T. Bryant, & M. Rioux (Eds.), *Staying Alive: Critical Perspectives on Health, Illness, and Health Care* (pp. 193–216). Toronto: Canadian Scholars' Press.

Burstrom, B., Diderichsen, F., Ostlin, P., & Ostergren, P. O. (2002). Sweden. In J. Mackenbach & M. Bakker (Eds.), *Reducing Inequalities in Health: A European Perspective* (pp. 274–283). London: Routledge.

Campaign 2000. (2004). *Honouring Our Promises: Meeting the Challenge to End Child and Family Poverty, 2003 Report Card on Child Poverty in Canada.* Toronto: Campaign 2000.

Canadian Public Health Association. (1996). *Action Statement for Health Promotion in Canada.* Retrieved July, 2002, from http://www.cpha/cpha.docs/ActionStatement.eng.html

Castles, F. G. (1998). *Public Policy: Patterns of Post-war Transformation*. Cheltenham, UK: Edward Elgar.

Coburn, D. (2004). Beyond the income inequality hypothesis: Globalization, neo-liberalism, and health inequalities. *Social Science & Medicine, 58*, 41–56.

Coburn, D. (2006). Health and Health Care: A Political Economy Perspective. In D. Raphael, T. Bryant, & M. Rioux (Eds.), *Staying Alive: Critical Perspectives on Health, Illness, and Health Care.* (pp. 59–84). Toronto: Canadian Scholars' Press.

Davies, L., & McMullin, J. A. (2001). *Social Policy, Gender Inequality and Poverty*. Ottawa: Status of Women Canada.

Eikemo, T. A., & Bambra, C. (2008). The welfare state: a glossary for public health 10.1136/jech.2007.066787. *J Epidemiol Community Health, 62*(1), 3–6.

Esping-Andersen, G. (1990). *The Three Worlds of Welfare Capitalism*. Princeton, NJ: Princeton University Press.

Esping-Andersen, G. (1999). *Social Foundations of Post-Industrial Economies*. New York: Oxford University Press.

Ferrera, M. (1996). The "Southern" Model of Welfare in Social Europe. *Journal of European Social Policy, 6*(1), 17-37.

Freiler, C., Rothman, L., & Barata, P. (2004). *Pathways to progress: Structural solutions to address child poverty*, from http://www.campaign2000.ca/res/dis.html

Friendly, M. (2004). Early childhood education and care. In D. Raphael (Ed.), *Social Determinants of Health Canadian Perspectives*. Toronto: Canadian Scholars' Press.

Hux, J., Booth, G., & Laupacis, A. (2002, Sept 18). *The ICES Practice Atlas: Diabetes in Ontario*. Retrieved September, 2002, from http://www.ices.on.ca/

Innocenti Research Centre. (2000). *A league table of child poverty in rich nations*. Florence: Innocenti Research Centre.

Innocenti Research Centre. (2005). *Child Poverty in Rich Nations, 2005. Report Card No. 6*. Florence: Innocenti Research Centre.

Jackson, A. (2004). The unhealthy Canadian workplace. In D. Raphael (Ed.), *Social Determinants of Health: Canadian Perspectives*. Toronto: Canadian Scholars' Press.

Jackson, A. (2005). *Work and Labour in Canada: Critical Issues*. Toronto: Canadian Scholars' Press.

Leibfried, S. (1992). Towards a European welfare state? On integrating poverty regimes into the European Community. In Z. Ferge & J. E. Kolberg (Eds.), *Social policy in a changing Europe*. Frankfurt: Campus Verlag.

Lewis, J. (1992). Gender and the development of welfare regimes. *Journal of European Social Policy, 2*(3), 159–173.

Lindstrom, B. (1992). Quality of Life: A Model for Evaluating Health for All. *Soz Praventivmed, 37*, 301–306.

McCracken, M., & Watson, G. (2004). *Women Need Safe, Stable, Affordable Housing; A Study of Social, Private and Co-op Housing in Winnipeg*. Winnipeg, MB: Prairie Women's Health Centre of Excellence.

Michalski, J. H. (2001). *Asking Citizens What Matters for Quality of Life in Canada: Results of CPRN's Public Dialogue Process*. Ottawa: Canadian Policy Research Networks.

Myles, J. (1998). How to Design a "Liberal" Welfare State: A Comparison of Canada and the United States doi:10.1111/1467-9515.00120. *Social Policy and Administration, 32*(4), 341–364.

Navarro, V. (Ed.). (2002). *The Political Economy of Social Inequalities: Consequences for Health and Quality of Life.* Amityville, NY: Baywood Press.

Navarro, V., & Shi, L. (2001). The Political Context of Social Inequalities and Health. *International Journal of Health Services, 31*(1), 1–21.

O'Connor, J. S. (1993). Gender, class and citizenship in the comparative analysis of welfare state regimes: Theoretical and methodological issues. *The British Journal of Sociology, 44*(3), 501–518.

Organisation for Economic Co-operation and Development (OECD). (2004). *OECD Employment Outlook 2004.* Paris: OECD.

OECD. (2005). *Society at a Glance: OECD Social Indicators, 2005 Edition.* Paris: OECD.

OECD. (2006). *Society at a Glance: OECD Social Indicators.* Paris: OECD.

OECD. (2007a). *Society at a glance. 2006 edition.* Paris: OECD.

OECD. (2007b). *Health at a Glance: OECD Indicators 2007.* Paris: OECD.

Pederson, A., & Raphael, D. (2006). Gender, race, and health. In D. Raphael, T. Bryant & M. Rioux (Eds.), *Staying Alive: Critical Perspectives on Health, Illness, and Health Care*, 139-158. Toronto: Canadian Scholars' Press.

Rainwater, L., & Smeeding, T. (1995). *Doing Poorly: The Real Income of American Children in a Comparative Perspective.* Retrieved from http://lissy.ceps.lu/wpapersentire .htm, then ftp://lissy.ceps.lu/127.pdf

Raphael, D. (2004). Introduction to the social determinants of health. In D. Raphael (Ed.), *Social Determinants of Health: Canadian Perspectives.* Toronto: Canadian Scholars' Press.

Raphael, D. (2007a). Canadian Public Policy and Poverty in International Perspective. In D. Raphael (Ed.), *Poverty and Policy in Canada: Implications for Health and Quality of Life.* Toronto: Canadian Scholars' Press.

Raphael, D. (2007b). The Politics of Poverty. In D. Raphael (Ed.), *Poverty and policy in Canada: Implications for Health and Quality of Life*, 335-364. Toronto: Canadian Scholars' Press.

Raphael, D. (2007c). Poverty and Health: Mechanisms and Pathways. In D. Raphael (Ed.), *Poverty and Policy in Canada: Implications for Health and Quality of Life*, 239-268. Toronto: Canadian Scholars' Press.

Raphael, D. (2007d). *Poverty and Policy in Canada: Implications for Health and Quality of Life.* Toronto: Canadian Scholars' Press.

Raphael, D. (2008). Public policy and population health in the USA: Why is the public health community missing in action? *International Journal of Health Services, 38*, 63–94.

Raphael, D., Brown, I., Renwick, R., & Rootman, I. (1997). Quality of Life: What are the Implications for Health Promotion? *American Journal of Health Behavior, 21*(2), 118–128.

Raphael, D., & Bryant, T. (2004). The welfare state as a determinant of women's health: Support for women's quality of life in Canada and four comparison nations. *Health Policy, 68*, 63–79.

Raphael, D., Renwick, R., Brown, I., & Rootman, I. (1996). Quality of life indicators and health: Current status and emerging conceptions. *Social Indicators Research, 39*, 65–88.

Sainsbury, D. (1996). *Gender, equality and welfare states.* Cambridge, UK: Cambridge University Press.

Saint-Arnaud, S., & Bernard, P. (2003). Convergence or resilience? A hierarchical cluster analysis of the welfare regimes in advanced countries. *Current Sociology, 51*(5), 499–527.

Scarth, T. (Ed.). (2004). *Hell and High Water: An Assessment of Paul Martin's Record and Implications for the Future.* Ottawa: Canadian Centre for Policy Alternatives.

Shapcott, M. (2004). Housing. In D. Raphael (Ed.), *Social Determinants of Health: Canadian Perspectives.* Toronto: Canadian Scholars' Press.

Statistics Canada. (2006). *Women in Canada: A Gender-Based Statistical Report.* Ottawa: Minister of Industry.

Swartz, M. (2004, September 25). The REAL unemployment figure: It's much higher than we're led to believe. *Toronto Star* D12.

Teeple, G. (2000). *Globalization and the Decline of Social Reform: Into the Twenty First Century.* Aurora, ON: Garamond Press.

Teeple, G. (2006). Foreword. In D. Raphael, T. Bryant & M. Rioux (Eds.), *Staying Alive: Critical Perspectives on Health, Illness, and Health Care*, 1-4. Toronto: Canadian Scholars' Press.

Townsend, M., & Hayes, K. (2007). *Women and the Employment Insurance program.* Ottawa: Canadian Centre for Policy Alternatives.

Tremblay, D. G. (2004). Unemployment and the labour market. In D. Raphael (Ed.), *Social Determinants of Health: Canadian Perspectives.* Toronto: Canadian Scholars' Press.

United Nations. (1995). *Commitments of the U.N. World Summit on Social Development.* Copenhagen: United Nations.

United Nations Development Programme (UNDP). (2007a). *Human development report 2007/2008. Fighting climate change: Human solidarity in a divided world.* New York: Palgrave Macmillan.

UNDP. (2007b). *Human Development Report 2007/2008: Fighting climate change: Human solidarity in a divided world.* New York: UNDP.

Vleminckx, K., & Smeeding, T. (Eds.). (2001). *Child Well-being, child poverty and child policy in modern nations.* Bristol, UK: The Policy Press.

Wilkins, R., Berthelot, J.-M., & Ng, E. (2002). Trends in mortality by neighbourhood income in urban Canada from 1971 to 1996. *Health Reports (Stats Can), 13*(Supplement), 1–28.

Deone Curling, Soma Chatterjee and Notisha Massaquoi

Women's Transnational Locations as a Determinant of Mental Health: Results from a Participatory-Action Research Project with New Immigrant Women of Colour in Toronto

Migrating to a new country can be a time of stress, uncertainty, and transition. For many immigrants, it is a process of transnational mobility to establish a new home in the host country and renegotiating one's role within families left behind in the country (or countries) of origin.[1] This physically and emotionally challenging trajectory involves losses in socio-economic status and social networks, separation from extended family, and discrimination manifesting itself at multiple levels in the host society. These stressors are particularly destructive given they may threaten the core of a person's identity and have been linked to mental-health challenges among immigrants in general and immigrant women in particular (Cassidy et al., 2004; Mawani, 2008; Smith, Lalonde, & Johnson, 2004; Zelkowitz et al.). Immigrant women in Canada report a higher incidence of depression compared with their Canadian-born counterparts (Schreiber, Stern, & Wilson, 1998; Zelkowitz et al., 2004) and are also at greater risk of experiencing mental-health challenges (Franks & Faux, 1990). In this chapter, we argue that women's migration as a transnational process may have serious emotional impacts, and that it is particularly crucial for mental-health-service providers to be aware of and understand the process of transnational mobility and adaptation.

In Canada, current immigration and settlement policies add to immigrant women's settlement challenges (Crawford, 2007) as there is a persistent and disturbing trend of economic marginalization of immigrant women in Canada. For instance, women are one-third as likely as men to be accepted into Canada as the principal applicant in the economic class. Only 10% of economic immigrants are women, while 37% of all immigrant women are classified as "spouses or dependents" of economic immigrants (Statistics Canada, 2006). In the category of family-class immigrants (i.e., those sponsored by close family members), 36% of all immigrant women are family-class immigrants (Statistics Canada, 2006).

In terms of financial status, only 32% of women in the family class are employed six months after their arrival, compared with 54% of men. Men who are classified as spouses or dependents are 8% more likely to be employed than women in the same class (of which more than two-thirds are unemployed) (Statistics Canada, 2006). Thirty-five percent of women who immigrated to Canada between 1991 and 2001 were living in a low-income household (Statistics Canada, 2006). Forty-two percent of female immigrants under the age of 15, almost three times as many as their non-immigrant counterparts (17%), was living in a low-income household (Statistics Canada, 2006). Because the vast majority of immigrants coming to Canada are classified as visible minorities,[2] it is evident that the Canadian immigration and settlement process is becoming a socio-economically marginalizing experience based on both race and gender.

Of particular concern, is the fact that very few immigrant women actually recognize and/or acknowledge that these processes of economic marginalization and discrimination can lead to mental-health challenges (Massaquoi, 2004). Starting with an account of a *transnational feminist framework*—our premise in this chapter—we demonstrate the need to integrate "transnationalism" into our understanding of immigration and women's mental health. This framework demonstrates how women are linked to both their communities of origin and their communities of resettlement through intricate flows of capital, labour, culture, ideologies, and knowledge production (Grewal & Kaplan, 1994). Using this framework as the lens to interpret our research, we see that immigration turns many women into transnational health promoters since the well-being of families, communities, and nations is ensured through long-distance caregiving in the country of origin, regardless of an immigrant woman's current location in Canada (Gastaldo, Gooden, & Massaquoi, 2005). Transnationalism, therefore, is a process that demands that we pay attention to the gendered power relations embedded in global migration and immigration. The social aspects of identity become embedded in geographic movement—with inevitable positive and negative encounters occurring as a result (Grewal et al. 2001; Massaquoi, 2004).

The chapter describes a mixed-methods (i.e., qualitative and quantitative) study designed to explore the various ways new immigrant women in Canada care for their mental health and well-being, and how that translates into health and well-being for their communities both here in Canada and abroad. Using a participatory-action research model, and administering the satisfaction-with-life scale to new immigrant women, the study documents how, amid a high degree of systemic discrimination, immigrant women manage to care for themselves, their families, and their communities.

Transnational Feminist Framework

A highly feminized movement of labour from the global South to the North underscores the Canadian nation-state's development and organization around capitalism, class formation, and the constant racializing and gendering of its political economy (Bannerji, 2000; Gabriel, 1996; Henry, 2005; Smith et al., 2004). As more and more "foreign" bodies cross the borders of the state, demarking and "otherizing" based on the Canadian notions of legitimacy, loyalty, and ownership becomes rampant and immigrants are increasingly seen as more marginal than central to Canada's continued growth. Immigrant women of colour have always been central to this otherizing discourse because the state devised an immigration system based along lines of race and gender (Carty, 1988; Thobani, 2000; Vallee, 2002). For instance, Canada absolutely relies on immigration, yet enacts immigration laws that pick and choose on the basis of a point system that is potentially limiting and alienating for women migrating from the South, for example. The current policy (the Immigration and Refugee Protection Act, 2001) positions women in subservient roles as sponsored spouses and does not adequately provide support in cases of sponsorship breakdowns. The context and surrounding of immigrants' arrival in Canada (when, from where, and the immigration status upon arrival) clearly articulates many things about their perceived worth, treatment, and their entitlement to what Canada has to offer (Gabriel, 1996; Javed 1995; Maceda-Villanueva, 1990). Still, this Western location remains an ideal for many, especially for many women, as it a waged setting, a comparatively accepting setting and, finally, a safe setting despite being at moral odds with the systemic injustices experienced by immigrant women, who, we know, are necessary to keep our Canadian cities running.

A transnational feminist framework places an immigrant woman at the centre of this phenomenon and calls for us to pay attention to the power relations embedded in global movements that split and place female bodies/ minds across borders. This fractured body/mind becomes a key determinant of immigrant women's physical and mental health. Theoretical frameworks designed to promote an understanding of immigration, racialization, and such must move beyond considering race only and engage in a discussion of the cultural differences in relation to gender, power relations, history, movement, resistance, and transformation. This translates into how we begin to understand transnational identities as reconstructed subjectivities that have been altered by the external forces associated with migration and reconstitution in new locales (Bammer 1994, Gastaldo, Gooden, & Massaquoi, 2005). Unfortunately, the literature on immigration and transnationalism frequently disregard these aspects of immigration, their ties with globalization, and how they play out in the lives of immigrant women.

Immigrant Women and Health Promotion: Limitations in Literature

Living transnationally and caring for themselves and their families in Canada and abroad impacts upon women's physical and mental health. However, little is known about immigrant women's strengths and their health-promotion strategies in everyday life. Important steps have been taken to create a more culturally sensitive health-care system, but research is still focused on the social and policy determinants of physical and mental health for racialized immigrants, their general health needs/practices, and cultural competency as necessary framework for service delivery with racialized immigrants. Very rarely does research focus on the women themselves; rather, they face silencing and erasure amid the broader immigration concerns/ questions dominating the research scene. Even when discussed, immigrant women are often looked upon as helpless victims of a larger system. Their various ways of coming to terms with the stressors of immigration and settlement and their innovative ways to restore and maintain community living both locally and transnationally are overlooked.

The role of transnationalism in shaping women's health needs and behaviours are a telling gap in this literature. Although some researchers have looked into the multiple wellness and healing strategies that women employ amid the restricting circumstances following immigration (Ahmad et al., 2004; Dyck & Dossa, 2007; Menjívar, 2002; Messias, 2002; Schmalzbaur, 2004; Spitzer et al. 2003; Tung, 2000), the self- and community-health-promoting behaviours of immigrant women in the transnational context have not been thoroughly investigated. The only literature to have seriously engaged with immigrant women's health-promotion strategies across countries/continents is the literature on transnationalism and on a feminized global labour force (Derose, Escarce, & Lurie, 2007; Meadows et al., 2001).

This is because live-in and live-out caregivers, house cleaners, and elderly caregivers are almost exclusively women immigrating to other countries for sustenance.

We push the boundaries of the literature by arguing that immigrant women in general, belonging to a variety of immigration, residential, and citizenship categories, play crucial community- and family-health-promotion roles (Gastaldo, Gooden, & Massaquoi, 2005) in home and host countries. It is well-documented that immigrants' health, especially the health of immigrant women, deteriorate while living in the host country (Women's Health in Women's Hands, 2005; Massaquoi, 2004. Many struggle to physically, emotionally, and spiritually support their immediate and distant families, an ongoing process that turns them into transnational mental-health promoters. Immigrant women tend to sacrifice their own emotional, physical, and financial well-being in order to care for family members. The trajectories of their lives and the structure, content, and strategies of their health-promoting behaviours are largely overlooked in the literature, as are their mental-health needs.

We further ground this chapter on an expanded notion of the social determinants of health. Based on the data from "Revisiting 'Personal is Political': Immigrant Women's Health Promotion," a community-based, participatory-action research project, we argue that transnational locations and responsibilities are crucial determinants of immigrant women's biomedical and psychological health, and should be incorporated into relevant mental-health-service frameworks. Multiple roles in multiple locations effect racialized immigrant and refugee women's emotional health, and this must be acknowledged and integrated into mental-health-service frameworks. The research project was designed to bring out these experiences.

"Revisiting 'Personal is Political': Immigrant Women's Health Promotion": Objectives, Design, and Methods

The "Revisiting 'Personal is Political'" research project was a multi-phased, mixed-method, feminist health-research initiative funded by the Canadian Institutes of Health Research. The objectives of the research were to:

a) illustrate the resources and strategies immigrant and refugee women employ to promote their own mental health;
b) examine the concepts of individual and collective empowerment as key elements for health promotion;
c) examine the key social determinants of health as a factor in the lives of immigrant and refugee women; and
d) identify the discourse of immigrant and refugee women for self-care and care of others.

Based on the principles of empowerment, immigrant women, health professionals, and academics worked together to attain an enhanced understanding of how gender, health, and the politics of everyday life are interwoven, and how to use this knowledge to promote immigrant women's health. As part of the selection criteria of the study, women had to have lived in Canada for less than three years. Given the difficulties with recruiting seniors (55 years and over) and Black women, the selection criteria was amended to include women who had lived in Canada for less than five years (for seniors), and those who had lived in Canada for less than six years and had landed immigrant or refugee status for less than three years (for Black women).

The Women's Health in Women's Hands Community Health Centre (WHIWH) in Toronto partnered with the Faculty of Nursing at the University of Toronto for the project. Flyers were posted around the centre and staff at the centre also helped to recruit women. Flyers were also sent out to numerous community agencies around the Greater Toronto Area whose clientele was largely refugees and/or immigrants. In order to reach a variety of immigrants, the flyers were printed in several languages: Hindi, Portuguese, French, Spanish, English, Urdu, and Swahili. Some women visiting the centre for personal reasons were also approached directly by members of the research team to screen for eligibility and interest in the study. Interested participants were also asked to notify friends if they met the selection criteria. The research coordinator then contacted each qualified individual via telephone to discuss the nature of the study, the potential risks and benefits of participation, and the right to withdraw at any time.

The project was divided into four phases. Thirty-three immigrant women between the ages of 25 and 67, from Mexico, Ukraine, Sierra Leone, Haiti, Taiwan, St. Lucia, Turkey, Kenya, Ethiopia, Cuba, Ukraine, China, India, and Brazil, participated in focus groups delivered as the first phase of the project. Interpreters were provided as necessary. The discussions explored issues regarding health and well-being in the context of displacement and gender and the strategies and resources being employed to promote health. The participants analyzed their own health status and provided accounts for the members. Participants also established personal and collective health-promotion goals and strategies.

Participants from the first phase were invited to participate in the second phase of the project. Thirteen group members from the first phase choose to continue with the project. In this phase, the women discussed their personal goals regarding health and well-being. They requested educational workshops such as public speaking, resumé writing, and interview skills to assist them in their personal health-promotion goals.

The third phase looked at reflection as a powerful tool for empowerment (Johns, 1999). The group evaluated the achievements and difficulties involved in the process of trying to assert greater control over their health.

In phase four, participants, in collaboration with the researchers and WHIWH staff, created a health-promotion program that promotes health and empowers other immigrant women to be implemented at the community health centre.

A variety of approaches to data collection were used to facilitate sensitive observation and interpretation of the women's experiences. The researchers understood that women's voices need to be preserved in the construction of knowledge and in advocating for social change (Malterud, 1993). Focus groups, a satisfaction-with-life scale (SWLS) were administered, and diaries were used to engage in in-depth explorations of issues concerning power relations and gender. Thus, the principles of empowerment were respected and the politics of knowledge production in research was also addressed.

Participatory methods of collection of data were used to inform the study. The focus groups helped identify key themes in women's immigration and health-promotion activities, and the participants had the opportunity to choose various methods of informing the study through photographs and/or diaries as a way to reflect on daily life and personal health-promotion strategies in their particular contexts. As the researchers recognized that some participants might not be comfortable articulating their experiences in writing, photography was offered as an option. Each participant also had the opportunity to photograph elements of their everyday living that were related to health promotion, such as work or leisure activities. Participants were also videotaped toward promoting a critical analysis of their everyday living. Those participants who did not wish to present images of their homes or neighbourhoods were encouraged to choose diary-writing. The keeping of personal diaries promoted self-reflection regarding activities of daily living. Those who found writing a challenge were given the option to call with or leave a recorded message of their comments, thus generating an oral diary. Both participants and researchers kept copies of the materials produced.

The SWLS (Pavot & Diener, 1993) was administered to measure women's cognitive judgments of well-being. The SWLS (Diener, Emmons, Larsen, & Griffin, 1985) is a short, five-item instrument designed to measure individual's subjective experience of well-being. In completing the SWLS, participants indicate their degree of agreement or disagreement with each item using a seven-point Likert scale (1 = strongly disagree to 7 = strongly agree). Scores on the SWLS range from five to thirty-five, with higher scores indicating greater life satisfaction. The SWLS was factor-analytically derived from a pool of 48 items (Diener et al., 1985). Diener et al. reported a two-month test-retest correlation coefficient of .82 and a coefficient alpha of .87. The SWLS was found to be free from the influences of social desirability.

88 Pathways, Bridges and Havens

Results and Discussion

The participants had varieties of reasons to immigrate. They included, but were not limited to, personal safety, educational goals for self and family, and better quality of life. Table 1 of the SWLS results quantifies the women's subjective well-being.

As is evident from Table 1, research participants had a generally positive response/attitude toward life. The focus-group data and phases two and three of the project corroborate the finding of the SWLS. The women were satisfied to have sacrificed their home country for a better future for their families. Some had prestigious professional jobs in their country of origin, but were willing to sacrifice their high standard of living for a better quality of life for themselves and family, Canada being considered a safe and peaceful country. They strongly believed that they and their families could have a future in Canada. However, all identified that leaving family members behind was extremely difficult, but acknowledged that it was crucial for the betterment of the family as a whole.

Participants identified that having a good paying job in their field, a connection with family here and in their home countries, and being proficient in English were important components in providing the most satisfaction in life. However, their persistence and determination to overcome barriers to achieving these goals were clearly evident. As revealed in the results of the SWLS and the data collected from the focus groups, photography, videos, and dairies also demonstrated the women's resistance to isolation and discrimination, their fight against unemployment and language barriers, and their overall struggles and determination to create a home for themselves and family in Canada. The project's methodology created a dialogue that allowed an in-depth exploration of power relations, place, and gender. The data revealed that many participants described living in a transnational social space in which they continued to be very active. The women

Table 1: Results from the SWLS			
Supposition	1	2	3
In most ways my life is close to my ideal	36.6%	9.09%	27.27%
The conditions of my life are excellent	0%	27.27%	36.36%
I am satisfied with my life	0%	36.36%	9.09%
So far I have gotten the important things I want in life	18.18%	63.63%	9.09%
If I could live my life over, I would change almost nothing	9.09%	27.27%	9.09%

1 strongly agree
2 agree
3 slightly agree
4 neither agree nor disagree
5 slightly disagree
6 disagree
7 strongly disagree

were invested in their daily life in Canada, which incorporated narratives of the transnational caring of family members in the country of origin. Using the narratives of these women, we add new dimensions to the field of transnationalism and mental-health counselling by exploring the context of migration, the experience of women as transnational migrants, and their role in the promotion of their own health and the health of others.

Themes such as resilience and strength; care-giving strategies for self, families, and communities; and transnational living recurred throughout the project.

Resilience and Strength

Resilience was a prominent trait among the women. Apart from their commitment to start new lives, this may have been due to various other factors, including the specific nature of the sample. For instance, some women fleeing from war and other forms of civil disturbances had found a safe haven in Canada for themselves and their children:

> Well, I came here this year because my country has war so we ran away from there … we came across Canada because Canada is safe…for better life and safety because I stop my school in Africa because of the war there … burning houses and killing people … here, I am safe, my kids are safe too and my husband, but still my family is in Africa. *Namoba, Sierra Leone, age 32*

> There is war in my country and I am half cast form Eritrea and Ethiopia so I can't stay in Eritrea and I can't stay in Ethiopia …in the war, they want to arrest me … so I flew to Kenya … I apply to Canada to get a better life, to get through school. *Senait, Ethiopia, 30*

4	5	6	7
9.09%	0%	9.18.18%	0%
0%	0%	27.27%	9.09%
9.09%	9.09%	27.27%	9.09%
0%	0%	9.09%	0%
0%	0%	45.45%	9.09%

The above quotations explain the high overall rating in the SWLS because their situation in their home country was untenable and did not provide them with the appropriate means to care for their families. Therefore, challenges such as "deskilling," language barriers, and missing family members identified in the focus groups were manageable and acceptable as compared with the realities of life in their home countries. The women noted that they did not foresee these challenges but they were still determined to make Canada their home. One participant expresses her experience within the quote below:

> [T]he experience here is like entering a bridge. When you get into a bridge you know there is an entrance and there is an exit. The problem with (my) experience is that (I) got into the bridge but (I) don't know whether (I) am at the beginning, middle or end of the bridge and where it is leading (me) … what keeps (me) going is the hope of exiting the bridge but it is a really hard process.
> *Martha, Mexico, 51*

Most women shared the feeling articulated in the above quote, stating that it has been a difficult journey immigrating to Canada but they still have a positive outlook regarding their future. As another woman explains:

> You come with dreams to this country but then you realize that there are many barriers, many doors that are closed to you and this affects you overall, the whole body, the whole person gets affected by this process but women here have a good thing, they have their rights respected and this gives you strength to achieve things.
> *Nicole, Haiti, 35*

Overall, Canada was seen as a place where families could have a future, safety, good education for their children, and opportunities in which they could generate income to send home to their family members. When challenges occurred, they tried to stay positive because their families depended on them, both in Canada and in their home countries. There was no room for doubt or giving up, as one participant describes:

> Sometimes I say I stay here for my children. I need to be strong, to be active, to be everything. *Ava, Turkey, 28*

The women also used creative ways in keeping resilient and strong through difficult times. For instance, many expressed that they used the English language to dissociate from their emotional pain so that they could continue to move forward. This is illustrated by this woman:

> I'm sorry, I choose to speak English because I do not feel too much in English my feelings, but I discover at this moment, yes in English, I feel pain. [Participant cries.] *Annie, Taiwan, 28*

Conversely, the English language was seen as a very important criterion in helping women feel settled in Canada. They believed that their ability to learn English would create a better life for them in Canada. They felt that being proficient in English would secure them good paying jobs that would provide for their families.

Self-Care and Care For Others

The women spoke as "we," not "I," when they referred to self-care. Making sure their family members were well taken care of gave them a sense of purpose and pride. Self-care was seen in the context of how it would benefit the family, not just themselves. Many saw themselves as natural caregivers and expressed that caring for others made them feel good about themselves. Nurturing family members and others was their way of nurturing themselves. One of the women explains:

> People around me, they trust me, I know they are comfortable with me and sometimes they are telling me their secrets and this way I am thinking if they are trusting me and telling me their secrets, I'm important for them and I see myself as important.
> *Anastasiya, Ukraine, 41*

Participants began to extend their caring by supporting each other and other immigrant women. They agreed that coming to community meetings/ gatherings and volunteering and supporting one another helped them cope with everyday stressors, and gave them continued strength in rebuilding their lives:

> What helps me is that...I started to do voluntary work at [a] heart and stroke hospital ... so you know going there you have a responsibility, you have something to do, something to aim for.
> *Hyacinth, St. Lucia, 27*

Many spoke about feeling alone and isolated in Canada. Getting involved in activities at community agencies and regularly socializing with others from their communities were strategies adopted to address isolation, as expressed by this woman:

> [G]oing to "Sistering" for company, for talk, for laughter, and this place has a big group of women from Latin America. They have English class, piano class, carpentry class for women ... and this place shows me how to use the computer. I learn how to make things for my home, flowers, sometimes for table, tablecloth with flower, so much. *Martha, Mexico, 51*

Transnational Living and Caregiving

Transnational living and caregiving were overarching themes throughout the discussions, as was evident in the women's everyday health promotion for themselves and their families. For many of the participants, immigrating to Canada did not release them of their multiple roles and family responsibilities. They were still expected to continue to perform their roles in the family. As experienced by this participant, her responsibilities as the first-born daughter in her family did not end when she migrated to Canada:

> I have brothers and sisters, but being the first born girl, I have the responsibility almost equal to my mom ... I wanted to have my own freedom. No matter what you do, it is forever. *Esther, Kenya, 51*

It was also apparent that many of the mothers in the group financially and emotionally support their children and other family members in their country of origin. Caring for their children became a transnational form of parenting in which the assistance of other women plays a vital role. It is not uncommon for mothers migrating to Canada to leave the direct care of their children in the hands of "other mothers" in their county of origin. The other mother plays a vital role in the preservation of transnational motherhood as mature women, usually grandmothers and great aunts, nurture and care for children. They become caretakers while their female relatives or friends are away trying to provide for their children and households.

The participants felt that finding appropriate employment in Canada while learning English and taking care of their children was especially challenging. They agreed that the province of Ontario does not provide a social structure in which they could successfully raise their children during the process of getting settled. Therefore, some felt that the most viable option was having their children stay behind in the country of origin, there being directly cared for by other members (the so-called other mothers) of the family while they establish themselves in Canada. One participant expressed her difficulty in deciding that it was best for her children to go back home.

> This summer I make a very difficult decision, it is difficult, I send my daughter back to China. *Sunny, China, 30*

Many of the women cared for their children and relatives back home by sending money and goods to help with the caregiving. Many spent their money on phone cards to be in constant communication with their family members. The women acknowledged that family brings them the most satisfaction and joy, but they grieve the loss of family members and friends who were left behind, as articulated by this woman:

> I am comfortable in Canada, me, my husband and my two sons, I
> think I more worry for my mother who lives in Ukraine.
> *Anastasiya, Ukraine, 41*

Being relatively stable and safe in Canada while their family members
back home did not have the resources and comforts that the participants
have access to was a root cause of the women's distress, and was compounded by survivor guilt:

> I feel sometime lonely, because for three years I didn't see my family
> and I am wondering about them now, because their life is not so
> easy but beside that I know I am not, not really lonely because I have
> family here, I have my daughter. *Habiba, India, 68*

The women also talked at length about home and compared and contrasted home with Canada. When asked if they feel like Torontonians, the
women responded with a range of feelings and understandings about the
meaning of home. However, they all associated home with the place they
and their families (i.e., children and extended families) came from.

> Anastayia said that it's too early to feel Torontonian because she has
> been here only for a year. If asked where she is from, she says she is
> from Ukraine but lives in Toronto. She said she will never forget her
> city by the Black Sea. This is where her roots are.
> *Anastayia, Ukraine, 41*

> Martha says Toronto is the only city she knows in Canada. She feels
> that in Canada she is from Toronto, but she always refers to her
> country of origin.
> *Martha, Mexico, 51*

Outcomes

The women not only supported each other throughout the project activities,
they also created resources to help other immigrant women and women
thinking about migrating to Canada. The creation of a website, the production of a documentary, and the publication of a book of poetry were various
media the women chose to communicate with other immigrant women in
like circumstances.

The website offered advice and key information to potential immigrant
women. The participants felt that the website needed to provide important
information to other women in the midst of deciding to migrate to Canada.
That daycare provision in Toronto is expensive, the importance of knowing

English before coming to Canada, and that professional employment is not easily accessible were some of the components that were added as crucial settlement information.

A documentary was produced to visually and verbally capture the everyday realities of being an immigrant in Canada. The women opened up their homes and lives to the world. For the participants, the film was a way to voice their experiences and help others in the process of settling in Canada. It also let other immigrant women know that they are not alone. The book of poetry *I Am Not the Woman I Used To Be* (Gastaldo, 2004) that came out of the monthly meetings was developed to share the women's experiences. The book truly reflected the participatory nature of the project. Some poems are written collaboratively by the participants and some are individual contributions, but all reveal the complexity of immigrant women's experiences. "In some, shared ideas are captured in a single poem, while in others multiple voices can be heard challenging each other." (Gastaldo, 2004). Overall, the poems captured the emotions expressed throughout the project by the women: sadness, distress, anger, joy, pleasure. The poems became a telling piece of these women's struggles and determination, their expectations from Canada and their disappointments, their recognition of the systemic barriers, and, also, their refusal to give up for the sake of families, children, and for those likely to follow them in the paths of migration as expressed in the following poem.

> We miss our homeland...
> Customs, foods, friends...
> We miss
> Celebrations, cultural traditions, music
> Our lives, we miss them...
> Yet leaving what we know, what was ours,
> We knew how long the road would be
> The difficulty situations we would have to face
> But we decided
> Now we have two places in our hearts
> One for our country
> It is hard, yes it is, but if we believe,
> We are able...we can keep alive the memories of our
> Previous life
> And we incorporate the new life,
> The new life we have chosen.
> (*Maria*, "Leaving What We Know," Cuba)

Conclusion

Resilience, emotional strength, and optimism nourish immigrant women's thirst for a better future for themselves and their family in Canada and back home. Experiences of isolation and unemployment compounded by the difficulties of providing financial and emotional support for family members in Canada and back home are part of immigrant women's experiences. The "Revisiting 'Personal is Political'" project used quantitative and qualitative methods to capture these everyday realities of immigrant and refugee women to demonstrate their resilience and strategies in taking care of themselves, their families, and their communities. However, the project also found that these transnational connections and responsibilities have a profound impact on the well-being and mental health of the women. The study clearly demonstrates that many immigrant women end up compromising their own mental health in order to care for family members in the country of origin. Sometimes, this is rooted in cultural belief of who they are as women: mother, wife, daughter, and/or sister.

Mental-health strategies that do not acknowledge that immigrant women's sense of well-being is situated in the context of multiple cultural identities can be harmful. For instance, the Western approach to counselling tends to address cultural variables in isolation from one another. Namely, they examine the woman within the context of mother, daughter, wife, provider, and nurturer separately and within the confines of Canadian borders, rather than addressing the interplay among these contexts nationally and internationally. Thus the lives of immigrant women are compartmentalized into fragmented cultural categories that do not mirror their real lives. To ignore a woman's connections to her country of origin is to ignore crucial components of her identity and well-being.

Therefore, mental-health care practitioners should strive to:

a)   Include immigrant and refugee women's transnational realities as a determinant of health.

b)   Acknowledge that women's resilience and transnational realities are central to the provision of appropriate care.

c)   Appreciate that women's understanding of self-care includes the well-being of their families across borders. This may be achieved by documenting and understanding women's lived realities.

An inclusive approach in the provision of mental-health services for immigrant women should locate the women within a broader picture as opposed to looking at them in fragments. A service framework respectful of the multiple and complex lived realities of immigrant women that arise out of their multiple roles, responsibilities, traditions, and knowledge is, therefore, imperative. Services cannot be absolute or constant, rather they need to be mobile and, above all, suited to the individual who identifies as an immigrant or refugee woman.

Notes

1. Transnationalism, for the purposes of this chapter, can best be described as the amplification of the social processes that facilitate cultural interconnectedness and mobility across space (Appadurai, 1996; Grewal et.al., 2001; Spivak, 1996).

2. According to the 2006 census, 16.2% identified as visible minorities (Statistics Canada, 2008).

References

Access to Primary Health Care for Black Women and Women of Colour. (2005). Unpublished raw data.

Ahmad et al. (2004). Voices of South Asian Women: Immigration and Mental Health. *Women & Health, 40*(4), 113-130.

Appadurai, A. (1996). *Modernity at Large: Cultural Dimensions of Globalization*. Minneapolis, MN: University of Minnesota Press.

Bammer, A. (1994). *Displacements: Cultural Identities in Question*. Indianapolis, IN: Indiana University Press.

Bannerji, H. (2000). *The Dark Side of the Nation*. Toronto: Canadian Scholars' Press.

Carty, L. (1988). "Visible Minority" Women—A Creation of the Canadian State. *Resources for Feminist Research, 17*(3), 39-42.

Cassidy, C., O'Connor, R. C., Howe, C., & Warden, D. (2004). Perceived discrimination and psychological distress: The role of personal and ethnic self-esteem. *Journal of Counseling Psychology, 51*(3), 329–339.

Crawford, C. (2007). Black Women, Racing and Gendering the Canadian Nation. In Notisha Massaquoi & Njoki Wane (Eds.), *Theorizing Empowerment: Canadian Perspectives on Black Feminist Thoought*. Toronto: Inanna Publications and Education Inc., 199-129.

Derose, K. P., Escarce, J. J., & Luries, N. (2007). Immigrants And Health Care: Sources of Vulnerability, *Health Affairs, 26*(5), 1258-1268.

Diener, E., Emmons, R. A., Larsen, R. J., & Griffin, S. (1985). The Satisfaction With Life Scale. *Journal of Personality Assessment, 49*(1), 71–75.

Dyck, I., & Dossa, P. (2007). Place, health and home: Gender and migration in the constitution of healthy space. *Health & Place, 13*, 691–701.

Franks, F. & Faux, S.A. (1990). Depression, Stress, Mastery and Social Resources in Four Thocultural Women's Groups. *Research in Nursing and Health, 13* (5), 283-292.

Gabriel, C. (1996). One or the Other? "Race," Gender, and the Limits of Official Multiculturalism. In Janine Brodie (Ed.), Women and Canadian Public Policy. Toronto: Harcourt Brace and Company, 173-195.

Gastaldo, D. (2004). *I'm Not the Woman I Used to Be: 30 Poems by Recent Immigrant Women*. Toronto: Women's Health in Woemn's Hands Community Health Centre.

Gastaldo, D., Gooden, A., & Massaquoi, N. (2005). Transnational Health Promotion: Social well-being across borders and immigrant women's subjectivities. *Wagadu: A Journal of Transnational Women's and Gender Studies* 2(2005), 1-16.

Grewal, I. & Kaplan, C. (1994). *Scattered Hegemonies: Postmodernity and Transnational Feminist Practices*. Minneapolis, MN: University of Minnesota Press.

Henry, F. & Taylor, C. (2005). *The Colour of Democracy: Racism in Canadian Society*. Toronto: Thompson Canada.

Javed, N.S. (1995). Life Themes of Immigrant Women of Colour in Canada. In J. Adleman & G. Enguidanos (Eds.). *Racism in the Lives of Women*. New York: Haworth Press.

Johns, C. (1999). Reflections as Empowerment? *Nursing Inquiry, 6*(4), 241-249.

Maceda-Villanueva, M. (1990). Focus on Immigrant Women: A Study of Immigrant Women's Needs and Programs. Toronto: Ontario Council of Agencies Serving Immigrants (OCASI).

Malterud, K. (1993). Strategies for empowering women's voices in the medical culture. *Health Care for Women International*, 14, 365–373.

Massaquoi, N. (2004). An African Child Becomes a Black Canadian Feminist. *Canadian Woman Studies/les cahiers de la femme, 23*(2), 140-144.

Mawani, F. N. (2008). Social Determinants of Depression among Immigrant and Refugee Women. In S. Guruge & E. Collins (Eds.), *Working with Immigrant Women: Issues and Strategies for Mental Health Professionals*, Toronto, ON: Enid Centre for Addiction and Mental Health.

Meadows, L. M., et al. (2001). Immigrant women's health. *Social Science & Medicine, 52*, 1451–1458

Menjívar, C. (2002). The Ties That Heal: Guatemalan Immigrant Women's Networks and Medical Treatment. *International Migration Review, 36*(2), 437–466.

Messias, D. K. (2002). Transnational Health Resources, Practices, and Perspectives: Brazilian Immigrant Women's Narratives. *Journal of Immigrant Health, 4*(4), 183-200.

Oamn-Martinez, J., Abdool, S.N., & Loiselle-Leonard, M. (2000). *Canadian Journal of Public Health, 91*(5), 394.

Pavot. W. & E. Diener. (1993). Review of the Satisfaction With Life Scale. *Psychological Assessment, 5*(2), 164–172.

Schmalzbauer, L., (2004). Searching for Wages and Mothering from Afar: The Case of Honduran Transnational Families *Journal of Marriage and Family, 66*(5), Research Library Core, pg. 1317-1331.

Schreiber, R., Stern, P. N., & Wilson, C. (1998) The context for managing depression and its stigma among black West Indian Canadian women. *Journal of Advanced Nursing*, 27, 510–517.

Smith, A., Lalonde, R. N., Johnson, S. (2004). Serial Migration and Its Implications for the Parent-Child Relationship: A Retrospective Analysis of the Experiences of the Children of Caribbean Immigrants. *Cultural Diversity and Ethnic Minority Psychology, 10*(2), 107–122.

Spitzer, D., et al. (2003). Caregiving in Transnational Context: "My Wings Have Been Cut; Where Can I Fly?" *Gender and Society, 17*(2), 267–286.

Statistics Canada. (2006, March). Women in Canada: A Gender-based Statistical Report, 5th edition. Ottawa. Retrieved from http://www.statcan.ca/english/freepub/89-503-XIE/0010589-503-XIE.pdf.

Statistics Canada. (2006, March). Longitudinal Survey of Immigrants to Canada: A Regional Perspective of the Labour Market Experiences. Ottawa. Retrieved from http://www.statcan.ca/english/freepub/89-616-XIE/2006001/bfront1.htm.

Thobani, S. (2000). Closing Ranks: racism and sexism in Canada's immigration policy. *Race & Class, 42*(1), 35–55.

Tung, C. (2000). The Cost of Caring: The Social Reproductive Labor of Filipina Live-in Home Health Caregivers. *Frontiers: A Journal of Women Studies, 21*(1/2), Asian American Women, 61–82.

Vallee, M. (2002). Unaccompanied Women Immigrating to Canada during the 1920s: Laying Down a Policy Founded on "Gender." *Recherches feministes, 15*(2), 65-85.

Women's Health in Women's Hands Community Health Centre. (2005). Access to Primary Health Care for Black Women and Women of Colour Report. Unpublished Data.

Zelkowitz, P., Shinazi, J., Katofsky, L., et al. (2004). Factors Associated with Depression in Pregnant Immigrant Women. *Transcultural Psychiatry, 41*(4), 445–464.

Peter Horvath and Pamela Wambolt

The Effects of Dysfunctional Motivational Components in Self-Regulation on Negative and Positive Affect in Women

Women worldwide experience major problems with mood disorders (Health Canada, 2002; Stewart, Gucciardi, & Grace, 2004). However, despite recognizing the influence of many antecedents and of moderating variables such as stress (Brems, 1995; Mazure, Keita, & Blehar, 2002; McGrath, Keita, Strickland, & Russo, 1990; Nolen-Hoeksema, 2006), we still do not really understand the processes through which mood disorders occur in women. The stud`y described in this chapter examined three forms of dysfunctions in the regulation of self-esteem or self-worth as possible antecedents for negative moods in women. The terms "self-esteem" and "self-worth" will be used interchangeably in this chapter and will be defined as the extent to which one perceives oneself to be relatively close to or distant from being the kind of person one wants to be, with respect to person qualities one values (Block & Robbins, 1993). Low self-esteem, variable self-esteem, and dysfunctions in the regulation of self-esteem have been associated with dysphoria and depression in both men and women (Roberts & Gotlib, 1997; Roberts & Monroe, 1999; Strauman, 1995). Dysfunctions in the regulation of self-worth have been proposed to be underlying processes in various forms of vulnerabilities for negative affect and depression (Campbell & Kwon, 2001;

Horvath, 2008; Horvath, Bissix, Sumarah, Crouchman, & Bowdrey, 2008). Possible forms of dysfunctions in the regulation of self-worth as vulnerabilities for depression are described in Beck's (1983) cognitive theory, the hopelessness theory of depression (Abramson et al., 2002), and Dykman's (1998) the motivational theory of validation-seeking, among others. Some of the main theories relevant to this proposal are reviewed below.

Research on dysfunctions in the regulation of self-worth is relevant for examining antecedents of negative affect and depression in women because the suppression of self-esteem and self-identity are particular problems associated with mood disorders in women (Jack, 1999; Jack & Dill, 1992). Our study examined the role of personality styles, hopelessness, and validation-seeking as forms of dysfunctions in the regulation of self-worth, and as possible antecedent variables of negative affect in women.

Sociotropy and Autonomy

Beck's (1983; Clark & Beck, 1991; Sacco & Beck, 1995) cognitive theory of depression proposed that two personality styles, sociotropy and autonomy, act as vulnerabilities for depression. According to cognitive theory, the vulnerability in these personal styles is based on the presence of particular schemas. Sociotropic individuals have a high need for the approval of others (Beck, 1983; Sacco & Beck, 1995). Autonomous individuals have a high need for independence and achievement.

Cognitive theory proposes that congruence between the personality vulnerability and a matching stress precipitates depression (Beck, 1983; Sacco & Beck, 1995). Sociotropic individuals are vulnerable to the development of depression when they experience social rejection. Autonomous individuals are vulnerable to the development of depression when they experience failure or loss of independence. The viability of Beck's cognitive theory of depression, however, has been questioned (Coyne & Whiffen, 1995). Support for the congruence theory of depression has been mixed, with more support found for the effects of matching stress on sociotropy than on autonomy (Clark, Beck, & Brown, 1992; Kwon & Whisman, 1998; Mazure, Bruce, Maciejewski, & Jacobs, 2000; Rude & Burnham, 1993).

Santor (2003) suggested that these personality styles may be vulnerabilities for the development of depression independent of life events. He suggested that they should be examined for their motivational and behavioural components. In support of this proposal, some studies have found sociotropy and autonomy to be associated with depressive symptoms independent of negative life events (Campbell & Kwon, 2001; Fairbrother & Moretti, 1998; Horvath et al., 2008). In addition, low self-esteem (Fairbrother & Moretti, 1998) and validation-seeking (Horvath et al., 2008) have been associated with some of the underlying vulnerabilities in these personality styles.

Campbell and Kwon (2001) conceptualized sociotropy and autonomy in motivational terms as goal-directed activities to attain self-worth. Extrinsic motivations to attain self-worth might be an aspect of the vulnerability in sociotropy and autonomy. These personality styles have been associated with validation-seeking or extrinsically oriented goal pursuits to attain self-worth (Horvath et al., 2008). Extrinsically oriented goal pursuits, reflecting contingencies of self-worth, result in negative affect and poor adjustment when not realized (Crocker, 2002; Crocker, Karpinski, Quinn, & Chase, 2003; Crocker, Luhtanen, Cooper, & Bouvrette, 2003; Deci & Ryan, 2000). Self-determination and intrinsic motivational orientations, on the other hand, are associated with well-being (Deci & Ryan, 2000; Ryan & Deci, 2000). Both sociotropy and autonomy appear to contain precarious forms of goal and coping orientations to acquire and maintain self-worth. Little research, however, has examined the possible self-regulatory or motivational components that might constitute the vulnerabilities for negative affect in these personality styles.

Optimism and Pessimism

Low expectation for goal attainment is another example of dysfunctions in the regulation of self-worth associated with vulnerabilities for negative affect and depression. Expectations can be positive or negative, optimistic or pessimistic. Low expectations for achieving desired goals have been associated with depressive symptoms and low self-esteem (Campbell & Kwon, 2001; Endler & Kocovski, 2000; Horvath et al., 2008; Kocovski & Endler, 2000; Tripp, Catano, & Sullivan, 1997). According to the hopelessness theory of depression, pessimistic expectations that highly desired outcomes will not occur or that highly aversive outcomes will occur is a proximal cause of depressive symptoms (Abramson et al., 2002; Abramson, Metalsky, & Alloy, 1989; Alloy, Just, & Panzarella, 1997). At the root of pessimistic expectations are dysfunctional conceptualizations of the self's ability to attain or control favourable outcomes. Pessimistic expectations are the result of the tendency to attribute the causes of negative outcomes internally to the self and the causes of positive events to external factors. Pessimism, therefore, is another candidate to examine as a possible form of the dysfunctional regulation of self-worth and as a vulnerability for negative affect.

Validation-seeking

Validation-seeking, the result of low self-esteem, is another form of dys-functional regulation of self-worth. Both low self-esteem (Kocovski & Endler, 2000; Tripp et al., 1997) and variability in self-esteem have been associated with depression (Kernis, Grannemann, & Mathis, 1991; Roberts & Gotlib, 1997). Difficulties with the regulation of self-esteem have been found to be vulnerabilities for the development of emotional disorders (Roberts & Monroe, 1999; Strauman, 1995). Research has also shown that depression-prone individuals engage in excessive negative self-evaluations when they fail some important task (Hyland, 1987; Pyszczynski & Greenberg, 1987). They tend to ruminate on their failures and do not disengage from their goals. One reason for this might be that such goals are important to their identity or self-esteem.

Low self-esteem leads to compensatory validation-seeking (Dykman, 1998). Individuals high on validation-seeking orient themselves to tasks and situations as a means to prove their self-worth. Research has suggested that the pursuit of self-esteem for its own sake, as reflected in validation-seeking, is a form of dysfunctional motivational orientation and dysfunctional self-regulation associated with emotional problems (Crocker & Park, 2004; Dykman, 1998). Validation-seeking has been associated with anxiety and depressive symptoms (Dykman, 1998; Horvath et al., 2008). Validation-seeking, therefore, is another good candidate to examine as reflecting a form of dysfunctional regulation of self-worth and as vulnerability for negative affect in women.

The Present Study

The present study examined three forms of dysfunction in the regulation of self-worth as vulnerabilities for negative affect in women. As stated above, such research is relevant for examining negative affect and depression in women because the suppression of self-identity and self-esteem are particular problems associated with the presence of negative affect in women. The present study examined personality styles, hopelessness, and validation-seeking as three forms of dysfunctional regulations of self-worth. Payne, Youngcourt, and Beaubien (2007) found that state goal or motivational orientations are somewhat better predictors of performance variables than trait goal orientations. Therefore, we evaluated pessimistic expectations and validation-seeking in their state form as they applied to the current situation.

We predicted that sociotropy and autonomy would be associated with negative affect in women. In addition, we hypothesized that pessimistic expectations and validation-seeking would also be associated with negative affect in women. Furthermore, we predicted that sociotropy and autonomy, pessimistic expectations, and validation-seeking would each interact with or moderate the impact of negative feedback on negative affect in women.

Method

Participants

The participants in the present study were 68 volunteer female students selected from a slightly larger sample ($N = 88$) that included both male and female students in undergraduate psychology courses. Based on their choice, the participants received either a bonus point toward the psychology course they had been recruited from or were entered into a draw to win an Apple iPod. The average age of the female participants in the study was 19.84 ($SD = 1.59$) with a range from 18 to 25 years. Sixty-four (94.1%) of the participants reported that they were single, three (4.4%) were living in common-law relationships, and one (1.5%) was married. When asked about employment, 51 (75.0%) indicated that they were students, 16 (23.5%) were employed part-time, and one (1.5%) was employed full time. The sample consisted of 61 (89.7%) Caucasians, one (1.5%) African-Canadian, and six (8.8%) who indicated "other" or gave no response. The mean number of years of post-secondary education was 1.71 ($SD = 1.12$), with a range from 0.0 to 4.0.

Procedure

In order to investigate the self-regulatory aspects of vulnerability for negative affect, a quasi-experimental design was employed. Participants were first administered measures for sociotropy and autonomy. They were then randomly assigned to three experimental feedback conditions that followed completion of a sequence task. All participants completed the same sequence task, but upon completion of the task received either positive, neutral, or negative feedback depending on which of these three experimental conditions they were assigned.

The independent variable was the type of feedback the participants received. Depending on the analysis, the moderating variables were sociotropy and autonomy, optimism/pessimism, or validation-seeking. The dependent variables were post-anxiety, dysphoria, and positive affect. Before the task, anxiety, dysphoria, and positive affect were assessed and after completing the task and receiving feedback, measures pertaining to validation-seeking, optimism/pessimism, anxiety, dysphoria, positive affect, and depression were administered. All measures used in the present study showed high internal reliability, with Cronbach's alpha coefficient ranging between .80 and .95.

Sequence Task

Participants were asked to complete a sequence task (adapted from Rottler, 2003) that involved eight rows of boxes. Each of the boxes contained x's that created a pattern along the row. Within each row one box was blank and the participants were required to determine the pattern of the row and fill in the missing x's. Upon completion of the task participants were given feedback regarding their performance. While there were correct responses to the sequences, feedback was instead based on random selection. Participants were given positive, negative, or neutral feedback depending on which category they were assigned as opposed to their actual performance on the task. They were told that success on the task was not based on finishing all of the items; rather, the experimenter determined success as only he or she knew if the contingencies for success or failure had been met.

Feedback

Standard positive, neutral, or negative feedback was given to participants in an attempt to keep each condition similar within the three experimental conditions. For example, individuals who were in the positive-feedback group were told, "Your performance on this task was excellent. Most people find this task very difficult, and you performed well above average in comparison to other people." Feedback given to those in the neutral group consisted of, "You did okay on this task today; most people can do a fair number of these tasks, and your performance was about average in comparison to other people." Finally, those in the negative-feedback group were told, "Your performance on this task was very poor. Most people find this task fairly easy, and you performed well below average in comparison to other people."

Measures

Demographic information—Participants began the experiment by completing general demographic questions on their gender, age, years of postsecondary education, employment, ethnic, and relationship status.

Moderating Variables

Sociotropy and autonomy—Personality styles were measured using the Personal Style Inventory (PSI; Robins et al., 1994). The PSI contains 48 self-report items measuring sociotropy and autonomy (24 items each). Participants rate each item on a scale from 1 (strongly disagree) to 6 (strongly agree). Sociotropy measures issues regarding interpersonal relations, including concerns about what others think, dependency, and the tendency to please others. Autonomy measures perfectionism/self-criticism, need for control, and defensive separation issues. Each of these scales has been shown to measure vulnerabilities for depression (Robins et al., 1994).

Optimism/pessimism—A measure of expectancies was designed for this study adapted from the Life Orientation Test-Revised (LOT-R; Scheier, Carver, & Bridges, 1994). It was used to assess participants' current levels of optimism and pessimism. Four of the ten items of the LOT-R are filler items, while three each of the remaining six items are used to measure optimism and pessimism. Respondents are asked to rate each item using a Likert-type scale ranging from 0 (strongly disagree) to 4 (strongly agree). Three of the items were negatively worded and were reverse-coded before scoring. For the current study, the items and instructions were modified to reflect participants' present or situational optimism and pessimism. Optimistic items included, "I expect the best when it comes to the uncertainty of my future," "I'm optimistic about my future," and "I expect more good things to happen to me than bad." Pessimistic items included, "If something can go wrong for me, it will," "I do not expect things to go my way," and "I do not count on good things happening to me." These were reversed before scoring. The overall score could range from extreme pessimism to extreme optimism (i.e., 0–24).

Validation seeking—Five items were adapted from the Goal Orientation Inventory (GOI, Dykman, 1998), a measure of self-validation-seeking. The items and instructions were modified to reflect participants' situational rather than dispositional (trait) validation-seeking. Respondents were asked to indicate their level of agreement to each statement using a Likert-type scale ranging from 1 (strongly disagree) to 7 (strongly agree). The items included, "My main motive in doing this task was to prove my self-worth, competence, or likeability," "How well I performed in this situation is a direct measure of my self-worth," and "How well I did on this task feels like a test of my self-worth." The remaining items are as follows, "My approach to this situation was one of needing to prove my self-worth," and "I viewed my difficulty with this task as an all-or-none test of my worth as a person."

Dependent Variables

Anxiety—A portion of the State-Trait Anxiety Inventory (STAI; Spielberger, 1983) was used to measure state anxiety in the current study before and after the sequence task. The test is a 40-item self-report measure using a four-point Likert-type rating scale ranging from 1 (not at all) to 4 (very much so). The inventory contains 20 questions to measure state anxiety and 20 for trait anxiety. However, only the 20 questions pertaining to state anxiety were used in the present study to measure the participants' reaction to the experimental manipulation. The State-Anxiety scale evaluates feelings of apprehension, tension, nervousness, and worry, which increase in response to physical danger and psychological stress. State anxiety was assessed in the participants immediately before and following the presentation of the experimental task and feedback.

Mood—Participants were asked to complete the Multiple Affect Adjective Checklist-Revised (MAACL-R; Zuckerman & Lubin, 1985) before and after the assigned sequence task and feedback. The MAACL-R is a 132-item checklist of adjectives used to evaluate subsets of affect. These include anxiety (A), depression (D), hostility (H), positive affect (PA), and sensation-seeking (SS). Two forms are available with this checklist. One measures state affect and the other measures trait affect. Only the form designed to gauge state affect was used for the present study. The directions for this form instruct participants to check only the words that describe how they currently feel as opposed to how they generally feel. The test also yields two summary scores, which are dysphoria (A + D + H) and positive affect/sensation-seeking (PA + SS). These two summary scores were the initial focus for the present study. With respect to the PA/SS scale, it was determined that is was best to use only the PA component of this scale after review of the reliability for these summary scales in the present sample. These two scales were used to gauge changes in the participants' levels of dysphoria and positive affect due to the experimental conditions.

Depressive Symptoms

The Center for Epidemiological Studies-Depression (CES-D; Radloff, 1977) was used to measure depressive symptoms. The CES-D is a 20-item self-report measure used to assess depressive symptoms in untreated community samples. The measure consists of a rating scale that ranges from 0 (rarely or none of the time) to 3 (most of the time). Individuals rate each item based on how often they have experienced symptoms during the past week. A score of more than 16 is the cut-off that indicates depression.

Results

Summary statistics for all measures are presented in table 1. All 68 participants responded to measures of autonomy, sociotropy, validation-seeking, pre-task anxiety, and depression. However, only 67 participants completed the pre- and post-task dysphoria, post-task anxiety, and optimism/pessimism measures. Aside from these uncompleted measures, there were no other missing data on these variables.

Overall, the sample showed some depression on the CES-D, likely due to school demands such as mid-term exams. The mean of the sample was just above 16, the raw-score cut-off for indication of depression on the CES-D (Radloff, 1977). The scores on sociotropy and autonomy personality styles, however, were similar to the means found for other undergraduate samples (Robins et al., 1994). Change scores for anxiety, dysphoria, and positive affect were calculated by subtracting pretest from post-test scores.

Table 1 Summary Statistics for all Major Measures (N = 68)				
Measure	Min.	Max.	M	SD
Autonomy	43	109	79.10	15.07
Sociotropy	55	137	94.94	16.20
Pre-task Positive Affect	0	21	8.57	6.17
Pre-task Dysphoria	0	22	3.72	5.07
Pre-task Anxiety	20	68	38.78	12.68
Post-task Positive Affect	0	20	7.07	5.67
Post-task Dysphoria	0	22	3.52	5.61
Post-task Anxiety	20	74	39.90	12.92
Validation Seeking	5	30	12.19	6.59
Optimism/Pessimism	3	24	15.57	4.38
Depression	0	47	17.44	11.03

Check of Experimental Manipulation Effects

The feedback on the tasks appears to have had the intended effects in the three experimental conditions. One-way analyses of variance compared the three experimental conditions against three measures of affect change from pretest to post-test (pretest scores subtracted from post-test scores). Table 2 presents the means of these three experimental conditions and the results of the analyses of variance.

All three measures of changes in affect were in the directions expected according to the three experimental feedback conditions (e.g., positive, neutral, and negative). However, changes in affect were significantly different among the three experimental conditions only on measures of positive affect [$F(2, 64) = 7.17, p < .01$] and anxiety [$F(2, 64) = 4.39, p < .05$], but not on dysphoria [$F(2, 64) = 2.35, p > .05$]. Tukey HSD post hoc tests of differences among the three experimental conditions indicated that the reduction in positive affect from pre-task to post-task was significantly greater in the negative-feedback group compared to both the positive- and neutral-feedback groups. There was no significant difference between the neutral- and positive-feedback groups on the measure of changes in positive affect. Tukey HSD post hoc tests of differences indicated that the increase in anxiety from pre- to post-task was significantly greater in the negative-feedback group in comparison with the positive-feedback group. There were no other significant differences among the three experimental conditions on changes in anxiety from pre- to post-task.

Correlational Analysis

Two-tailed Pearson correlations were conducted to examine significant associations among the major variables (see table 3). Sociotropy was positively correlated with validation-seeking, depressive symptoms, and increased anxiety from pretest to post-test. Significant negative correlations were found between sociotropy and optimism and positive affect change. Autonomy was positively correlated with validation-seeking and depressive symptoms, and negatively correlated with optimism. Optimism was negatively correlated with depressive symptoms. Validation-seeking was also

Table 2
One-way Analyses of Variance Comparing the Three Experimental Feedback Conditions on Change Scores in Positive Affect, Dysphoria, and Anxiety from Pre-task to Post-task (N =67)

	Positive		Neutral		Negative		
	M	SD	M	SD	M	SD	F
Positive Affect	0.43	3.67	-0.85	3.53	-4.35	5.34	7.17**
Dysphoria	-1.71	2.19	-0.27	2.79	1.50	7.80	2.35
Anxiety	-2.82	8.49	0.04	7.47	6.00	13.15	4.39*

Notes. * p < .05. ** p < .01. *** p < .001.

Table 3 - Correlation Matrix for All Main Measures and Affect Change Scores (N = 68)

	1	2	3	4	5	6	7	8
1. Sociotropy	—	.19	-.28*	.32**	-.29*	.24*	.09	.33**
2. Autonomy		—	-.44***	.26*	.10	.09	-.04	.43***
3. Optimism			—	-.11	-.10	.08	.21	-.63***
4. Validation				—	-.21	.31	.29*	.24*
5. Positive affect change					—	-.67***	-.47***	-.07
6. Anxiety change						—	.64***	-.05
7. Dysphoria change							—	-.15
8. Depression								—

* p < .05. ** p < .01. *** p < .001.

significantly associated with depressive symptoms and increases in anxiety and dysphoria from pretest to post-test. All affect change measures were significantly correlated with each other in the expected directions, but were not correlated with depressive symptoms.

Effects of Personality Styles and Feedback on Affect

Following the recommendation of Baron and Kenney (1986), hierarchical multiple regressions were used to test the moderating effects of personality styles on feedback in predicting affective reactions. The regressions predicted post-test anxiety, dysphoria, and positive affect after controlling for pretest levels of the same affect. As there were three experimental levels, the feedback categorical variables were first dummy coded into k-1 variables, each with two levels, according to the recommendations of Tabachnick and Fidell (2001). Each hierarchical multiple regression had six steps. At the first step, the pretest affect measure was entered into the regression, followed by personality style, then the two dummy-coded feedback variables, and finally the two-personality style by feedback interactions. The effects of sociotropy and autonomy were tested separately. In all regression analyses, the pretest measure of affect was significantly associated with the post-test measure of the same affect.

The effects of sociotropy and task feedback on measures of affect were tested as follows: The first regression tested the effects of the predictor variables on post-test positive affect. Both sociotropy and negative feedback were found to be significant predictors of a reduction in positive affect. There were no other significant individual predictors. However, the final regression step with all the predictor variables in the equation was significant.[1]

The second regression tested the effects of the predictor variables on post-test anxiety. Sociotropy, negative feedback, and the sociotropy by negative-feedback interaction were significant predictors of an increase in anxiety (see table 4). The final regression step with all the predictor variables in the equation was significant.

Significant interaction effects between moderators and negative feedback were further examined by follow-up analyses to determine the source of the interaction according to the recommendations of Aiken and West (1991) and O'Connor (1998). The general principle is that high, medium, and low levels of the interacting variables are estimated by calculating the mean and by either adding or subtracting one standard deviation. These values are then substituted into the regression equation, which are then used to predict the dependent variable at all possible combinations of high, medium, and low levels of the interacting variables. In the present study, O'Connor's (1998) program was used to examine significant interactions. The program generated plots of the dependent variable at low, average, and high levels of the moderator, and at two SDs below and two SDs above the mean of the independent variable.

In the follow-up analysis of the significant interaction between sociotropy and negative feedback predicting post-test anxiety, the simple slope standardized betas indicated that those who were moderate and high in sociotropy experienced significantly greater anxiety when they received negative feedback, in contrast with those who received other types of feedback. See figure 1, which depicts the slopes of this interaction.

Table 4
Hierarchical Multiple Regression Predicting Post-Test Anxiety by Sociotropy, Positive Feedback, Negative Feedback, and their Interactions (N = 66)

	B	SE B	ß
Step 1			
Pre-Anxiety	0.69	0.09	0.68***
Step 2			
Sociotropy (S)	0.24	0.07	0.31**
Step 3			
Positive Feedback (P)	-3.62	2.35	-0.13
Step 4			
Negative Feedback (N)	6.01	2.55	0.21*
Step 5			
S x P	1.53	2.64	0.06
Step 6			
S x N	5.01	2.39	0.23

Note. R^2 = 0.46 for Step 1 (p < .001). ΔR^2 = 0.09 for Step 2 (p < .01). ΔR^2 = 0.02 for Step 3 (p > .05). ΔR^2 = 0.04 for Step 4 (p <.05). ΔR^2 = 0.00 for Step 5 (p > .05). ΔR^2 = 0.03 for Step 6 (p < .05). *p < .05. ** p < .01. *** p < .001.

The next regression tested the effects of the predictor variables on post-test dysphoria. Except for the pretest, none of the predictor variables were significant. However, the final equation with all the variables was significant.

The effects of autonomy and task feedback on post-test measures of affect were tested as follows. The first regression tested the effects of the predictor variables on positive affect. Positive feedback was a significant predictor of positive affect. Negative feedback significantly predicted a reduction in positive affect. The final step with all the predictor variables in the equation was significant. There were no other individually significant effects.

The second regression tested the effects of the predictor variables on post-test anxiety. Both autonomy and negative feedback were significant predictors of increased anxiety. Positive feedback was a significant predictor of a reduction in anxiety. The final regression step with all the predictor variables in the equation was significant. There were no other individual significant effects.

The final regression tested the effects of the predictor variables on post-test dysphoria. Positive feedback significantly predicted a decrease in dysphoria. The final step with all the predictors in the equation was significant. There were no other individual significant effects.

Figure 1. Effect of the Interaction of Sociotropy with Negative Feedback on Post-Test Anxiety.

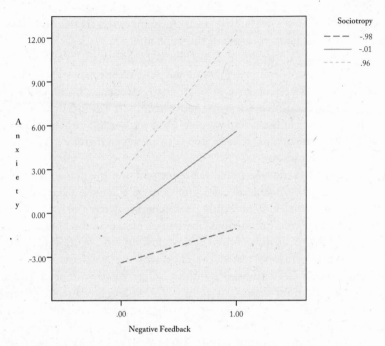

Effects of Personality Styles and Feedback on Optimism and Validation-seeking

Hierarchical multiple regressions were used to test the effects of feedback, personality styles, and their interactions on optimism and validation-seeking as dependent variables. Each hierarchical multiple regression had five steps. At the first step, personality style was entered into the regression equation, then into the two dummy-coded feedback variables, and finally into the two personality styles by feedback interactions. The effects of sociotropy and autonomy were tested separately on optimism and validation-seeking. Sociotropy and autonomy were each associated with pessimism and validation-seeking. However, there were no significant effects for feedback or their interactions with personality styles on optimism or validation-seeking.

Effects of Optimism, Validation-seeking, and Feedback on Affect

As before, hierarchical multiple regressions were used to test the moderating effects of optimism and validation-seeking on feedback in predicting reactions in affect. The regressions predicted post-test anxiety, dysphoria, and positive affect after controlling for pretest levels of the same affect. Each hierarchical multiple regression had six steps. At the first step, the pretest affect measure was entered into the regression, followed by optimism or validation-seeking, then the two dummy-coded feedback variables, and finally the two-personality variable by feedback interactions. The effects of optimism and validation-seeking were tested in separate regressions. In all regression analyses, the pretest measure of affect was significantly associated with the post-test measure of the same affect.

The effects of optimism and task feedback on measures of affect were tested as follows. The first regression tested the effects of the predictor variables on post-test positive affect. Positive feedback significantly predicted increased positive affect. Negative feedback significantly predicted decreased positive affect. There were no other significant individual predictors. However, the final regression step with all the predictor variables in the equation was significant.

The second regression tested the effects of the predictor variables on post-test anxiety. Positive feedback significantly predicted a decrease in anxiety. Negative feedback significantly predicted an increase in anxiety. There were no other significant individual predictors. However, the final regression step with all the predictor variables in the equation was significant.

The third regression tested the effects of the predictor variables on post-test dysphoria. Optimism significantly interacted with negative feedback to predict an increase in dysphoria. The final regression step with all the predictor variables in the equation was significant. There were no other significant individual predictors.

The significant interaction effect was further examined by follow-up analyses to determine the source of the interaction as before, using O'Connor's (1998) program. In the follow-up analysis of the significant interaction between optimism and negative feedback predicting post-test dysphoria, the simple slope standardized betas indicated that those who were moderate and high in optimism experienced significantly greater dysphoria when they received negative feedback, in contrast with those who received other types of feedback.

The effects of validation-seeking and task feedback on measures of affect were tested as follows. The first regression tested the effects of the predictor variables on post-test positive affect (see table 5). Positive feedback and the interaction of validation-seeking with positive feedback significantly predicted increased positive affect. Negative feedback significantly predicted decreased positive affect. There were no other significant individual predictors. However, the final regression step with all the predictor variables in the equation was significant.

In the follow-up analysis of the significant interaction between validation-seeking and positive feedback predicting post-test positive affect, the simple slope standardized betas indicated that those who were moderate and high in validation-seeking experienced significantly greater positive affect when they received positive feedback, in contrast with those who

Table 5
Hierarchical Multiple Regression Predicting Post-Test Positive Affect by Validation Seeking, Positive Feedback, Negative Feedback, and their Interactions (N = 66)

	B	SE B	β
Step 1			
Pre-Positive Affect	0.65	0.08	0.71**
Step 2			
Validation (V)	-0.13	0.07	-0.15
Step 3			
Positive Feedback (P)	2.36	1.02	0.19*
Step 4			
Negative Feedback (N)	-3.86	1.06	-0.31**
Step 5			
V x P	2.00	0.94	0.19*
Step 6			
V x N	-1.04	1.02	-0.12

Note. $R^2 = 0.50$ for Step 1 ($p < .001$). $\Delta R^2 = 0.02$ for Step 2 ($p > .05$). $\Delta R^2 = 0.04$ for Step 3 ($p < .05$). $\Delta R^2 = 0.08$ for Step 4 ($p < .01$). $\Delta R^2 = 0.02$ for Step 5 ($p < .05$). $\Delta R^2 = 0.01$ for Step 6 ($p > .05$). *$p < .05$. **$p < .01$. ***$p < .001$.

Figure 2. Effect of the Interaction of Validation-Seeking with Positive Feedback on Post-Test Positive Affect.

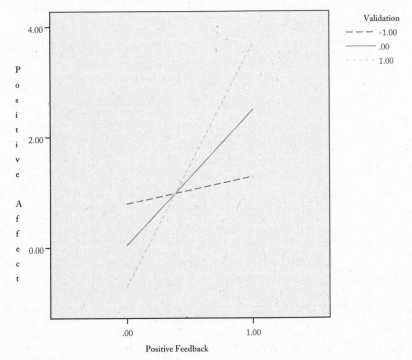

Table 6
Hierarchical Multiple Regression Predicting Post-Test Anxiety by Validation Seeking, Positive Feedback, Negative Feedback, and their Interactions (N = 66)

	B	SE B	β
Step 1			
Pre-Anxiety	0.69	0.09	0.68***
Step 2			
Validation (V)	0.48	0.17	0.25**
Step 3			
Positive Feedback (P)	-4.91	2.31	-0.18*
Step 4			
Negative Feedback (N)	5.97	2.59	0.21*
Step 5			
V x P	-4.93	2.31	0.020*
Step 6			
V x N	4.22	2.49	0.21

Note. $R^2 = 0.46$ for Step 1 ($p < .001$). $\Delta R^2 = 0.06$ for Step 2 ($p < .01$). $\Delta R^2 = 0.03$ for Step 3 ($p < .05$). $\Delta R^2 = 0.03$ for Step 4 ($p < .05$). $\Delta R^2 = 0.03$ for Step 5 ($p < .05$). $\Delta R^2 = 0.02$ for Step 6 ($p > .05$). *$p < .05$. **$p < .01$. ***$p < .001$.

Figure 3. Effect of the Interaction of Validation-Seeking with Positive Feedback on Post-Test Anxiety.

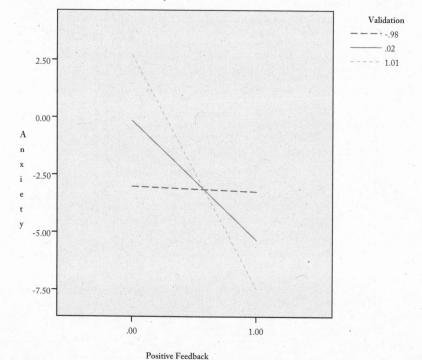

Positive Feedback

Table 7
Hierarchical Multiple Regression Predicting Post-Test Dysphoria by Validation Seeking, Positive Feedback, Negative Feedback, and their Interactions (N = 66)

	B	SE B	β
Step 1			
Pre-Dysphoria	0.65	0.11	0.59***
Step 2			
Validation (V)	0.23	0.08	0.28**
Step 3			
Positive Feedback (P)	-2.23	1.11	-0.19*
Step 4			
Negative Feedback (N)	1.94	1.26	0.16
Step 5			
V x P	-1.67	1.14	-.016
Step 6			
V x N	2.65	1.20	0.30*

Note. R^2 = 0.35 for Step 1 ($p < .001$). ΔR^2 = 0.08 for Step 2 ($p < .01$). ΔR^2 = 0.03 for Step 3 ($p < .05$). ΔR^2 = 0.02 for Step 4 ($p > .05$). ΔR^2 = 0.02 for Step 5 ($p > .05$). ΔR^2 = 0.04 for Step 6 ($p < .05$). *$p < .05$. **$p < .01$. ***$p < .001$.

received other types of feedback. See figure 2, which depicts the slopes of this interaction.

The second regression tested the effects of the predictor variables on post-test anxiety (see table 6). Validation-seeking and negative feedback significantly predicted an increase in anxiety. Positive feedback and the interaction of validation-seeking with positive feedback significantly predicted a decrease in anxiety. There were no other significant individual predictors. However, the final regression step with all the predictor variables in the equation was significant.

In the follow-up analysis of the significant interaction between validation-seeking and positive feedback predicting post-test anxiety, the simple slope standardized betas indicated that those who were moderate and high in validation-seeking experienced significantly less anxiety when they received positive feedback, in contrast with those who received other types of feedback. See figure 3, depicting the slopes of this interaction.

The third regression tested the effects of the predictor variables on post-test dysphoria (see table 7). Validation-seeking and the interaction of validation-seeking with negative feedback significantly predicted an increase in dysphoria. Positive feedback significantly predicted a decrease in dysphoria. The final regression step with all the predictor variables in the equation was significant. There were no other significant individual predictors.

In the follow-up analysis of the significant interaction between validation-seeking and negative feedback predicting post-test dysphoria, the simple slope standardized betas indicated that those who were moderate and high in validation-seeking experienced significantly greater dysphoria when they received negative feedback, in contrast with those who received other types of feedback. See figure 4, depicting the slopes of this interaction.

Figure 4. Effect of the Interaction of Validation-Seeking with Negative Feedback on Post-Test Dysphoria.

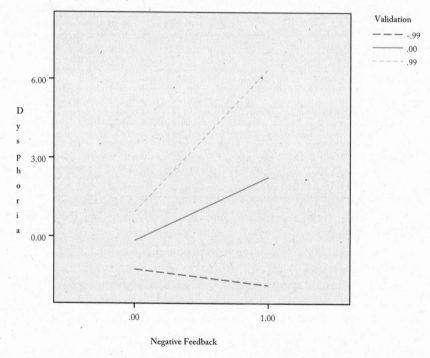

Negative Feedback

Discussion

The results of the present study indicated that overall task feedback was effective and produced affect change. Analysis of change scores revealed that positive affect decreased and anxiety increased in response to negative feedback. The regression analyses also indicated that negative feedback reduced positive affect and increased anxiety. Positive feedback increased positive affect, and lowered anxiety and dysphoria.

The results indicated that affect change was associated with vulnerable personality styles by themselves as well as by the response of vulnerable personality styles to stressful feedback. The evidence was stronger for sociotropy than autonomy. Sociotropy was associated with lower positive affect and increased anxiety. Sociotropy also increased the adverse effect of negative feedback on anxiety. Autonomy was associated only with higher anxiety by itself. There were no interactions of either personality styles with positive feedback.

Based on the present results and past research showing the similarity between personality styles and low self-esteem, we might speculate that individuals with vulnerable personality styles might be sensitive to failure experiences, with dependency, self-criticism, and avoidance as possible reactions. Sociotropic individuals might react to failure with excessive reassurance-seeking (Joiner & Metalsky, 2001). Like low-self-esteem individuals, they might be motivated to avoid failure (Brown & Dutton, 1995) and tend to ruminate on them (Dodgson & Wood, 1998). Also like depression-prone individuals, they might engage in excessive negative self-evaluations when they fail some important task (Hyland, 1987; Pyszczynski & Greenberg, 1987). These reactions to failure tend to prolong rather than diminish negative affect (Fichman, Koestner, Zuroff, & Laurel, 1999).

The present study also investigated whether validation-seeking and pessimistic expectations might be reactions to stress of individuals with vulnerable personality styles. The results suggested that this was not the case. Sociotropy and autonomy were both related to pessimistic expectations and validation-seeking. However, the results suggested that these two motivation orientations were neither a consequence or a reaction of the personality styles to stress. Rather, the association of the personality styles and these two motivation orientations are more likely to be due to shared or similar underlying personality processes.

Validation-seeking was associated with increased anxiety and dysphoria. Validation-seeking also increased the adverse effect of negative feedback on dysphoria. Counter to expectation, optimism also increased the adverse effect of negative feedback on dysphoria. This was likely the result, however, of the anomaly of the particular regression analysis, as optimism by itself was not related to any affect change in any of the analyses. Validation-seeking also showed a unique reaction to positive feedback. Those high on validation-seeking showed an increase in positive affect and a reduction in anxiety in reaction to positive feedback. The results suggest that validation-seeking is different than personality styles like sociotropy, which showed reactions only to negative feedback. Whereas personality styles seem to show sensitivity mostly to failure, those high in validation-seeking are also sensitive to positive feedback and a boost to their self-esteem. The results suggest, therefore, that the two forms of dysfunctional regulations of self-worth might be different, with mostly avoidance of loss of self-worth present in sociotropy, and both avoidance and approach processes present in validation-seeking.

The present findings were not totally consistent with the congruency theory of the development of emotional disorders as proposed by Beck's cognitive theory (Beck, 1983; Clark & Beck, 1991; Sacco & Beck, 1995). Although in the case of sociotropy this personality style did moderate negative feedback to increase anxiety, increase in negative affect was not dependent on events matching a personal style, as required by congruency theory (Beck, 1983; Clark & Beck, 1991; Sacco & Beck, 1995). Other studies have shown similar findings (Clark, Beck, & Brown, 1992; Kwon & Whisman, 1998; Mazure, Bruce, Maciejewski, & Jacobs, 2000; Rude & Burnham, 1993). There were no congruency effects for autonomy. These personality styles appear to be associated with negative affect regardless of the presence of matching negative events. Therefore, cognitive-theory explanations of the processes by which these personality styles influence the development of emotional disorders need to be reconsidered.

Difficulties with the regulation of self-worth have been shown to lead to emotional problems and depression (Roberts & Monroe, 1999). Overall, our findings are consistent with the proposal that dysfunctional regulations of self-worth are related to negative affect in women. It has been proposed that sociotropy and autonomy are associated with a preoccupation with the use of extrinsic goals to acquire self-worth (Campbell & Kwon, 2001). In our study, these personality styles showed significant correlations with both validation-seeking and pessimistic expectations. Validation-seeking is the tendency to be preoccupied with self-concerns and to prove one's self-worth (Dykman, 1998). Extrinsic motivation orientations in these personality styles and in validation-seeking expose the person's self-worth to the vagaries of circumstances. Extrinsically oriented goal pursuits have been associated with negative affect and poor adjustment when not realized (Crocker, 2002; Crocker, Karpinski, Quinn, & Chase, 2003; Crocker, Luhtanen, Cooper, & Bouvrette, 2003). Our findings also indicated that individuals with a validation-seeking orientation are especially sensitive to external events as they reacted to both negative as well as positive feedback. Extrinsic motivational orientations might also displace the individual's ability to acquire and make use of intrinsic interests (Crocker & Park, 2004; Deci & Ryan, 2000). Intrinsic motivational orientations tend to reflect self-determination and are associated with well-being (Ratelle, Vallerand, Chantal, & Provencher, 2004; Ryan & Deci, 2000). Sociotropy and autonomy were also associated with pessimism. Pessimism also reflects perceived difficulties with the acquisition of goals that have implications for self-worth. According to the hopelessness theory of depression, pessimism originates in the tendency to attribute the causes of negative outcomes to oneself but the causes of positive outcomes to external factors (Abramson et al., 1989).

Executive processes are involved in the self-regulation of affect. Self-mastery executive processes have been shown to directly influence self-esteem (Neiss et al., 2005). Self-esteem, in turn, mediates the association between the executive self or self-mastery and negative affect. It has been suggested that higher rates of depression in women might be the result of lack of executive control over the frames of reference by which self-worth is evaluated (Horvath, 2008). Women tend to adopt external fames of reference to evaluate themselves or their self-worth, which makes them vulnerable to dysphoria (Moretti, Rein, & Wiebe, 1998). More evidence for the central role of control over the evaluation of self-worth in negative affect comes from research on depression in women. For example, research has shown that "silencing the self" or lack of control over self-expression and self-worth is associated with depression in women (Jack, 1999; Jack & Dill, 1992). Women have less access to the levers of power through which social position and success is acquired. The fact that women have less social power might result in their having less control over the criteria by which they are evaluated. Fewer opportunities might also lead to fewer alternate sources of satisfaction to rely on in case of loss or stress, making women more vulnerable to affective disorders (Champion & Power, 1995).

Some limitations of the study need to be considered. The sequence task and feedback were aimed more at achievement than at social needs and goals. The feedback also appears to have had only a moderate degree of impact. We also did not measure diagnosed mood disorders in clinical populations. Consequently, one must be cautious of generalizing the present findings to an understanding of the causes of mood disorders in women. However, our findings were consistent with past research, and helped to clarify some issues that had remained ambiguous and unresolved. Accordingly, we can view the present findings as helping to extend our understanding of the role of motivational and self-regulation processes in the onset of negative and positive mood in women.

Note

This study was partially based on the Master's thesis of Pamela Wambolt and was supported by a Social Sciences and Humanities Research Council of Canada Small Institutional Grant held by the first author.

References

Abramson, L. Y., Alloy, L. B., Hankin, B. L., Haeffel, G. J., MacCoon, D. G., & Gibb, B. E. (2002). Cognitive vulnerability-stress models of depression in a self-regulatory and psychobiological context. In I. H. Gotlib & C. L. Hammen, (Eds.), *Handbook of depression* (pp. 268–294). New York: Guilford.

Abramson, L. Y., Metalsky, G. L., & Alloy, L. B. (1989). Hopelessness depression: A theory-based subtype of depression. *Psychological Review, 96,* 358–372.

Aiken, L. S., & West, S. G. (1991). *Multiple regression: Testing and interpreting interactions.* Newbury Park, CA: Sage.

Alloy, L. B., Just, N., & Panzarella, C. (1997). Attributional style, daily life events, and hopelessness depression: Subtype validation by prospective variability and specificity of symptoms. *Cognitive Therapy and Research, 21,* 321–344.

Baron, R., & Kenney, D. (1986). The moderator-mediator distinction in social psychology research: Conceptual, strategic and statistical considerations. *Journal of Personality and Social Psychology, 51,* 1173–1182.

Beck, A. (1983). Cognitive therapy of depression: New perspectives. In P. J. Clayton & J. E. Barrett (Eds.), *Treatment of depression: Old controversies and new approaches* (pp. 265–283). New York: Raven.

Block, J., & Robbins, R. W. (1993). A longitudinal study of consistency and change in self-esteem from early adolescence to early adulthood. *Child Development, 64,* 909–923.

Brems, C. (1995). Women and depression: A comprehensive analysis. In E. E. Beckman & W. R. Leber (Eds.), *Handbook of depression* (2nd ed., pp. 539–566). New York, NY: Guilford Press.

Brown, J., & Dutton, K. (1995) The thrill of victory, the complexity of defeat: Self-esteem and people's emotional reactions to success and failure. *Journal of Personality and Social Psychology, 68,* 712–722.

Campbell, D. G., & Kwon, P. (2001). Domain-specific hope and personal style: Toward an integrative understanding of dysphoria. *Journal of Social and Clinical Psychology, 20,* 498–520.

Champion, L., & Power, M. (1995). Social and cognitive approaches to depression: Towards a new synthesis. *British Journal of Clinical Psychology, 34,* 485–503.

Clark, D. A., & Beck, A. T. (1991). Personality factors in dysphoria: A psychometric refinement of Beck's sociotropy-autonomy scale. *Journal of Psychopathology and Behavioral Assessment, 13,* 369–388.

Clark, D., Beck, A., & Brown, G. (1992). Sociotropy, autonomy, and life event perceptions in dysphoric and nondysphoric individuals. *Cognitive Therapy and Research, 16,* 635–652.

Coyne, J. C. & Whiffen, V. E. (1995). Issues in personality as diathesis for depression: The case of sociotropy-dependency and autonomy-self-criticism. *Psychological Bulletin, 118,* 358–378.

Crocker, J. (2002). Contingencies of self-worth: Implications for self-regulation and psychological vulnerability. *Self and Identity, 1,* 143–149.

Crocker, J., Karpinski, A., Quinn, D. M., & Chase, S. K. (2003). When grades determine self-worth: Consequences of contingent self-worth for male and female engineering and psychology majors. *Journal of Personality and Social Psychology, 85,* 507–516.

Crocker, J., Luhtanen, R. K., Cooper, M. L., & Bouvrette, A. (2003). Contingencies of self-worth in college students: Theory and measurement. *Journal of Personality and Social Psychology, 85,* 894–908.

Crocker, J., & Park, L. E. (2004). The costly pursuit of self-esteem. *Psychological Bulletin, 130,* 392–414.

Deci, E. L., & Ryan, R. M. (2000). The "what" and "why" of goal pursuits: Human needs and the self-determination of behavior. *Psychological Inquiry, 11,* 227–268.

Dodgson, P., & Wood, J. (1998). Self-esteem and the cognitive accessibility of strengths and weaknesses after failure. *Journal of Personality and Social Psychology, 25,* 178–197.

Dykman, B. (1998) Integrating cognitive and motivational factors in depression: Initial tests of a goal-orientation approach. *Journal of Personality and Social Psychology, 74,* 139–158.

Endler, N. S., & Kocovski, N. L. (2000). Self-regulation and distress in clinical psychology. In M. Boekaerts, P. R. Pintrich, & M. Zeidner (Eds.), *Handbook of self-regulation* (pp. 569–599). San Diego, CA: Academic Press.

Fairbrother, N., & Moretti, M. (1998). Sociotropy, autonomy, and self-discrepancy: Status in depressed, remitted depressed, and control participants. *Cognitive Therapy and Research, 22,* 279–296.

Fichman, L., Koestner, R., Zuroff, D., & Laurel, G. (1999). Depressive styles and the regulation of negative affect: A daily experience study. *Cognitive Therapy and Research, 23,* 483–495.

Health Canada. (2002). *A report on mental illnesses in Canada.* Ottawa.

Horvath, P. (2008). Introduction: Women, depression, and the struggle for control over the evaluation of self-worth. *Journal of Prevention and Intervention in the Community, 35,* 1–3.

Horvath, P., Bissix, G., Sumarah, J., Crouchman, E., & Bowdrey, J. (2008). Motivational orientation, expectancies, and vulnerability for depression in women. *Journal of Prevention and Intervention in the Community, 35,* 19–32.

Hyland, M. (1987). Control theory interpretation of psychological mechanisms of depression: Comparison and integration of several theories. *Psychological Bulletin, 102,* 109–121.

Jack, D. C. (1999). Silencing the self: Inner dialogues and outer realities. In T. Joiner & J. C. Coyne (Eds.), *The interactional nature of depression: Advances in interpersonal approaches* (pp. 221–246). Washington, DC: American Psychological Association.

Jack, D. C., & Dill, D. (1992). The Silencing the Self Scale: Schemas of intimacy associated with depression in women. *Psychology of Women Quarterly, 16,* 97–106.

Joiner, T., & Metalsky, G. (2001). Excessive reassurance seeking: Delineating a risk factor involved in the development of depressive symptoms. *Psychological Science, 12,* 371–378.

Kernis, M. H., Grannemann, B. D., & Mathis, L. C. (1991). Stability of self-esteem as a moderator of the relation between level of self-esteem and depression. *Journal of Personality and Social Psychology, 61,* 80–84.

Kocovski, N. L., & Endler, N. S. (2000). Self-regulation: Social anxiety and depression. *Journal of Applied Biobehavioral Research, 5,* 80–91.

Kwon, P., & Whisman, M. A. (1998). Sociotropy and autonomy as vulnerabilities to specific life events: Issues in life event categorization. *Cognitive Therapy and Research, 22,* 353–362.

Mazure, C., Bruce, M., Maciejewski, P., & Jacobs, S. (2000). Adverse life events and cognitive-personality characteristics in the prediction of major depression and antidepressant response. *American Journal of Psychiatry, 157,* 896–903.

Mazure, C. M., Keita, G. P., & Blehar, M. C. (2002). *Summit on women and depression: Proceedings and recommendations.* Washington, DC: American Psychological Association. Retrieved from: http://www.apa.org/pi/wpo/women&depression.pdf

McGrath, E., Keita, G. P., Strickland, B. R., & Russo, N. F. (1990). *Women and depression: Risk factors and treatment issues: Final report of the American Psychological Association's National Task Force on Women and Depression.* Washington, DC: American Psychological Association.

Moretti, M., Rein, A., & Wiebe, V. (1998). Relational self-regulation: Gender differences in risk for dysphoria. *Canadian Journal of Behavioural Science, 30,* 243–252.

Neiss, M. B., Stevenson, J., Sedikides, C., Kumashiro, M., Finkel, E. J., & Rusbult, C. E. (2005). Executive self, self-esteem, and negative affectivity: Relations at the phenotypic and genotypic level. *Journal of Personality and Social Psychology, 89,* 593–606.

Nolen-Hoeksema, S. (2006). The etiology of gender differences in depression. In C. M. Mazure & G. P. Keita (Eds.), *Understanding depression in women: Applying empirical research to practice and policy* (pp. 9–43). Washington, DC: American Psychological Association.

O'Connor, B. P. (1998). SIMPLE: All-in-one programs for exploring interactions in moderated multiple regression. *Educational and Psychological Measurement, 58,* 833–837.

Payne, S. C., Youngcourt, S. S., & Beaubien, J. M. (2007). A meta-analytic examination of the goal orientation nomological net. *Journal of Applied Psychology, 92,* 128–150.

Pyszczynski, T., & Greenberg, J. (1987). Self-regulatory perseveration and the depressive self-focusing style: A self-awareness theory of reactive depression. *Psychological Bulletin, 102,* 122–138.

Radloff, L. (1977). The CES-D scale: A self-report depression scale for research in the general population. *Applied Psychological Measurement, 1,* 385–401.

Ratelle, C. F., Vallerand, R. J., Chantal, Y., & Provencher, P. (2004). Cognitive adaptation and mental health: A motivational analysis. *European Journal of Social Psychology, 34,* 459–476.

Roberts, J. E., & Gotlib, I. H. (1997). Temporal variability in global self-esteem and specific self-evaluation as prospective predictors of emotional distress: Specificity in predictors and outcome. *Journal of Abnormal Psychology, 106,* 521–529.

Roberts, J., & Monroe, S. (1999). Vulnerable self-esteem and social processes in depression: Toward an interpersonal model of self-esteem regulation. In T. Joiner & J. Coyne (Eds.), *The interactional nature of depression: Advances in interpersonal approaches* (pp. 149–187). Washington, DC: American Psychological Association.

Robins, C., Ladd, J., Welkowitz, J., Blaney, P., Diaz, R., & Kutcher, G. (1994). The Personal Style Inventory: Preliminary validation studies of new measures of sociotropy and autonomy. *Journal of Psychopathology and Behavioral Assessment, 16,* 277–300.

Rottler, A. (2003). Rottus' Sequence Test. Retrieved July 13, 2006, from http://www
.bricks-game.de/seqtest/rst_neu2.html

Rude, S., & Burnham, B. (1993). Do interpersonal and achievement vulnerabilities
interact with congruent events to predict depression? Comparison of DEQ, SAS, and
combined scales. *Cognitive Therapy and Research, 17*, 531–548.

Ryan, R. M., & Deci, E. L. (2000). Self-determination theory and the facilitation of
intrinsic motivation, social development, and well-being. *American Psychologist, 55*,
68–78.

Sacco, W. P., & Beck, A. T. (1995). Cognitive theory and therapy. In E. E. Beckham &
W. R. Leber (Eds.), *Handbook of depression* (2nd ed., pp. 329–351). New York: Guilford
Press.

Santor, D. (2003). Proximal effects of dependency and self-criticism: Conceptual and
methodological challenges for depressive vulnerability research. *Cognitive Behaviour
Therapy, 32*, 49–67.

Scheier, M., Carver, C., & Bridges, M. (1994). Distinguishing optimism from neu-
roticism (and trait anxiety, self-mastery, and self-esteem): A reevaluation of the Life
Orientation Test. *Journal of Personality and Social Psychology, 67*, 1063–1078.

Spielberger, C. D. (1983). *Manual for the State-Trait Anxiety Inventory (STAI)*. Palo
Alto, CA: Consulting Psychologists Press.

Stewart, D. E., Gucciardi, E., & Grace, S. L. (2004). Depression. *BMC Women's Health*,
4(Suppl. 1), S19. Retrieved from http://www.biomedcentral.com/1472-6874/4/S1/S19

Strauman, T. J. (1995). Psychopathology form a self-regulation perspective. *Journal of
Psychotherapy Integration, 5*, 313–321.

Tabachnick, B., & Fidell, L. (2001). *Using multivariate statistics* (4th ed.). Needham
Heights, MA: Allyn & Bacon.

Tripp, D. A., Catano, V., & Sullivan, M. J. L. (1997). The contributions of attributional
style, expectancies, depression, and self-esteem in a cognition-based depression model.
Canadian Journal of Behavioural Science, 29, 101–111.

Zuckerman, M., & Lubin, B. (1985). *Manual for the Multiple Affect Adjective Checklist-
Revised (MAACL-R)*. San Diego, CA: Educational and Industrial Testing Service.

Kathryn D. Lafreniere, Donna M. Eansor,
Joanna Kraft, and Elsa Sardinha

The Health Consequences of Negotiating Work–Life Balance in the Legal Profession: A Focus on Women's Resilience

"Work–life balance" is a catchphrase of the early twenty-first century, capturing the struggle of Canadian families to balance the demands of paid work with caregiving responsibilities. Striking this balance generates a work–life conflict that involves both role overload (having too much to do and not enough time) and role conflict (feeling pulled apart by conflicting demands) (Baruch, Biener, & Barnett, 1987). Accomplishing work–life balance in the legal profession, specifically in legal practice, poses a formidable challenge. The present study examined the experience and consequences of work–family and family–work conflict in a large stratified sample of Canadian women lawyers.

Perceptions about work–life balance vary greatly between older, established lawyers and newer-generation lawyers. Older lawyers tend to be willing and able to work long hours and to service their clients at a moment's notice, whereas younger lawyers are less so inclined. In a recent Catalyst study, newer lawyers cited an environment supportive of work and family commitments as a factor for strong consideration in the choice of a potential law firm (Catalyst, 2005). To recruit young lawyers, many law firms have been promising a work–life balance, yet many lawyers see this as the "great lie." A lawyer from a national firm says: .

> The associates who leave are most upset with the lie ... that the work-life balance can exist ... They get upset with the image that we hold out, that we can accommodate any type of individual as long as they are smart. We can't. The model itself does not allow it. Don't tell them that we have a work-life balance. We don't. (McPhee, 2007, p. 38)

Work–life balance in the legal profession is difficult to attain, as setting schedules and determining workflow depends on client demand. Lawyers provide services to clients when clients need service, and that often requires late nights and work on weekends. Established lawyers often argue that work–life balance can be achieved "through sheer will and ... compromise" (McPhee, 2007, p. 38), although most of these same lawyers admit that firms are moving away from endeavouring work–life balance.

There are numerous reasons why law firms should be moving toward, and not away from, work–life balance. One is that lawyers are likely to stay with a firm long term if their perceptions of their work–life balance are positive. This will reduce turnover of both female and male associates, although a greater percentage of women have been quitting private practice in record numbers since the early 1990s: 62% of female associates and 47% of male associates surveyed expect to leave their firms in the next five years. Law firms are abuzz with talk of retention strategies as financial advisors recommend gender equality and work–life balance because it makes good business sense. In terms of dollars, associate turnover costs firms $315,000 for a four-year associate (or approximately twice the average associate's annual salary) every time an associate leaves the firm (Catalyst, 2005). One of the most compelling reasons for poor retention is that lack of work–life balance is systemic and constricts gender equality in the legal profession. Under the law, women have a constitutional right to be treated equally and without discrimination in employment. The Ontario Human Rights Code requires law firms to provide environments that allow women to advance without barriers based on gender.[1]

Women are not advancing in the legal practice because of barriers that are intricately connected with gender. Compared with their male counterparts, women earn less income (Cooper, Brockman, & Hoffart, 2004) and occupy fewer partnership positions (Kay, Curry, & Masuch, 2004; Kay, Masuch, & Curry, 2004), are less likely to be in positions of seniority or supervision, experience low levels of autonomy, and have little policy decision-making power (Cooper et al., 2004; Kay, et al., 2004; Rhode, 2001b). Moreover, the retention of women in private practice has reached a critical stage; there is a significantly higher rate of attrition for women than men in private practice (Catalyst, 2005), and the attrition rate of women of colour is more alarming (Rhode, 2001b). The number of women leaving private practice means that fewer women will advance to positions where they can facilitate change within the profession that will lead to the advancement of women lawyers. "Women cannot move up the ladder in sufficient volume to influence significant change, and the few who do either grow weary of fighting against the current, or become co-opted over time" (Cooper et al., 2004, p. 168). As a result, in 2008 the Law Society of Upper Canada identified the issue of retaining women in private practice as a priority and has proposed strategies to address the issue, including the creation of the Retention of Women Working Group (Law Society of Upper Canada [LSUC], 2008).

Women are leaving the legal practice in droves and central to this attrition is the work–life conflict (Cooper et al., 2004; LSUC, 2008). Women continue to provide the bulk of caregiving in our society, whether it is for children, aging parents, relatives, or family members with disabilities. For example, over 70% of informal caregiving for individuals with dementia is provided by women (Alzheimer Society of Canada, 2005). Professional women, including lawyers, experience the highest levels of work–life conflict by substantive margins (Duxbury & Higgins, 2001; Rhode, 2001a). Both women and men lawyers devote the same amount of time per week practicing law, yet male lawyers spend less than half, and in some cases as little as one-fourth, of the time as women engaged in informal caregiving (Cooper et al., 2004; Kay, Curry, et al., 2004). A woman lawyer observed, "Women lawyers have a tough time balancing work and family. Men don't! I see it over and over and they never *get it*." (Kay, Curry, et al., 2004, p. 81). The experiences of inequality of women in the legal profession, including work–life conflict, inadequate pay, and occupying lower ranking positions within the profession, are stressors that can elevate the risk of a woman lawyer experiencing mental-health problems. Health research has shown that these stressors are associated with vulnerability to higher risk and greater incidence of mental-health problems (World Health Organization, 2001). Work–life conflict alone is a leading cause of stress, distress, and mental-health problems, including depression (Duxbury, Higgins, & Johnson, 1999; Rosenfield, 1999). Women lawyers might be particularly susceptible to these health problems, as other scientific evidence suggests that they are among the most high-risk groups in Canada and the United States to experience mental-health problems. Lawyers, both men and women, experience elevated mental-health risks (Sells, 1994). For example, a research study conducted by John Hopkins University determined that lawyers topped the list of 104 occupations suffering from major depressive disorder, at a rate of 3.6 times higher than non-lawyers (Syverud & Schiltx, 1999). Women are more likely to experience certain types of mental-health problems than are men. Globally, for example, women are nearly twice as likely to experience depression than men, a finding which runs across all socio-economic levels (Department of Mental Health and Substance Abuse, 2002). Health scientists have linked poor mental health with patterns of direct and systemic discrimination within the family and within the workplace (Kay, 1989), including work–life conflict. Discrimination in the legal profession based on gender and other characteristics is pervasive and well-documented (Cooper et al., 2004; Kay, 1989; Kay, Curry, et al., 2004; Rhode, 2001b).

Stressors, including work–life conflict, inadequate pay, and occupying lower ranking positions within the profession, are determinants of health and amenable to change (Public Health Agency of Canada, n.d.). One of the key elements of the so-called population approach is the examination of the determinants of health and their interactions in a population or subpopulation. The goal of this element is to "frame" health issues in terms of their causes. Once risks to mental health are identified, workplace-intervention strategies can be developed and implemented. The Public Health Agency of Canada acknowledges that not all eight key elements will be addressed at the same time and by the same individuals and agencies. Research that addresses any of the elements is a contribution to gaps that exist in current knowledge.

Legal organizations, including law firms, can craft well-structured management practices to eliminate the existence of these stressors in the workplace and create a neutral opportunity field for women lawyers. Women will successfully integrate into the profession and advance appropriately, and resilience to mental-health problems will simultaneously be achieved as positive supportive environments act as a buffer against the risks of ill health. The retention of women in private legal practice serves as an example of where workplace structures might operate to create this neutral opportunity field. Some legal organizations, including law firms, have created policies that include flexible hours and/or reduced hours with reduced pay, extended maternity and paternity leaves, and child-care benefits to address work–life conflict. Firms with these policies report the highest retention rates (LSUC, 2008).

At the same time, despite these efforts many women lawyers are reluctant to access law-firm policies crafted to address work–life conflict. A recent Catalyst study (2003) revealed that only 25% of women felt that they could use flexible work arrangements without career penalties, while many other women reported unfriendly environments and strong challenges to their professional commitment when they did access these policies. A real fear of being ostracized and experiencing backlash exists. One woman lawyer in their study said:

> I have what many working mothers in this profession might consider the ideal job—work in a child-focused field of public law, no billing pressures, an assured salary, some promotion abilities ... Yet I have

developed a pervasive resentment for what I have "given up" in order
to accommodate work and family, while my colleagues seem to have
developed their own resentment for precisely the same reason—what
they have each had to assume in order to accommodate my work and
my family! We all pass each other in the hallway, dissatisfied with the
arrangement, while the executive staff gives itself a collective pat on
the back. (Kay, Curry, et al., 2004, p. 82)

Women who are mothers, unlike men who are fathers, are often as-
sumed to lack the commitment required for partnerships and senior positions, resulting in negative performance evaluations for these women
(Rhode, 2001b). The perception is that women contribute less time on the
job than their male counterparts, but data clearly shows that this is not so
(Kay, Curry, et al., 2004). Memories of women leaving the office early pre-
dominate, while memories of the nights women have worked late are dim
(Rhode, 2001b).

Wallace (1999) examined work-to-non-work conflict in a large Canadian sample of married male and female lawyers and found that female lawyers reported significantly higher levels of work overload than male lawyers,
although male lawyers reported working longer hours. Results of her study
showed that the actual number of hours worked was not an important predictor of work-to-non-work conflict, but rather the perception of excessive
demands was the most critical determinant of work-to-non-work conflict
for both women and men. Work settings were an important factor that
influenced women's experiences of work-to-non-work conflict, and working in a law firm resulted in greater time-based conflict and role strain for
women. Interestingly, Wallace's results also showed that having preschool
children actually led to reductions in strain-based conflict for women. Wallace speculated that many of these mothers might have the presence of
external help in assisting with child care and home responsibilities, and
suggested that simultaneously meeting the demands of young children and
a demanding and prestigious professional career might contribute to positive feelings of fulfillment and satisfaction in these women, based on their
abilities to successfully navigate their multiple roles.

One variable that might influence women's experience trying to negotiate a work–life balance in the legal profession is that of *resilience*. Psychological resilience refers to a set of dynamic processes that allow an individual to adapt to and move beyond adversity or threatening situations
(Dalton, Elias, & Wandersman, 2001). Resilience involves transactions between the person and their environment, in that factors in the environment,
such as the presence of supportive others, tangible services, and resources,
can help to foster resilience in people who are experiencing challenges or
threats. At the same time, considering resilience as a personality variable
can help to clarify relationships between experiences of workplace stress

and health consequences (Ferris, Sinclair, & Kline, 2005). Although there is little agreement on the definition of resilience, it is commonly contrasted with vulnerability to adversity, and some theorists place vulnerability and resilience at opposite ends of a single continuum (Jackson, Firtko, & Edenborough, 2007). Qualities associated with resilience include resourcefulness, problem-solving abilities, flexibility, and optimism, and factors such as empowerment and self-care are key aspects of developing personal resilience (Jackson et al., 2007).

Previous research has shown resilience to be a protective factor that mediates between occupational stressors and negative outcomes such as burnout and symptomatology. For example, Glasberg, Eriksson, and Norberg (2007) found that low social support from co-workers and low levels of resilience were associated with emotional exhaustion in a sample of 423 Swedish healthcare personnel, who experienced high levels of occupational stress, such as heavy work demands, high work–life conflict, and lack of time to provide adequate care. Similar findings were reported by McCallister, Dolbier, Webster, Mallon, and Steinhardt (2006) in a study that examined protective factors (including dispositional resilience and co-worker and supervisor support) in relation to job satisfaction and work stress in a large sample of American government employees and technology workers. Their findings indicated that resilience and support from supervisors and co-workers significantly predicted job satisfaction and were negative predictors of work stress. McCallister et al. suggested that interventions that particularly target increasing supervisor support and foster personal resilience have the greatest influence on increased job satisfaction.

The Present Study

The present study examined whether workplace stressors and high levels of work–life conflict led to negative consequences, including decreased job satisfaction and burnout, in a sample of Canadian women lawyers. In addition, we wanted to examine the mental-health consequences of these women's work experiences, including an examination of women's levels of depression and anxiety, as well as whether women's levels of resilience reduce the impact of negative workplace experiences. Questionnaires containing measures of work–family conflict, job satisfaction, burnout, mental-health symptomatology, resilience, and demographic characteristics were mailed to a random sample of women lawyers from the provinces of Alberta, Ontario, New Brunswick, and Nova Scotia.

This study investigated the following hypotheses:

1) It was predicted that women lawyers who reported higher levels of work–family conflict and family–work conflict would experience greater perceived stress, burnout, mental-health symptomatology, and lower levels of job satisfaction.

2) High personal resilience was expected to mediate the relations between work–family conflict (or family–work conflict) and negative mental-health outcomes.

We also examined the impact of women's unique circumstances on work–family conflict, family–work conflict, and the outcome variables (perceived stress, burnout, mental-health symptoms, and job satisfaction) to address the following research questions: Does being married (or living with a partner) influence women's experience of work–life balance and its outcomes? Does having children, particularly small children living at home, increase women's levels of work–family and family–work conflict and their negative consequences? Do women lawyers who are older and those with more years of practice in the legal profession experience less work–family conflict and fewer negative consequences? Do women who work in law firms experience greater work–family conflict and more negative consequences, as compared with women employed in other legal settings? Additionally, we examined the supports and family-friendly policies that women identified in their workplaces, and assessed whether women lawyers would be comfortable in accessing these services and supports.

Method

Participants

The participants were 277 women lawyers who ranged in age from 27 to 77 years, with a median age of 38. The majority of respondents were employed in law firms as counsel or associates (38.3%) or as partners (15.5%). Other women were employed as industry or corporate counsel (14.8%), government lawyers (10.8%), and sole practitioners (9.0%). The remaining women were employed in various settings including legal-aid clinics, as union lawyers or labour arbitrators, as in-house counsel to non-profit organizations, or were recently retired from the practice of law. Most women (58%) had practiced law for 10 or fewer years. The majority of women identified as heterosexual (95.7%), were married or living with a partner (72.9%), and reported having one or more children (56.0%).

Most women identified their ethnic or cultural group as English Canadian (52.7%), followed by British (7.2%), and French Canadian (6.9%). The remainder identified as eastern (5.1%), western (3.2%), or southern European (2.5%); Far Eastern (2.9%); Aboriginal (2.5%); Scandinavian (2.2%); and a number of other diverse cultural groups including Middle Eastern, African, Caribbean, Latin American, South American, and Australian, with fewer than 1.5% of respondents in each of these groups. Annual incomes ranged from less than $24,000 (1.1%) to greater than $500,000 (2.2%), with the majority of women indicating annual earnings in the $50,000 to $99,999 range (39.4%), followed by the $100,000 to $149,999 range (25.3%).

Participant Recruitment

This study is part of a larger investigation that employed a mail-out survey to assess the impact of workplace stressors, including gendered elements of the work environment, on the mental health of women in the legal profession. Questionnaires were mailed in September 2007, to a random sample of 1,234 women lawyers from the provinces of Alberta, Ontario, New Brunswick, and Nova Scotia based on lists obtained from the Canadian Bar Association. Most returns were received in October and November 2007. Eleven questionnaires were returned unopened because the recipient was no longer at the posted address. A total of 277 completed questionnaires were returned, yielding an overall response rate of 22.6%. Response rates varied by province, with the highest rate of response obtained from Nova Scotia (30.1%) and the lowest from New Brunswick (17.8%). Ontario and Alberta had response rates of 22.8% and 18.0%, respectively.

Measures and Procedure

The entire questionnaire took approximately 35 to 45 minutes to complete and contained detailed demographic questions that included a number of questions regarding professional background (e.g., areas of practice, years practicing, current position, hours worked per week, characteristics of the work setting)[2] and personal background (including sex, age, ethnicity, relationship status, sexual orientation, number of children, and income). Included in each questionnaire package were an informed consent letter, the questionnaire, a postage-prepaid return envelope, and an individually wrapped teabag with a sticker that said "Please enjoy this cup of tea while you complete our survey. Thank you for your help!" Dillman's Tailored Design Method (Dillman, 2000) suggests including a token incentive to maximize response rates to mail-out surveys.

In addition to the demographic questions, the questionnaire included the following measures:

Work–family conflict and family–work conflict scales.
Work–family conflict and family–work conflict were measured using Netemeyer, Boles, and McMurrian's (1996) scale. This measure consists of five
items assessing work–family conflict and five items assessing family–work
conflict, measured on a seven-point Likert-type scale (strongly disagree to
strongly agree). Work–family conflict refers to job-related demands that
interfere with home and family life, while family–work conflict concerns
the conflict that arises from demands from family and home life impacting
upon work-related duties. Both work–family conflict and family–work conflict have been found to be reliable and valid measures of work–life conflict
in numerous previous studies, and the measures showed strong internal-
consistency reliability (Cronbach's alpha = .94 for work–family conflict and
= .90 for family–work conflict) in the present sample.

Job-satisfaction survey.
Job satisfaction was assessed using Spector's (1985) Job Satisfaction Survey.
This measure is comprised of sub-scales assessing satisfaction with workplace experiences, including pay, promotion, supervision, benefits, contingent rewards, operating procedures, co-workers, nature of work, and communication. To shorten the measure and make it more uniformly applicable
to women lawyers employed in diverse legal settings, we eliminated the pay,
benefits, and communication sub-scales, which yielded a 24-item instrument of total job satisfaction. The abbreviated measure showed good internal consistency (α = .91) in the current sample.

Maslach Burnout Inventory.
This indicator (Schaufeli, Leiter, Maslach, & Jackson, 1996) includes a 16-
item inventory that has been successfully used in research on occupational
groups that included lawyers (e.g., Langballe, Falkum, Innstrand, & Aasland, 2006) and was used in the present study to assess three sub-factors of
burnout: emotional exhaustion, cynicism, and reduced professional efficacy.
The internal consistency of the sub-scales was adequate in the present study
(α = .92 for emotional exhaustion, α = .83 for professional efficacy, and α =
.88 for cynicism).

Perceived-stress scale.
This 14-item scale is widely used as a measure of non-specific appraised
stress. Cohen, Kamarck, & Mermelstein (1983) reported high internal-
consistency reliability for the measure, with alpha coefficients of .84 to .86
reported for standardization samples. Previous studies have supported the
convergent and predictive validity of the Perceived Stress Scale, based on
correlations with life-events stress, depression, use of health services, and
health behaviours (Cohen & Williamson, 1988). Internal-consistency reliability of this measure was strong (α = .89) in the present study.

Symptom Assessment–45 Questionnaire.

The SA-45 questionnaire involves a brief measure of psychiatric symptomatology suitable for use in both clinical and non-clinical samples (Strategic Advantage, 2000). In the present study, each of the following five-item subscales was assessed: anxiety, depression, hostility, interpersonal sensitivity (symptomatic feelings about oneself in relation to others, such as feelings of inferiority or unease), obsessive-compulsive (includes difficulty making decisions, repetitive checking, and doing things slowly to ensure they are correct), paranoid ideation (includes feelings that others cannot be trusted, and beliefs that others fail to give credit for one's achievements), and somatization (presence of vague bodily symptoms). Internal consistency was adequate for all of the sub-scales in the present study, with Cronbach's alpha coefficients as follows: anxiety = .72, depression = .84, hostility = .74, interpersonal sensitivity = .81, obsessive-compulsive = .80, paranoid ideation = .82, and somatization = .72.

Resilience Scale

The instrument (Wagnild & Young, 1993) consists of 25 items measured on a seven-point Likert-type scale that assess resilience as an individual personality characteristic that reflects ability to adapt and persevere despite stressful circumstances. A Cronbach's alpha coefficient of .90 indicated strong internal-consistency reliability in the present sample.

The questionnaire also included some open-ended questions regarding reasons why women might feel more or less comfortable accessing workplace benefits and supports, challenges confronting women in the legal profession, and included other comments respondents might wish to make about their workplace experiences.

Results

The data contained few missing values on any single variable and showed a random pattern of missing values. A statistical technique known as "listwise deletion," or "complete-case analysis," was used when missing data exceeded 20% of the items for a particular scale. Otherwise, missing data was handled through imputing the scale means for the missing items. The inspection of skewness and kurtosis of each variable resulted in the deletion of only a few outliers. Cronbach's alpha coefficients (reported in the "Measures and Procedure" section) indicated that all scales and sub-scales showed adequate internal consistency ($\alpha > .70$). The present study adopted a conservative p value of .01 to define statistical significance for the correlation analyses due to the large number of correlational analyses that were run.

Correlations between work–family conflict and family–work conflict and the outcome variables are shown in table 1. Higher levels of work–family conflict were positively related to higher levels of perceived stress, emotional exhaustion, cynicism, anxiety, depression, interpersonal sensitivity, obsessive-compulsiveness, paranoid ideation, and somatization, and were negatively related to job satisfaction. A relatively similar pattern occurred for family–work conflict, except that family–work conflict was also significantly and positively related to professional inefficacy, and family–work

Table 1
Work–Family Conflict and Family–Work Conflict Correlations with Outcome Variables (N = 277)

Outcome Variable	Work–Family Conflict		Family–Work Conflict	
	r	p	r	p
Perceived Stress	.42	< .001	.35	< .001
Turnout				
Emotional Exhaustion	.57	< .001	.27	< .001
Professional Inefficacy	.08	ns	.16	< .01
Cynicism	.30	< .001	.21	< .005
SA-45 Symptoms				
Anxiety	.31	< .001	.17	< .01
Depression	.22	< .001	.19	< .005
Hostility	.12	ns	.12	ns
Interpersonal Sensitivity	.21	< .001	.20	< .005
Obsessive-Compulsive	.19	< .005	.22	< .001
Paranoid Ideation	.21	< .005	.09	ns
Somatization	.16	< .01	.02	ns
Job Satisfaction	-.30	< .001	-.17	< .01

conflict was not significantly related to paranoid ideation or to somatization. Thus, the hypothesis that women who experience greater work–family conflict would experience more stress, burnout, symptomatology, and lower job satisfaction was supported.

To examine our second hypothesis, that high personal resilience would mediate the relations between work–family conflict (or family–work conflict) and negative mental-health outcomes, we conducted a series of correlational and regression analyses between work–family conflict, family–work conflict, and the outcome variables. Resilience was found to correlate significantly and negatively with work–family conflict, $r(274) = -.21, p < .005$, family–work conflict, $r(274) = -.22, p < .001$, and with all of the outcome measures except for somatization, with correlations ranging from $r(271) = -.17, p < .01$ for paranoid ideation to $r(271) = -.56, p < .001$ for perceived stress. Resilience was positively associated with job satisfaction, $r(274) =$

.25, $p < .001$. According to Baron and Kenny (1986), a mediation effect occurs when the following happens: (1) the independent variable is significantly related to the mediator, (2) the independent variable is significantly related to the dependent variable, (3) the mediator is significantly related to the dependent variable when the dependent variable is regressed on the independent variable and the mediator, and (4) the relation between the independent variable and the dependent variable becomes non-significant when the mediator is added to the regression model. Using Baron and Kenny's procedure, it was determined that resilience mediated the relation between family–work conflict and depression, as well as the relation between family–work conflict and anxiety, and the relation between family–work conflict and job satisfaction, providing partial support for our second hypothesis. Although resilience was significantly correlated with work–family conflict and most of the outcome measures, it did not fully mediate the relations between work–family conflict and any of the outcome variables, in that adding resilience to the regression model did not render the relations between work–family conflict and the outcome measures non-significant.

The impact of women's unique circumstances on the outcome variables was examined in a number of ways. Comparisons of women who were married or cohabiting versus those who were single, women with children versus women who were childless, and women with small children at home versus women with no small children were made through a series of independent samples t-tests. Means, standard deviations, and t-test findings for these analyses are displayed in table 2. Women who were married or co-

TABLE 2 Significant t-test Findings for Current Relationship Status and Child Status							
	Married/ Cohabiting		Currently Single				
	M	SD	M	SD	t	df	p
Work–Family Conflict	24.52	7.90	21.98	7.97	-2.35	273	.019
Family–Work Conflict	17.03	7.94	14.01	6.84	-2.87	272	.004
	Children		No Children				
	M	SD	M	SD	t	df	p
Family–Work Conflict	18.06	8.26	13.90	6.49	-4.47	241	<.001
Anxiety	7.72	2.39	8.60	3.56	2.17	157	.032
Depression	8.50	3.59	9.62	4.31	2.16	184	.032
Interpersonal Sensitivity	7.57	2.77	8.84	3.66	2.96	171	.004
	Children Under 6		None Under 6				
	M	SD	M	SD	t	df	p
Family–Work Conflict	21.63	8.06	15.00	7.94	-5.83	275	<.001
Resilience	136.11	17.67	142.75	16.86	2.51	272	.013

habiting were significantly higher than those who were currently single on both work–family conflict and family–work conflict. Women with children (irrespective of whether the children lived at home) were higher on family–work conflict, but were significantly lower on anxiety, depression, and interpersonal sensitivity (which reflects problematic feelings about oneself in relation to others). Women with children at home under the age of six were significantly higher on family–work conflict, as compared with women without young children at home, but showed no other significant differences from the other women apart from being significantly lower in resilience (reflecting increased vulnerability in this group). Interestingly, women with young children at home did not differ from other women in terms of increased perceived stress, anxiety, or depression.

In addition, we examined differences between women who worked as employees or associates in law firms (n = 106, or 38.3% of the total sample)[3] and women who worked in other legal settings on work–family conflict, family–work conflict, and the outcome variables through a series of independent samples t-tests. Means, standard deviations, and t-test findings for these analyses are displayed in table 3. Women who worked in law firms were higher in work–family conflict (but not in family–work conflict) and showed more severe levels of all three components of burnout. They were also higher in anxiety, interpersonal sensitivity, and paranoid ideation. Women who worked in law firms also reported working significantly longer weekday hours, on average.

Correlational analyses were conducted to determine the impact of hours worked and hours engaged in child care upon work–family conflict, family–work conflict, and the outcome measures. Women who worked longer weekday hours were higher in work–family conflict, r (224) = .35, p < .001, and in emotional exhaustion, r (222) = .25, p < .001. Women who worked more overtime hours at the office were also higher in work–family conflict, r (235) = .24, p < .001. Women who reported more hours engaged

Table 3 Significant t-Test Findings for Law-Firm vs. Other Work Settings							
	Law Firm		Other Settings				
	M	SD	M	SD	t	df	p
Work–Family Conflict	26.25	6.67	22.79	8.15	-3.37	203	.001
Emotional Exhaustion	17.90	6.60	15.41	7.77	-2.51	209	.013
Professional Efficacy	26.06	6.13	28.23	5.43	2.77	208	.006
Cynicism	14.43	8.03	9.88	7.53	-4.22	207	<.001
Anxiety	8.52	3.04	7.69	2.94	-2.02	210	.045
Interpersonal Sensitivity	8.72	3.32	7.78	3.23	-2.08	210	.039
Paranoid Ideation	8.59	3.62	7.62	3.28	-2.05	209	.042
Hours Worked per Weekday	9.36	1.38	8.65	1.70	-3.03	172	.003

in child care were higher on family–work conflict, r (128) =.28, p < .005. Interestingly, engaging in more hours of work or child care did not relate significantly to any other problematic outcomes (e.g., increased perceived stress, depression, or anxiety) or to job satisfaction.

Women who were older, and those with more years of practice, had significantly more positive outcomes. Specifically, age was positively correlated with resilience, r (263) = .22, p < .001, and with professional efficacy, r (263) = .32, p < .001. Age was negatively correlated with perceived stress, r (263) = −.21, p < .005, cynicism, r (263) = −.23, p < .001, depression, r (264) = −.22, p < .001, hostility, r (264) = −.18, p < .005, interpersonal sensitivity, r (264) = −.27, p < .001, obsessive-compulsiveness, r (264) = −.20, p < .005, and paranoid ideation, r (264) = −.18, p < .005. Women who had spent more years engaged in the practice of law were higher in resilience, r (269) =.17, p < .01, and professional efficacy, r (270) =.28, p < .001, and were lower in cynicism r (268) = −.16, p < .01, and depression, r (271) = −.21, p < .005. Women were asked about the presence of a number of benefits and family-friendly policies in their workplaces. While a majority of women reported that their workplaces supported continuing legal education (82.7%), had dental plans (82.3%), long-term disability (72.9%), sick leaves (71.8%), and offered some flexibility in hours (58.8%), fewer women reported the presence of workplace policies that might serve to reduce work–family conflict, including unpaid maternity leaves (50.5%), part-time work (46.2%), unpaid paternity leaves (37.5%), job-sharing (14.1%), child-care benefits (4.7%), and daycare facilities (4.0%). It should be noted that the percentages reported above indicate the proportion of women responding "yes," that their workplaces had these policies, while the remainder reported either "no" or "not sure." A separate question asked about the degree (on a five-point scale, from 1, "very comfortable," to 5, "very uncomfortable") to which women would feel comfortable accessing the benefits that were applicable to them. A majority of women reported that they would be very comfortable (47.3%) or comfortable (28.2%) with accessing these services and benefits, although 5.5% indicated that they would be uncomfortable or very uncomfortable accessing them. Comfort/discomfort with accessing these benefits was assessed in relation to work–family conflict, family–work conflict, and the other outcome measures through correlational analyses. Discomfort with accessing benefits was found to be positively related to higher levels of work–family conflict, r (251) =.25, p < .001, family–work conflict, r (250) =.19, p < .005, perceived stress, r (249) =.30, p < .001, emotional exhaustion, r (250) =.26, p < .001, cynicism, r (249) =.30, p < .001, depression, r (251) =.27, p < .01 anxiety, r (251) =.21, p < .005, paranoid ideation, r (251) =.35, p < .001, interpersonal sensitivity, r (251) =.32, p < .001, obsessive-compulsiveness, r (251) =.20, p < .005, and negatively related to job satisfaction, r (247) = −.36, p < .001. Unfortunately, it appears that the women who would benefit from workplace services and supports the most are the least likely to feel comfortable with accessing them.

Discussion

The findings of this study supported the hypothesized relationship between higher levels of work–family conflict and family–work conflict, and the experience of greater perceived stress, burnout, and mental-health symptomatology. As predicted, higher levels of work–family and family–work conflict also impacted negatively on job satisfaction. Personal resilience was negatively associated with work–family conflict, family–work conflict, and the mental-health outcome measures, and was positively related to job satisfaction. In addition, resilience mediated the relation between family–work conflict and three of the outcome measures (depression, anxiety, and job satisfaction), supporting the idea that resilience can serve a stress-buffering function, reducing the negative impact of family–work conflict on health consequences.

When we examined women's characteristics that might influence their experience of work–family and family–work conflict, an interesting pattern of results emerged. Women who were married or living with a partner did experience more work–family and family–work conflict than women who were single, but married women were not at increased risk of experiencing higher levels of burnout, perceived stress, depression, anxiety, or other symptomatology relative to single women. Thus, apart from an awareness that work demands impact on their home lives, and that demands from home influence their work lives, marriage in and of itself did not seem to influence women's stress and mental-health symptoms. It is possible that the potential stress that is associated with increased work–family and family–work conflict is mitigated for these women by the emotional and instrumental support they receive from their husbands or partners.

When we examined the impact of children on women's work–life balance, the findings were interesting and somewhat surprising. Women with children (of any age, and irrespective of whether the children lived at home) were higher on family–work conflict, but not on work–family conflict. In other words, women with children reported that demands from their home life impacted on their ability to perform their duties at work, but not that work demands interfered with their home and family life. While women in our study tended to work long hours and experience stressful outcomes of work–family conflict in general, it may be that women who are mothers are reluctant to admit that work interferes with their home and family life. At the same time, they do identify that the demands from home impact on their life at work.

In answering the open-ended questions, most women tended not to talk about the impact of their career upon their family life, and chose instead to relate their concerns about how having children could negatively affect their careers. For example, one woman said, "I am concerned about what will happen when I am ready to have kids. I work, but I want to spend quality time with my family and I don't want to feel bad about it" (28-year-old married participant). In the words of another respondent, "I also struggle with work-life balance; although I was only called to the Bar three years ago and feel it's relatively early on in my career. The priority in my life seems to be work—often at the expense of the other aspects of my life" (48-year-old married participant).

Women with children were found to report less anxiety, depression, and interpersonal concerns relative to women without children. Even in the case of women with children at home under the age of six, there were few negative outcomes beyond increased family–work conflict. While these results might seem surprising and somewhat counterintuitive, they replicate the findings of Wallace (1999), who found that having preschool children led to reduced strain-based conflict for women. Wallace suggested that women's abilities to successfully meet the demands of multiple roles might lead to greater fulfillment and satisfaction that has a stress-buffering effect. Some of the narrative accounts from women in our study would seem to support this idea. For example,

> I have found law a great profession. It was always interesting and a
> vehicle to take one in many directions. I did combine my in house
> career with a family of 4 children. I was able to work part time for a
> number of years when my children were small and I found support
> for doing this in several companies. I have also found my experiences
> as a mother useful in managing people over the years, and in being
> able to read a situation, and handle it accordingly. (58-year-old mar-
> ried participant)

Comparisons of women in our study who worked in law firms versus women who were engaged in other areas of legal practice showed that women employed in law firms were higher on work–family conflict (but not family–work conflict), as well as showing higher levels of all three components of burnout (emotional exhaustion, professional inefficacy, cynicism). Women in law firms also showed higher levels of symptomatology, including greater anxiety, interpersonal sensitivity, and "paranoid ideation" (which reflects things like mistrusting others and believing that one isn't being given credit for one's accomplishments), and tended to work longer hours. These findings are consistent with the results reported by Wallace (1999), who found that women working for law firms reported more time-based conflict (in which the time spent on one role interferes with the time spent on the competing role) and more strain-based conflict (when women are preoccupied with one role while trying to fulfill the demands of an other role), as compared to women employed as lawyers in other work settings.

Many of the narrative accounts of the women in our study supported the idea that women working in law firms are at increased risk of work–life conflict, and a number of women indicated that they had left or intended to leave their jobs in a law firm in order to achieve a more positive work–life balance. Some examples are listed below:

> This might be the highest stress profession in the world. Frankly, I am considering changing professions when I have children because I do not believe that it is possible for me to have an active home life and work full-time as a lawyer. (29-year-old married participant)

> My career took me to in-house counsel work in the life insurance industry as I knew that I wanted to have a family. (58-year-old married participant)

> I am very disillusioned with the practice of law and I am considering leaving the profession altogether. My firm just keeps taking and taking more out of me, and has no appreciation of how difficult it is to be a lawyer and a mother and a wife, run a house, and stay sane. I believe this is because I work with a bunch of selfish old men who all have stay at home wives and have never had to juggle the same things I do. (34-year-old married participant)

Not all women's experiences in law firms were negative, however, and some women gave examples of workplaces that were quite supportive of having a family:

> All the staff at my firm are women. There are only 3 male lawyers. It is a positive environment. All the lawyers are married or cohabitating. Many of the young lawyers have young families. I think since many of us are in the same boat we can understand each other. We all want to do well. We work hard and can have fun. We all think family is important and take the time for our families and ourselves. (35-year-old married participant)

Findings from the present study indicated that working longer hours was not associated with substantial negative mental-health outcomes, and primarily influenced work–family conflict alone. Not surprisingly, working longer weekday hours was related to emotional exhaustion as well as work–family conflict. Working more overtime hours increased work–family conflict, and engaging in more hours of child care was related to family–work conflict. Engaging in longer workdays, more overtime, or more child-care hours was not related to increases in perceived stress, depression, anxiety, or to decreased job satisfaction. These findings are in contrast to those of Wallace (1999), who found that the actual number of hours worked did not have a significant impact on work–family conflict. While our study did find a significant correlation between hours worked and work–family conflict, we also found that hours worked did not relate to most of the negative mental-health consequences of work–family conflict, and our overall pattern of results (including our qualitative findings) is consistent with Wallace's conclusion that it is the perception of work demands that is more influential in determining the negative effects of work–family conflict.

Most women in our investigation reported the presence of a number of workplace supports and family-friendly policies in their work environments. In contrast to the Catalyst study (2003) that reported that only 25% of women felt that they could use flexible work arrangements without being penalized, the majority of women in our sample indicated that they would feel comfortable using at least some of these supports. There was still a significant minority (24.5%) of women who did not indicate that they would be comfortable accessing these services. Disturbingly, it was the women who would appear to be in most need of support who felt least comfortable in accessing these policies and services. Discomfort with accessing services was related to higher levels of work–family conflict, perceived stress, emotional exhaustion, cynicism, depression, anxiety, paranoid ideation, interpersonal sensitivity, obsessive-compulsiveness, and lower job satisfaction.

Creating an environment in which women feel comfortable accessing these policies is a challenge that requires an attitudinal and cultural change of significant magnitude within the profession. Social expectations as to child-care and family responsibilities are at the centre of stereotypes and bias that often operate at unconscious levels, even among members of the profession that are fully committed to the equality of women (Taylor & Willson, 2003). Several examples illustrate the way in which these stereotypes and biases influence advancement decisions for women and generate work–life conflict. They serve to illustrate the pervasive and imbedded attitudes that exist about women and caregiving in the legal profession.

> Although our firm has an informal maternity leave policy, it is not a written policy yet. Therefore, each time an associate has been pregnant, she has had to approach the partnership to ask for and negotiate paid/unpaid maternity benefits. A written policy would make this a more comfortable process. (31-year-old married participant)

> In my first job I was dismissed because I had children. This was very devastating. I am committed to providing a workplace that is accommodating to parents. I take the long view—if we provide flexibility when needed, we get loyalty when needed. (52-year-old previously married participant)

I know one associate who is on flex time 4 days per week, and she is criticized for being uncommitted. There is pressure for her to leave. (43-year-old married participant)

I would worry that benefits such as unpaid maternity leave, part time work or flex time work would negatively impact my position at firm; entrance to partnership, bonus, etc. (30-year-old married participant)

I have faced severe discrimination since the birth of my first child for taking what my boss refers to as 2 "protracted leaves" = maternity/parental leave. Single women without children who do half the work that I do have been promoted over me with no rationale. Employer has told me to make sure my husband gets a vasectomy. When I told my boss I was pregnant with 2nd child, response was "Jesus Christ, you can't be serious!" Was on the brink of filing a human rights complaint but wanted to continue working in my field so decided not to pursue. This is the only office in [my region] where I can do [my area of specialization]. So have chosen to put up with the discrimination. (37-year-old married participant)

One positive finding in the present study was that a great deal of the difficulties and stresses of an early career in the legal profession seem to lessen as women lawyers get older and have more years of experience in their careers. Women showed more resilience and professional efficacy with increased age and years of practice. Women who were older also experienced less cynicism, perceived stress, depression, hostility, interpersonal sensitivity, obsessive-compulsiveness, and paranoid ideation. It is interesting that some components of burnout (cynicism and professional inefficacy) actually appear to lessen over time, when one might expect lawyers with many years' experience to be more burned out. While greater experience with the profession undoubtedly reduces early feelings of professional inefficacy, it is older age that is likely to empower women, build confidence, and foster resilience. In the words of one of our participants:

Much of the reason my experience has been so positive, I believe, is the fact that I came to the profession late in life. I started law school at 36 years of age and was called to the Bar at 40 years of age. I have more confidence than younger women; am less intimidated by senior lawyers; do not have to juggle child-bearing and work; am willing to limit billable hours even if it means I may not be invited into the partnership. These benefits greatly reduce my stress level, in my view. (48-year-old married participant)

On the whole, the findings from the present study portray a picture of women's experience in the legal profession as almost inevitably involving significant challenges to maintain a healthy work–life balance. Work–family and family–work conflict were a pervasive experience of the women in our investigation. Despite its predominance in the lives of female lawyers, work–family conflict does not always lead to negative health consequences. Many of the women in our study seemed to be engaged in their work lives and family with great enthusiasm and energy for both. With increasing age, women in the legal profession tend to become more resilient and better able to overcome its inherent stressors.

This study has important implications for both women in the legal profession and the workplace settings that employ them. At the same time, there are some limitations that need to be considered when interpreting the findings. The study adopted a cross-sectional design, and thus we cannot infer anything about the actual processes that women in the legal profession undergo over time, except for anecdotal information gleaned from the responses to the open-ended questions. Future research that tracks women lawyers over time to observe the ways in which they either adapt to or resist their work environments in response to their changing personal circumstances would be extremely useful. Although our sample involved some regional stratification, it would be useful to replicate the study with an even broader sample of Canadian women lawyers, perhaps through the use of a web-based survey. Despite these limitations, the present study significantly adds to the existing literature on how women negotiate the complexities of achieving work–life balance in a demanding profession.

Notes

1. Ontario Human Rights Code, R.S.O. 1990, c. H.19. s. 5(1), s. 5(2).

2. Many of the professional background items were adapted from items used in the Turning Points and Transitions study of Ontario lawyers (Kay, Curry, et al., 2004).

3. For the purposes of these analyses, we excluded women who were partners in law firms since their situation differs considerably from other women employed in law firms.

References

Alzheimer Society of Canada. (2005). *Patterns of caring for people with dementia in Canada.* Retrieved June 3, 2008, from http://www.alzheimer.ca/english/disease/stats-caregiving.htm

Baron, R. M., & Kenny, D. A. (1986). The moderator-mediator variable distinction in social psychological research: Conceptual, strategic, and statistical considerations. *Journal of Personality and Social Psychology, 51*(6), 1173–1182.

Baruch, G. K., Biener, L., & Barnett, R. C. (1987). Women and gender in research on work and family stress. *American Psychologist, 42*(2), 130–136.

Catalyst. (2003, August). *Viewpoints – A series based on Catalyst Research: Workplace flexibility isn't just a women's issue.* Retrieved June 3, 2008, from http://www.catalyst-women.org/files/view/Workplace%20Flexibility%20Isn't%20Just%20a%20Women's%20Issue.pdf

Catalyst. (2005). Beyond a reasonable doubt: Building the business case for flexibility, *The Catalyst Series on Flexibility in Canadian Law Firms.* Retrieved June 3, 2008, from http://www.catalystwomen.org/files/full/Flex%20in%20Canadian%20Law%20full%20report.pdf

Cohen, S., Kamarck, T., & Mermelstein, R. A. (1983). A global measure of perceived stress. *Journal of Health and Social Behavior, 24,* 385–396.

Cohen, S., & Williamson, G. (1988). Perceived stress in a probability sample of the United States. In S. Spacapan & S. Oskamp (Eds.), *The social psychology of health* (pp. 31–67). Newbury Park, CA: Sage.

Cooper, M., Brockman, J., & Hoffart, I. (2004, January 26). *Final report on equity and diversity in Alberta's legal profession.* Retrieved June 3, 2008, from the Law Society of Alberta Web site: http://www.lawsocietyalberta.com/files/reports/Equity_and_Diversity.pdf

Dalton, J. H., Elias, M. J., & Wandersman, A. (2001). *Community psychology: Linking individual and communities.* Belmont, CA: Wadsworth.

Department of Mental Health and Substance Abuse. (2002). *Gender disparities in mental health.* Retrieved June 3, 2008, from the World Health Organization Web site: http://www.who.int/mental_health/media/en/242.pdf

Dillman, D. A. (2000). *Mail and internet surveys: The tailored design method* (2nd ed.). Toronto: Wiley.

Duxbury, L., & Higgins, C. (2001). *Work-life balance in Canada: Making the case for change.* Retrieved June 3, 2008, from http://www.asiapacificresearch.ca/caprn/cjsp_project/duxbury_final.pdf

Duxbury, L., Higgins, C., & Johnson, K. L. (1999). An examination of the implications and cost of work-life conflict in Canada. Retrieved June 3, 2008, from the Health Canada Web site: http://www.phac-aspc.gc.ca/dca-dea/publications/duxbury_e.html

Ferris, P. A., Sinclair, C., & Kline, T. J. (2005). It takes two to tango: Personal and organizational resilience as predictors of strain and cardiovascular disease in a work sample. *Journal of Occupational Health Psychology, 10*(3), 225–238.

Glasberg, A. L., Eriksson, S., & Norberg, A. (2007). Burnout and 'stress of conscience' among healthcare personnel. *Journal of Advanced Nursing, 57*(4), 392–403.

Jackson, D., Firtko, A., & Edenborough,, M. (2007). Personal resilience as a strategy for surviving and thriving in the face of workplace adversity: A literature review. *Journal of Advanced Nursing, 60*(1), 1–9.

Kay, F. (1989). *Women in the Legal Profession* (Osgoode Hall). Toronto: Law Society of Upper Canada.

Kay, F. M., Curry, P., & Masuch, C. (2004, September). *Turning points and transitions: A longitudinal study of Ontario lawyers from 1975 to 2002.* Retrieved June 3, 2008, from the Law Society of Upper Canada Web site: http://www.lsuc.on.ca/media/oct2604_turning_points.pdf

Kay, F. M., Masuch, C., & Currey, P. (2004). *Diversity and change: The contemporary legal profession in Ontario*. Retrieved June 3, 2008, from the Law Society of Upper Canada Web site: http://www.lsuc.on.ca/media/oct 2604_diversity_and_change.pdf

Langballe, E. M., Falkum, E., Innstrand, S. T., & Aasland, O. G. (2006). The factorial validity of the Maslach Burnout Inventory-General Survey in representative samples of eight different occupational groups. *Journal of Career Assessment, 14*(3), 370–384.

Law Society of Upper Canada (2008). *Retention of women in private practice working group*. Retrieved June 3, 2008, from http://www.lsuc.on.ca/media/retentionofwomen .pdf

McCallister, K. T., Dolbier, C. L., Webster, J. A., Mallon, M. W., & Steinhardt, M. A. (2006). Hardiness and support at work as predictors of work stress and job satisfaction. *American Journal of Health Promotion, 20*(3), 183–191.

McPhee, J. (2007, March). The great lie. *Canadian Lawyer,* 36–39.

Netemeyer, R. G., Boles, J. S., & McMurrian, R. (1996). Development of work-family conflict and family-work conflict scales. *Journal of Applied Psychology, 81*(4), 400–410.

Public Health Agency of Canada. (n.d.). *The population health template working tool*. Retrieved June 3, 2008, from the Population Health Web site: www.phac-aspc.gc.ca/ ph-sp/phdd/pdf/template_tool.pdf

Rhode, D. L. (2001a). *Balanced lives changing the culture of legal practice*. Retrieved June 3, 2008, from Women in the Legal Profession: A Keck Center Clearinghouse Web site: http://womenlaw.stanford.edu/model.policies.html

Rhode, D. L. (2001b). *The unfinished agenda: Women and the legal profession*. Retrieved June 3, 2008, from the ABA Commission on Women in the Profession Web site: http://www.abanet.org/ftp/pub/women/unfinishedagenda.pdf

Rosenfield, S. (1999). Gender and mental health: Do women have more psychopathology, men more or both the same (and why?). In A. V. Horwitz & T. L. Scheid (Eds.), *A Handbook for the study of mental health* (pp. 348–360). New York: Cambridge University Press.

Schaufeli, W. B., Leiter, M. P., Maslach, C., & Jackson, S. E. (1996). Maslach Burnout Inventory-General Survey (MBI-GS). In C. Maslach, S.E. Jackson, & M. P. Leiter, *MBI Manual* (3rd ed.). Mountain View, CA: Consulting Psychologists Press.

Sells, B. (1994). *The soul of the law: Understanding lawyers and the law*. Rockport, MA: Element.

Spector, P. E. (1985). Measurement of human service staff satisfaction: Development of the Job Satisfaction Survey. *American Journal of Community Psychology, 13*, 693–713.

Strategic Advantage. (2000). *Symptom Assessment–45 Questionnaire (SA-45) technical manual*. Toronto: Multi Health Systems.

Syverud, K. D., & Schiltx, P. J. (1999). On being a happy, healthy and ethical member of an unhappy unhealthy and unethical profession. *Vanderbilt Law Review, 52*, 871–951.

Taylor, I, & Willson, S. (2003, September). Canada's top 25 women lawyers. *Lexpert Magazine,* 68–98.

Wagnild, G. M., & Young, H. M. (1993). Development and psychometric evaluation of the Resilience Scale. *Journal of Nursing Measurement, 1*, 165–178.

Wallace, J. E. (1999). Work-to-nonwork conflict among married male and female lawyers. *Journal of Organizational Behavior, 20,* 797–816.

World Health Organization. (2001). *The world health report – Mental health: New understanding, new hope.* Retrieved June 3, 2008, from the World Health Organization Web site: http://www.who.int/whr/2001/en/whr01_en.pdf

Jennifer J. Nicol

Managing Chronic Illness
with the Companionship of Music

Introduction

Given the prominence of social support as a concept in stress and coping theory (Carlson, 2000), it is not surprising that social-support networks have been identified as a key determinant of health (Health Canada, 2008; World Health Organization, 2008). A transactional understanding of stress and coping (e.g., Lazarus & Folkman, 1984) emphasizes the relationship between individuals and their environments, and defines stress within the context of appraisals, demands, and resources. When a demand (stressor) is appraised as taxing or exceeding individuals' resources, stress is experienced. Within this framework, health is understood as being positively impacted by coping resources, which are antecedent conditions that reduce vulnerability to stressors. Social support exemplifies a coping resource that reduces vulnerability to stressors.

Social support is linked with psychological and physiological benefits in terms of health outcomes (Cobb, 1976; Cohen & Syme, 1985), and in the particular context of adjusting to chronic illness (e.g., Penninx, Kriegsman, van Eijk, Boeke, & Deeg 1996). Chronic illness has obvious physical impacts (e.g., pain, fatigue, activity limitations), but also psychological impacts that are equally if not more significant (Hwu, 1995), especially as characterized by feelings and experiences of loss (Charmaz, 1983; Schaefer, 1995). Further challenges arise with the uncertainty and unpredictability of chronic illness, often an implicit movement and progression that may only be identified with hindsight (Thorne & Paterson, 2000). Social support has significant practical implications for those adjusting to chronic illness (Symister & Friend, 2003).

Social support has generally be understood in terms of support that is provided by human beings to other human beings, as is illustrated in the following definition: "Social support is all those forms of support provided by other individuals and groups that help individuals cope with life" (Reber, 1995, p. 734). Other scholars have differentiated between the needs satisfied by social support. For example:

> Social support is the process (e.g., perception or reception) by which resources in the social networks are brought to bear to meet the functional needs (e.g., instrumental and expressive) in routine and crisis situations. (Lin & Westcott, 1991, pp. 215–217)

Expressive needs are accessing someone who can share, understand, and empathize; instrumental needs are accessing someone who can help carry out specific tasks.

More recently, perceived social support has been emphasized. Lubkin (1998) argued that "Perception is key to the experience of social support. Social support is not determined by number of people, but by the perception of oneself as connected to others" (p. 213). The perception of being in relationship and connected with others has very different implications for operationalizing the concept of social support, and raises the possibility of social support that is experienced without face-to-face human interaction.

For example, a growing literature identifies the relational and community-building functions served by the arts. A survey (Cooley, 2003) on the arts and culture in medicine and health reported that:

> Engaging in both community arts programs and more formal cultural performances have both been shown to have positive effects including the following: reduced feelings of fear, anxiety and social isolation; improved social networks and new friendships; stronger community identification and pride; development of community networks; and generation of physical and social community renewal. (p. 6)

Themes that ran through a number of studies investigating intersections between the arts and health included coping skills, social connectedness, and a sense of control and mastery over life circumstances (Cooley, 2003). These are all factors that affect health.

A promising program of research at the University of Saskatchewan is driven by the following research questions: How does music enhance the actions of everyday life as negotiated across varied circumstances and populations? And, secondarily, how do spontaneous everyday uses of music extend understanding about coping? Two particular studies, discussed below, implicate everyday solitary music listening as a social process that aids women in coping with the challenges of chronic physical illness, and provide evidence that social support may be experienced through interactions with inanimate phenomena, such as music.

Study One

The first study was a qualitative inquiry that focused on lived experience and lived meaning (Nicol, 2002). Van Manen's (1990) hermeneutic-phenomenological research method was used to investigate the experience and meaning of six women's everyday music-listening experiences. Purposeful sampling, implemented with a snowballing strategy, was used to recruit participants living independently in the community. The six women who volunteered were aged 41–78 years (mean = 58 years) and had lived 2–20 years (mean = 10 years) with diseases that included osteoarthritis, macular degeneration, and spinal stenosis (i.e., illnesses associated with aging); acute transverse myelitis (a disease that affects the spinal cord, causing motor and sensory dysfunction); as well as chronic fatigue syndrome and fibromyalgia (poorly understood diseases more common in women). For the purposes of the study, the six were identified with pseudonyms: Storm, May, Celia, Iris, Jean, and Laurie.

Although some diversity existed across the women's socio-demographic characteristics (e.g., North American, European, and Asian heritages were represented, with two speaking English as a second language; high-school to postsecondary education levels completed; socio-economic status ranged from income assistance to comfortable retirement; two worked full time and four were unemployed; three were single, two were married, and one was widowed; two lived alone and four lived with others [spouse, sibling, roommates]; musical tastes included classical, top 40, folk, jazz, blues, golden oldies , gospel, hymns), these demographics were not intentional in terms of the study's design and are offered for descriptive purposes only. The key concern was that they were all women who had lived at least two years with an illness, which was managed, not cured, and who identified music listening as a significant activity in their lives.

Multiple in-depth individual interviews provided a primary source of data. Interviews ranged from one to three hours in duration and were taped and transcribed. All conversations were introduced to the women as knowl-edge-generating endeavors in which the women and I were motivated by a common curiosity about the phenomenon of everyday music listening. The emphasis and focus was placed on the participants' lived experiences, and the interviews were open-ended and largely unstructured. A few common questions were asked of each woman (e.g., "Tell me how listening to music is part of your life and how this relates to your chronic illness?" "Do you remember when you first became aware of the importance of music listen-ing in your life?" "Can you tell me about that experience?"), but my general task was to keep us attuned to the phenomenon of listening to music and to continuously encourage participants to use examples and anecdotes to convey what listening to music was like for them in their everyday lives. All the women were given a journal at the end of the first interview and invited to write about any insights, experiences, or thoughts pertinent to music lis-tening that occurred between the first and second interviews. The journals were private and optional. Three of the six women kept journals; two gave me their written material, and another read from hers during her second interview.

Analysis included phenomenological questioning, reflecting, and writ-ing, as well as guided existential reflection based on the four "life-world existentials" of lived body, lived time, lived space, and lived relationship (van Manen, 1990). These existential themes are reported in the phenomeno-logical literature and are believed to characterize the life world of all human beings (Merleau-Ponty, 1962; van Manen, 1990); thus, they help reveal how we live and experience ourselves as human beings. For example, we are al-ways bodily in the world, so lived body always informs or is part of an expe-rience. Similarly, we experience subjective time and live with an awareness of the past, present, and future; we perceive the dimensions of the world in terms of felt space; and we experience ourselves as in relationship and con-nected. Because these existential themes tend to be experienced pre-ver-bally, they can be used heuristically to aid in phenomenological analysis.

In this study, it was apparent that music altered the women's percep-tions of body, time, space, and relationship in ways that were significant given their chronic illness. When they listened to the "right music," their bodies sometimes animated with music, which, irrespective of their bodies actual capabilities, allowed them to experience grace, energy, sensuality, or steadiness; they sometimes got lost in music time and experienced a break from the measured time of pained bodies, restricted spaces, and solitude; and sometimes they expressed and managed feelings because of music's ability to create spaces that are spacious, calm, comforting, nostalgic, angry, cathartic—or whatever they needed. Last, when the women listened to the right music, they experienced companionship. With music the women were not alone. Furthermore, they might be reminded of others, they might feel understood, and they might experience themselves as whole rather than partially ill versions of themselves.

The relational qualities of the women's music-listening experiences were surprising and multi-faceted. The most obvious aspect of relationality was music as a shared interest. Listening to music was a way to be together that provided a focus for conversation, activity, and planning. Jean said,

> my husband and I plan our trips around going to places that have
> different operas ... so it becomes a project that we set out to do ...
> If we're going to an opera that we don't know, we go through the
> libretto several times and listen to it at the same time.

When Iris and her sister felt bored, one would say, "Let's listen to some music," and the music listening became their shared project. Celia and her friends shared music—compiling and sending tapes back and forth, inexpensively expanding their music collections.

But shared projects in music listening were about more than just activity. Storm talked about music linking the generations in her family: "I've always had music in my life: my mother, my father. There was always music in the house. My daughters too, they don't play instruments either but they love listening to music." Music listening evoked a felt understanding of family, the music representing and being associated with feelings of love and belonging, denoting and marking a place where she and intimates gathered.

Music revealed the women, making them visible in music to both themselves and others, which generated special bonds and relationships. For example, Celia's friends were actually doing more than just expanding a collection of music when they compiled and forwarded tapes to Celia. Rather, her friends were sharing themselves in music with her, as well as demonstrating an understanding of Celia in music—what she may or may not like. Similarly, the relationship between Iris and her sister also played out in music, the music of favoured songs and radio stations:

> We'll take turns. After we listen to her radio station, we'll listen to
> mine. So it works out pretty good. I mean we have similar tastes.
> Sometimes it's funny because we'll choose the same tape. She'll say
> "let's play that" and then I'll say "I was just going to say that
> too!" So it's pretty good because our lives are close, pretty similar.

If her sister liked her song when they listened to it, and if they both choose the same song, then Iris was delighted. She offered herself in song and her sister accepted. Iris knew who she was by the music she liked; she knew who her sister was by the music her sister liked; and she knew the strength of their relationship by the music they shared. Chronic illness had not changed this.

The women also reported being brought into relationship with themselves. Celia described listening and remembering passion, a known feeling, but one normally obscured by illness and fatigue:

> It's very sensual music. Lots of people would call it sexual but I call it sensual. It's quite romantic in its own way and I think what it does is remind me and bring out those aspects of myself in my own personality.

In that moment, Celia was more than a fragmented, partial person defined by illness, she was whole and complete in all of her history. This holistic experience of self was especially meaningful given the loss of former perceptions of self because of illness.

The varied aspects of the music—lyrics, instruments, musicians, composers—provided other sources of relational experiences. This was revealed in small words and turns of phrase as well as in more detailed anecdotes. Laurie, for example, talked about having music "with me in the bath," having a song that was "just mine"; May talked about "listening to my music"; and Jean talked about how music "reaches in and takes you out," how the "voice really seemed to reach me," and how "opera is my big love." Laurie also spoke of feeling either connected or disconnected by what she heard in a musician's playing:

> When I listen to people is when I hear them. If I can hear them in the music, it's coming from what I call true musicality. It's not always the technique, it's the intent of it. If I hear a recording of this wonderfully played Bach piece, it doesn't do it for me. I feel no connection with the music person. They are just playing notes. And I seem to be able to tell that.

Whether this was true or not was unimportant. What was important was Laurie's perception of being in relationship, of being played for, and of recognizing a musician's gift offered in music. Celia described a similar interactive experience with solitary music listening:

> Listening experiences kind of accordion themselves, they build on themselves. So if I listen to a lot of Celtic music, my ear will fine tune itself so that I know what I'm listening for. And if there's a little musical joke then I can pick up on it. Like if they play 2 bars of *Mary Had A Little Lamb* on the bagpipe? I can hear it and then it's gone, like a musical gesture. And it's like being included in some way in what they're doing. Like the music reaches out and encompasses me in some way. So I'm a participant as opposed to a monitor.

Celia experienced herself as a participant in the musicians' music making. In her solitude, sitting on her couch, alone in the living room, separate from a world of bustling people with places to go and work to do, Celia listened to music and felt part of something beyond herself. Music was able to offer a companionship and presence at times when people could not.

As mentioned, the relational aspects of the women's music-listening experiences were unexpected and surprising. They also struck me as the most important aspect of the women's music-listening experiences given their chronic illness. Storm referred to music as her savior:

> Music is my savior, it keeps me sane. It's the first thing I turn on in the morning and the last thing I turn off at night. Music is something you can't take away from a person and that's what's nice. It will always be there.

May similarly talked about her tape recorder at her bedside as "always there, ready to go … when I wake up stressed and overwhelmed," and Jean referred to music as a constant presence in her life, her personal lifesaver:

> Music was the one thing I still had, especially during this last year when I'd get a depression with fibromyalgia and think, "what's the point of life?" Music has been a lifesaver. Music is the greatest joy I have.

In sum, music appeared to be a long-standing part of these six women's lives and was experienced as a trusted, loyal, and intimate companion who seemed to aid in accommodating the later arrival of an uninvited and unpredictable chronic illness. These findings led me to think about the concept of social support. I had initially conceptualized music listening as a coping strategy and a coping resource; that is, both a behavior that manages emotional distress (i.e., emotion-focused) or alters the source of stress (i.e., problem-focused), and an antecedent condition that reduces vulnerability to stressors (Lazarus & Folkman, 1984). The discovery of relational experiences evoked with music listening suggested something akin to the concept of social support, which, as mentioned previously, is a coping resource broadly understood as "all those forms of support provided by other individuals and groups that help an individual cope with life" (Reber, 1995, p. 734). According to Study One participants, music listening led them to experience themselves as known, understood, and not alone, which seems strikingly similar to the understanding of social support as meeting one's expressive needs by accessing someone who can share, understand, and empathize (Lin & Westcott, 1991). Perhaps it was unnecessarily restrictive to assume that only humans can provide social support?

I returned to the research literature to search out other studies on the subject. I found a small body of qualitative research that identified solitary music listening as a complex, meaningful experience used intentionally, and intuitively, to meet goals and needs, which included social needs (De Nora, 1999; Hays & Minichiello, 2005; Nelson, 1994; Pederson, 1994). I also located a quote from poet Robert Browning, stating that "Who hears music feels their solitude peopled at once" (as cited in Wallace & McKowen, 1996, p. 92), as well as participant quotes from a variety of sources that echoed Study One's findings that music listening is a significant relational experience for women with chronic illness. Boal-Palheiros and Hargreaves (2001) cited a teenage girl who described music listening as an experience in which "You feel you have company" (p. 112). Another teenage girl said,

> Music, it's kind of like a best friend. 'Cause like, if nobody's there for me, when nobody was there for me, I always had my music, always. No matter what was going on in my life, I always had my music. (Meeting Youth in Music, unpublished raw data)

A male university student interviewed by Nelson (1994) said:

> Music is always there whenever you want it; it gives you everything without wanting anything back. I could say music is the perfect spouse, the perfect thing you can be with all your life, with no problems, no conflicts. (p. 126)

Curiosity piqued, I undertook a second study, which is still in progress.

Study Two

The second study uses Charmaz's (2006) constructivist grounded theory to further investigate the phenomenon of music listening as a social process for women living with chronic illness. The study's purpose is to extend the current literature by exploring and theoretically clarifying the role of solitary music listening as a social process in women's adjustment to chronic illness. Whereas the hermeneutic phenomenology of Study One was descriptive and focused on lived experience, the grounded theory of Study Two is explanatory and focuses on inductively generating a mid-range theory of the phenomenon.

To date, 14 women diagnosed with physical conditions that are managed rather than cured have been interviewed about their experiences with solitary music listening as a social process. Their ages range from 48 to 81 years, their heritages are varied (North American, European, Cree, Francophone), and they have lived 2–30 years with chronic illness. Data are being analyzed and a mid-range theory being constructed using grounded theory coding (initial, focused, axial, and theoretical coding), memoing, theoretical sampling, saturation, and sorting (Charmaz, 2006). Unlike the first study, in which a conversational tone and open structure was used in interviews to generate rich descriptions of music listening, Study Two's interviews are more structured and directive. Specific questions are posed and explored, as well as continuously adapted to incorporate data analysis that occurs concurrently with data collection.

Preliminary findings are summarized in tables 1, 2, and 3. The quotes listed in table 1 continue to underscore the importance of music listening in women's adjustment to chronic illness, whether for concrete practical reasons (e.g., "It's an activity that I can do on alone") or more existential reasons ("Music makes me know the world is bigger than me," or, paraphrasing another, it feeds me when I'm starving).

Table 1
Participant Quotes on the Importance of Music Listening in the Context of Chronic Illness

- *Without music, I wouldn't be alive*
- *Hey, I'm starving here. I need some music*
- *Giving myself a gift with music*
- *Doing more than nothing with music*
- *Life gets worrisome with illness, music gives me a break from worrying and relaxes me*
- *It's an activity that I can do alone*
- *I get really worn out so music is one of the filler [activities] I can do to recover*
- *If music has been part of your life, it's part of your coping*
- *Music makes me know the world is bigger than me*
- *Everything else is changing and unpredictable and you don't know what is going to happen, but the rhythm is always there and that has been a strengthening thing for me to feel*
- *Feeling tired, having a headache and can't do anything else so I choose music*

Table 2 presents statements that confirm and further illuminate the social processes experienced with solitary music listening. Similar to Study One, listening to music evokes relational meanings of belonging, being connected, and experiencing companionship, support, and reassurance. These meanings may be attached to evoked memories; perceived resonance with the musician, music or composer/songwriter; or transcendent experience of being in relationship with nature, humanity, or a spiritual entity.

Table 2
Participant Quotes Pointing to Social Processes Associated with Solitary Music
Listening

- *Music's just like having a friend in the room with you*
- *Feeling close to something bigger than me that is in control*
- *Feel safe, less alone and cared for*
- *Not alone because there's sound*
- *Music brings loved ones near*
- *Somebody knows I'm hurting*
- *Music reassures me, comforts me, connects me to my soul, a perfect part of me versus my imperfect and unwhole ill self*
- *Music helps me reconnect inside to a sense of positive energy*
- *Music brings the world a little closer to me*
- *It was a nice surprise to have that connection with my family happen for me…in this piece of music*

Tables 1 and 2 parallel the findings in Study One that sought to describe and evoke the lived experience and meaning of music listening for women living with chronic illness. Table 3 begins to extend Study One by introducing a level of analysis that will help generate an explanatory midrange theory. The question stems listed in the left column of table 3—who, when, where, what, how, how much, and why—are used to help identify actions and reveal significant processes in the data (Charmaz, 2006). The middle column of table 3 places those words in the context of this particular study of the music-listening phenomenon, and the column on the far right provides some early answers. The next step is to use these building blocks to start conceptualizing relationships between codes and explore hypotheses that will integrate into a theory, and determine whether social support is an extant concept deserving inclusion or not, that is, supported in the inductive analytic process or not.

Implications

These two studies coupled with the extant research literature underscore the value of (a) continuing to investigate experiences of solitary music listening as a social process, (b) re-considering the understanding of social support as restricted to human interactions, and (c) explicitly including music and the arts in discussions of health. The relational experiences associated with solitary music listening in the particular context of women living with chronic illness seem readily conceptualized as social support that is perceived and evoked without face-to-face, direct human interaction. Future research may identify similar experiences specific to other aesthetic media and inanimate objects. Including the arts as a health determinant requires further research

Table 3
Building Blocks of an Explanatory Model of Solitary Music Listening as a Social Process

WHO?	Who are the women using solitary music listening to help manage chronic illness?	• Those whose lives have involved music • Those with access to music
WHEN?	When do these women engage in solitary music listening and experience social processes?	• Want to improve/enhance an activity • Want company • Want to get out of their head • As part of a routine or ritual • Too tired to do anything else • Need to manage/express feelings • Want to do something other than nothing
HERE?	Where do these women engage in solitary music listening and experience social processes?	• At home • In nature • On the couch • In the car • In bed • In particular places (rooms)
WHAT?	What makes solitary music listening helpful for these women?	• The "right" music • Being able to determine how long to listen • Having the right volume • Being familiar with the music • Having choice and control over listening experience
HOW?	How is solitary music listening experienced and handled by these women?	• Intuitively • Intentionally • Absentmindedly • Habitually • Automatically • With care and intention
HOW MUCH?	How much solitary music listening is enough?	• Until a song or CD is over • Until a treatment is finished • Until satiated • Until feel better • Until fall asleep
WHY?	Why is solitary music listening important to these women?	• Works when nothing else does • Can be in charge of • Is familiar • Feels good • Is constant and reliable • Evokes memories of important people, places, past activities • Makes everything okay

and active dialogue between people working at the intersections of the arts, health, and health care. Inherent challenges include the different paradigms and cultures that typically characterize medical and artistic endeavors. Cooley (2003) commented that the impacts of the arts are multi-dimensional and require varied research methodologies and conceptualizations.

> They seem to be complex and multi-faceted, arising from some of most fundamental characteristics of arts-based activities—their ability to offer creative, integrative experiences and opportunities for connection to other individuals and deeper connections with one's communities. Thus, to disaggregate the effects of what is by nature an integrative and connecting experience is to risk missing much of its value. (p. 48)

However, holistic understandings of health have increased receptivity to different ways of knowing and researching. As health is recognized as more than a physical state, and the psychological, social, spiritual, and environmental aspects of health are considered, doors open for exciting collaborations across varied disciplines.

Note

This chapter is based on a paper given at the 19th Institute of the Section on Women and Psychology of the Canadian Psychological Association (Halifax, Nova Scotia, June 11, 2008). Acknowledgments to the Social Sciences and Humanities Research

Council of Canada who funded Study One and to the Saskatchewan Health Research Foundation who funded Study Two.

References

Boal-Palheiros, G. M., & Hargreaves, D. J. (2001). Listening to music at home and at school. *British Journal of Music Education, 18*(2), 103–118.

Carlson, J. G. (2000). Background and overview to stress and health: Research and clinical applications (pp.1–26). In D. T. Kenny, J. G. Carlson, F.G. McGuigan, & J. L. Sheppard (Eds.), *Stress and health: Research and clinical applications.* Amsterdam: Harwood Academic.

Charmaz, K. (1983). Loss of Self: A Fundamental Form of Suffering in the Chronically Ill, *Sociology of Health and Illness, 5*(2), 168–195.

Charmaz, K. (2006). *Constructing grounded theory: A practical guide through qualitative analysis.* Thousand Oaks, CA: Sage

Cobb, S. (1976). Social support as a moderator of life stress. *Psychosomatic Medicine, 38,* 300–314.

Cohen, S., & Syme, S. L. (Eds.). (1985). *Social support and health.* Orlando, FL: Academic Press.

Cooley, N. J. (2003). Arts and culture in medicine and health. Retrieved May 28, 2008, from http://bcartscouncil.ca/pdf/ASurveyResearchPaper.pdf

DeNora, T. (1999). Music as a Technology of the Self. *Poetics, 27*, 31–56.

Hays, T., & Minichiello, V. (2005). The meaning of music in the lives of older people: A qualitative study, *Psychology of Music, 33*(4), 437–451.

Health Canada (2008). What makes Canadians Healthy or unhealthy? Retrieved July 29, 2008, from http://www.phac-aspc.gc.ca/ph-sp/determinants/determinants-eng.php

Hwu, Y. J. (1995). The Impact of Chronic Illness on Patients, *Rehabilitation Nursing, 20*, 221–225.

Lazarus, R. S., & Folkman, S. (1984). *Stress, appraisal, and coping.* New York: Springer.

Lin, N., & Westcott, J. (1991). Marital engagement/disengagement, social networks, and mental health (pp. 213–237). In Eckenrode, J. (Ed.), *The social context of coping.* New York: Plenum Press.

Lubkin, I. M. (1998). *Chronic illness: Impact and interventions* (4th ed.). Toronto: Jones and Bartlett.

Merleau-Ponty, Maurice (1962). *Phenomenology of Perception.* C. Smith (translator). Routledge & Kegan Paul.

Nelson, D.C. (1994) *The phenomenological study of music listening experiences: Methodological, clinical, and practical implications.* Pepperdine University, California. (PhD thesis).

Nicol, J.J. (2002). *In the Company of Music and Illness: The Experience and Meaning for Music Listening for Women Living with Chronic Illness.* Vancouver, BC: University of British Columbia Press.

Pederson, T.L. (1994) *A Phenomenological Investigation of Music Listening in Daily Life.* California, United States of America. California School of Professional Psychology (PhD thesis).

Penninx, B. W. J., Kriegsman, D. M., van Eijk, J., Boeke, A. A., Deeg, D. J. H. (1996). Differential effect of social support on the course of chronic disease: A criteria-based literature study. *Families, Systems & Health, 14*(2), 223–244.

Reber, A.S. (1995). The Penguin dictionary of psychology (2nd ed.). New York: Penguin.

Saarikallio, S., & Erkkilä, J. (2007). The role of music in adolescents' mood regulation.

Schaefer, K. M. (1995). Women living in paradox: Loss and discovery in chronic illness. *Holistic Nursing Practice, 9*(3), 63–74.

Symister, P., & Friend, R. (2003). The influence of social support and problematic support on optimism and depression in chronic illness: A prospective study evaluating self-esteem as a mediator. *Health Psychology, 22*(2), 123–129.

Thorne, S. E., & Paterson, B. L. (2000). Two decades of insider research: What we know and don't know about chronic illness experience. *Annual Review of Nursing Research, 18*, 3–25.

van Manen, M. (1990) *Researching Lived Experience.* London, ON: Althouse Press.

Wallace, S., & McKowen, S. (1996). A music lover's diary. Willowdale, ON: Firefly Books

World Health Organization (2008). The determinants of health. Retrieved July 29, 2008, from http://www.who.int/hia/evidence/doh/en/

Brigitte C. Sabourin, Sherry H. Stewart

Patterns of Depression: Substance Use Disorder Comorbidity In Women Seeking Addictions Treatment

Substance-use disorders (SUDs) and major depression are two of the most prevalent psychiatric disorders, both associated with substantial personal and societal costs (Grant et al., 2004). There is wide consensus that the two disorders are highly comorbid (Grant et al., 2004; Helzer & Pryzbeck, 1987; Regier et al., 1990; Swendsen & Merikangas, 2000). The comorbidity relationship can be quantified using an odds ratio (OR), which specifies the odds that someone who suffers from one disorder also suffers from a second disorder (Sabourin & Stewart, 2007). For example, an OR of 1.0 would indicate no relationship between disorders, reflecting that a person has the same odds of developing a second disorder whether or not they suffer from the first disorder. Higher ORs (i.e., > 1.0) reflect stronger relationships between disorders. Conversely, ORs of less than 1.0 reflect a decreased probability of suffering from a second disorder given the presence of the first disorder. The OR for someone with a drug-use disorder to also be diagnosed with major depression has been found to be anywhere from 2.0 to 6.9 (Swendsen & Merikangas, 2000). In addition, the OR for an individual with an alcohol-use disorder (AUD) to suffer from a major depressive episode at some point in their lifetime has been found to be 4.8 (Grant et al., 2004; Schuckit et al., 1997). These rates are much higher than chance.

Independent versus substance-induced depression

The fourth edition of the *Diagnostic and Statistical Manual of Mental Disorders* (DSM-IV; American Psychiatric Association [APA], 1994) makes the distinction between two types of depressive episodes in relation to SUD: independent and substance-induced depression. Independent depression is said to develop prior to the onset of the SUD, or during a prolonged period of abstinence, whereas substance-induced depression is believed to occur due to the direct physiological effects of substance abuse (APA, 1994). Although independent depression is less prevalent than substance-induced depression (Schuckit et al., 1997), it is associated with poorer outcomes, including more frequent relapses to substance abuse and higher suicide rates (Brown, Evans, Miller, Burgess, & Mueller, 1997; Ramsey, Kahler, Read, Stuart, & Brown, 2004; Swendsen & Merikangas, 2000). Furthermore, in contrast to individuals with independent depression, those with substance-induced depression are expected to experience a substantial remission from depressive symptoms within four to six weeks of sobriety (Schuckit, et al., 1997).

Several studies have found that women with SUDs are more likely to suffer from comorbid independent depression compared with men with SUDs (Helzer & Pryzbeck, 1987; Schuckit et al., 1997; Zilberman, Tavares, Blume, & el-Guebaly, 2003; for a review, see also Sinha & Rounsaville, 2002). A widely cited population-based study found that in the case of AUDs, 66% of female comorbid clients suffer from independent major depression, relative to only 22% of male comorbid clients (Helzer & Pryzbeck, 1987). These gender differences in types of comorbid depression (independent vs. substance induced) would be expected to lead to differing severity of psychopathology and treatment outcomes for women versus men with comorbid SUD and depression.

Depression outcome following SUD treatment

Several studies have directly investigated the effects of SUD treatment on levels of depression in comorbid clients (see Swendsen & Merikangas, 2000). Some studies with AUD clients found that depression does not remit following AUD treatment (e.g., Penick, Powell, Liskow, Jackson, & Nickel, 1988). A few studies, on the other hand, found that for a majority of clients depression tends to remit following AUD treatment; unfortunately, these studies reported only on men with AUD and depression comorbidity (Brown et al., 1995; Brown & Schuckit, 1988). Brown et al. (1995) reported that in men there is a clear difference in depression outcome between AUD clients with independent and substance-induced depression. Specifically, the study found that for men with a primary AUD and secondary depression (i.e., the equivalent of substance-induced depression but using order of onset to determine the primary vs. secondary disorder), depression tends to remit following a few weeks of AUD treatment. On the other hand, men with primary depression and a secondary AUD (i.e., the equivalent of independent depression) do not show evidence of remitting from depression following AUD treatment. More research is needed to determine whether this pattern is replicated with comorbid women. If a similar pattern does exist with women and with other forms of SUDs, more comorbid women would be expected to have poorer depression outcomes following SUD treatment than comorbid men due to the former group's higher prevalence of independent depression (Helzer & Pryzbeck, 1987; Zilberman et al., 2003). Nevertheless, the existing studies do support the notion that independent depression represents a more complex clinical picture for comorbid SUD and depression clients that may need specialized intervention dealing specifically with the comorbid depression.

Comorbid depression and client SUD outcome

There is still a substantial amount of controversy over whether comorbid depression puts a client at higher risk of poorer SUD-treatment outcome and for SUD relapse. Although several studies have found clear evidence in support of poorer SUD outcomes for such comorbid clients (Charney, Paraherakis, & Gill, 2001; Greenfield et al., 1998; Hasin et al., 2002; Loosen, Dew, & Prange, 1990; McKay et al., 2002), some studies found that comorbid depression had no effect on SUD outcome (Miller, Hoffmann, Ninonuevo, & Astrachan, 1997; Siqueland et al., 2002). Still other studies found that, for the case of both AUDs and other SUDs, a diagnosis of depression improved treatment outcome (Charney, Paraherakis, Negrete, & Gill, 1998; Rounsaville, Dolinsky, Babor, & Meyer, 1987; Schuckit & Winokur, 1972). Miller et al. (1997) found that although a diagnosis of depression had no effect on SUD-treatment outcome, attendance in peer-support groups and formal aftercare provided by the treatment program significantly increased abstinence rates. It is possible that depressed patients may have attended more of these types of support services, improving their SUD outcomes. Feelings of dysphoria are believed to motivate depressed patients to attend more treatment (McKay, 2005), improving their short-term outcome. In explaining the findings that depression improved AUD-treatment outcome (Rounsaville et al., 1987, Schuckit & Winokur, 1972), it is possible that these comorbid clients were suffering from a less severe or less chronic form of alcoholism, as was found in Schuckit and Winokur. Thus, it is important to determine level of SUD severity in comorbid clients to predict probable treatment outcome. Finally, Rounsaville et al. (1987) found that clients who were depressed at treatment outset had higher depression levels at follow up, putting them at increased risk for longer-term alcoholism relapse (McKay, 2005; Sinha & Rounsaville, 2002). In fact, experiencing ongoing depressive symptoms can be a contributing factor to SUD relapse (Brown et al., 1998).

Findings regarding the role of gender in the relationship between depression and SUD-treatment outcome differ according to the substance being studied. At least one study suggests that gender does not contribute to the relationship between depression and AUD-treatment outcome (Walitzer & Dearing, 2006). However, in the case of cocaine dependence, mood may play a different role in explaining relapse for men and women. Women tend to be more likely than men to cite negative mood states as a reason for relapse to cocaine use (McKay, Rutherford, Cacciola, Kabasakalian-McKay, & Alterman, 1996), which suggests that symptoms of depression might be a greater risk factor for relapse for women than for men for at least certain types of SUDs.

Relationship of anxiety disorders to depression: SUD comorbidity

Anxiety disorders are common psychiatric disorders (i.e., lifetime prevalence of 28.8%; Kessler et al., 2005) that are highly comorbid with both depression and SUD. The National Comorbidity Survey (NCS; see Kessler, Nelson, McGonagle, Edlund, et al., 1996) reported a 12-month OR of 2.6 for individuals suffering from any anxiety disorder to also suffer from alcohol dependence, and a 12-month OR of 3.6 for drug dependence. Similarly, the 12-month OR was 4.2 for individuals who suffer from major depression to also suffer from an anxiety disorder (Kessler, Nelson, McGonagle, Liu, et al., 1996). The NCS (see Kessler et al., 1997) also examined gender differences in comorbidity between AUDs and anxiety disorders. Women with certain anxiety disorders (i.e., social phobia, simple phobias, posttraumatic stress disorder) had higher ORs of alcohol abuse than did men with these anxiety disorders, demonstrating a closer relationship between anxiety disorders and SUD for women than for men. Furthermore, there is wide consensus that the presence of comorbid anxiety disorders often result in less effective SUD treatment and higher rates of relapse for SUD individuals (Kushner, Abrams, & Borchardt, 2000; Zvolensky & Schmidt, 2004). Thus, the presence of anxiety disorders in individuals with comorbid depression and SUD may be a further indication of a more complex clinical picture with poorer prognosis following SUD treatment. And the extant literature suggests that the additional complexity of anxiety disorder comorbidity may be a particularly relevant problem for women struggling with co-occurring depression and SUD.

The present study

In view of the complicated clinical picture of individuals with SUDs who also suffer from comorbid depression, and the paucity of research exploring the ways in which women's experiences differ from those of men, the present study's goal was to further examine gender differences in patterns of depression and SUD comorbidity in individuals seeking addiction treatment. Specifically, the study explored rates of comorbid independent and substance-induced depression in both women and men with SUDs who sought treatment. Also, gender differences were examined in severity of SUDs associated with both independent and substance-induced comorbid depression, and in the specific influence of comorbid depression on screening positive for comorbid anxiety disorders—an index of clinical complexity.

It was hypothesized that SUD women would be more likely than SUD men to suffer from independent depression. That is, it was expected that depression symptoms would begin before the onset of substance-use problems and/or remain during periods of abstinence for more SUD women than SUD men. Also, because anxiety disorders have been shown to be more closely linked to both depression and SUDs for women than for men, it was hypothesized that SUD women who screened positive for depression would also screen positive for more anxiety disorders than their male counterparts. Further, it was hypothesized that the gender differences observed in a number of anxiety disorders would be more pronounced for individuals suffering from independent depression, which is associated with more severe psychopathology, compared with those suffering from substance-induced depression, which is associated with less severe psychopathology.

The inconsistencies reported in previous literature on the relationship between comorbid depression and SUD severity may have been due to a failure to consider the distinction between independent depression (i.e., associated with more severe psychopathology) and substance-induced depression (i.e., associated with less severe psychopathology), and also to a failure to consider the effects of gender on the link between comorbidity and clinical severity. Thus, it was hypothesized that comorbid independent depression would be associated with a more severe SUD presentation (i.e., more severe clinical presentation) than comorbid substance-induced depression, and, again, especially for women.

Method

Participants

Forty men and 36 women entering addiction treatment through Community and Counselling Support Services (CCSS), Addiction Prevention and Treatment Services (APTS), and Capital Health District, all located in Halifax, Nova Scotia, were recruited to participate in the study. Any individual entering treatment at CCSS was eligible for the study except for individuals receiving treatment for a driving-while-intoxicated (DWI) charge, as they are often mandated to treatment and thus makes up a very different population (Brown, 2007).

Socio-demographic characteristics are presented in table 1. Study participants' mean age was 37.5 years (SD = 11.4, range = 19–63 years). Over half of the participants who indicated their education level had at least some university-level education (50.9%). One-third (33.3%) of those who reported their income reported a current income level under $10,000 per annum, with 60% reporting under $20,000 per annum. There were no significant differences between men and women in age, t (72) = 1.55, p = .13; education level, $\chi^2(1, N = 57)$ = 4.82, p = .31; or income level, $\chi^2(1, N = 45)$ = 0.28, p = .96.

Table 1 Participant Education and Income Levels			
	N	%	
Highest Level of Education Completed			
Elementary School	2	2.6	
Junior High School	7	9.2	
High School	9	11.8	
Trade School	1	1.3	
Community College	7	9.2	
Some University	14	18.4	
University	15	19.7	
Other	2	2.6	
Did Not Specify		19	25.0
Annual Family Income			
Up to $10,000	15	19.7	
$11,000 – $20,000	12	15.8	
$21,000 – $30,000	2	2.6	
$31,000 – $40,000	3	3.9	
$41,000 – $50,000	2	2.6	
$51,000 – $60,000	5	6.6	
$61,000 – $70,000	3	3.9	
More Than $70,000	3	3.9	
Did Not Specify	31	40.8	

Measures

Screening questionnaire.
We used the Psychiatric Diagnostic Screening Questionnaire (PDSQ; Zimmerman & Mattia, 2001), a 111-item self-administered questionnaire designed to screen for DSM-IV Axis I disorders (APA, 1994), including major depression, AUDs, and drug-use disorders. The PDSQ has been found to have excellent psychometric properties in a variety of clinical populations, including SUD populations (Castel, Rush, Kennedy, Fulton, & Toneatto,

2007; Magruder, Sonne, Brady, Quellos, & Martin, 2005; Zimmerman & Mattia, 2001; Zimmerman, Sheeran, Chelminski, & Young, 2004). Zimmerman and Mattia (2001) reported internal-consistency and one-week test/re-test reliability to be 0.88 and 0.92, respectively, for the major depression sub-scale; 0.87 and 0.89 for the alcohol-abuse/dependence sub-scale; and 0.89 and 0.93 for the drug-abuse/dependence sub-scale—the three scales of primary interest in the present study. Six sub-scales screening for anxiety disorders were also used in the present study. These sub-scales had internal consistencies ranging from 0.83 to 0.94, and one-week test/re-test reliabilities ranging from 0.79 to 0.86. Correlations between the PDSQ sub-scales and other established scales measuring the same symptom domain were 0.77 for major depression, 0.62 for alcohol abuse/dependence, and 0.53 for drug abuse/dependence, and ranged from 0.64 to 0.73 for anxiety disorders, suggesting adequate convergent validity.

Participants completed the PDSQ answering "yes" or "no" to questions pertaining to feelings and behaviours related to various psychiatric disorders. The PDSQ included questions such as "Were you less interested in almost all of the activities you are usually interested in?" (from the major depression scale), "Did you think that you were drinking too much?" (from the AUDs scale), and "Did anyone in your family think or say that you were using drugs too much, or that you had a drug problem?" (from the drug-use-disorders scale). Two minor changes were made to the PDSQ. First, all questions inquiring about clients' feelings and behaviours over the past six months were modified to inquire about the past month (cf. Kushner et al., 2005) in order to obtain a more current clinical picture. Second, four questions were added to the PDSQ to assess independent versus substance-induced depression. Three questions assessing order of onset (i.e., the first distinguishing feature between independent and substance-induced depression according to the DSM-IV [APA, 2000]) asked participants to state the ages at which they first began experiencing: (1) depression symptoms, (2) alcohol problems and (3) drug-use problems. An additional question was inserted at the end of the depression sub-scale, asking participants to indicate whether symptoms of depression were ever experienced even when abstaining from alcohol or drugs (i.e., the second distinguishing feature between independent and substance-induced depression according to the DSM-IV [APA, 2000]).

A PDSQ cut-off score of 11 out of a possible 21 items endorsed was used to determine positive screening for depression during the two weeks prior to entering addictions treatment. This cut-off has been shown in a previous study to have 85% sensitivity and 82% specificity when compared with diagnoses made using a structured diagnostic interview (Castel et al., 2007). Because all participants were entering treatment for alcohol and/or drug addiction, and some participants entered treatment after a detoxification period lasting up to one month, their attendance at CCSS was taken as evidence of an SUD, regardless of their PDSQ scores on the alcohol or drug sub-scales, which assess for drinking or drug-use behaviours and consequences during the previous month only. Finally, an index of alcohol- or drug-use severity was calculated by adding the number of drug and alcohol problems endorsed (cf., Conrod et al., 2000; Zimmerman, 2002).[1]

Procedure

Participants were first contacted to participate in the present study during a group orientation session when they first entered addiction treatment at CCSS. After providing informed consent, they completed the PDSQ and an author-compiled demographic questionnaire. The questionnaires took approximately a half hour to complete.

Data Analysis

All analyses were conducted using the statistical software program SPSS for Windows, version 15.0. Descriptive statistics are presented as means and standard deviations for continuous variables and as raw numbers and percentages for categorical variables. Group differences were tested using factorial univariate analysis of variables and t-tests for continuous variables, and Pearson chi-square (χ^2) for categorical variables. Associations between continuous measures were examined using Pearson bivariate correlations. All tests were two-tailed unless otherwise specified (i.e., one-tailed tests were used when directional predictions had been made a priori).

Results

Comparisons in rates and indices of independent versus substance-induced comorbid depression

The number of SUD men and women who screened positive for comorbid depression is shown in table 2. For the purposes of this paper, however, analyses are based on clients' experiences with symptoms of depression rather than on meeting certain cut-off points for a possible diagnosis of depression. In a classic paper, Persons (1986) discusses several advantages to studying psychological phenomena at a symptomatic rather than a "syndromal" (i.e., diagnostic) level (see also Sabourin & Stewart, 2007).

The difference between independent and substance-induced depression was determined using order of onset of depression symptoms and substance-use problems, and the presence of symptoms of depression when abstaining from substance use. It was expected that women would be more likely than men to suffer from independent depression symptoms. Over two-thirds

(70%) of female participants, compared with slightly over half (60%) of male participants, had experienced depressive symp-

Table 2 Frequencies for Positive Screen for Depression	Men	Women	Total
Screen Positive for Depression	20	23	43
Screen Negative for Depression	20	13	33
Totals	40	36	76

toms prior to the onset of substance-use problems; and over three-quarters (81%) of female participants, compared with slightly over two-thirds (72%) of male participants, reported experiencing symptoms of depression even when abstaining from alcohol or drugs, although these differences were not statistically significant: $\chi^2(1, N = 38) = 0.55$, $p = .26$, and $\chi^2(1, N = 51) = 0.46$, $p = .34$ (one-tailed; see table 3 for frequencies). However, when examining differences in independent versus substance-induced depression within genders, women were more likely to self-report having suffered from depression symptoms before the onset of substance-use problems, $\chi^2(1, N = 23) = 3.52$, $p = .03$ (one-tailed) for women, compared with $\chi^2(1, N = 15) = 0.60$, $p = .44$ for men. Also, although for both women and men there was a larger number of participants who self-reported experiencing depression symptoms even during periods of abstinence as opposed to while using substances—$\chi^2(1, N = 26) = 9.85$, $p = .002$, for women, and $\chi^2(1, N = 25) = 4.84$, $p = .03$ for men—this pattern appears to be stronger for women than for

Table 3
Frequencies for Order of Onset and Experiencing Symptoms of Depression Even When Abstaining from Drugs or Alcohol by Gender

	Onset of Depression Symptoms[a]		
	Before SUD	After SUD	Total[b]
Men	9 (60.0%)	6 (40.0%)	15
Women	16 (69.6%)*	7 (30.4%)*	23
Total Sample	25	13	38

	Symptoms of Depression When Abstaining[a]		
	Yes	No	Total[b]
Men	18 (72.0%)**	7 (28.0%)**	25
Women	21 (80.8%)***	5 (19.2%)***	26
Total Sample	39	12	51

NOTE: Means with similar superscripts indicate a significant within-gender group difference: *$p < .05$, **$p < .05$, ***$p < .005$ (one-tailed tests).

[a]All clients who endorsed symptoms of depression, even if they failed to meet the recommended cut-off for screening positive for a major depressive episode, were included in these counts.

[b]Although all clients endorsed at least one symptom of depression, not all clients responded to the additional items that distinguished between independent and substance-induced symptoms of depression.

men, as indexed by larger effect sizes for women (χ^2 = .38, a moderate effect size) than for men (χ^2 = .19, a small effect size; see table 3 for frequencies).

Comparisons in severity associated with comorbid depression and substance-use disorders.

The number of comorbid anxiety disorders present (e.g., social phobia, post-traumatic stress disorder, panic disorder, generalized anxiety disorder) was used as a measure of clinical complexity, especially given the close relationship between anxiety disorders and both depression and SUD. Results suggested that women with comorbid depression had a more complex clinical picture than their male counterparts, having experienced a greater number of comorbid anxiety disorders during the month prior to when the study was conducted, $F(1, 41) = 10.54$, $p = .002$ (see figure 1). This gender difference did not exist, however, for participants who screened negative for depression, $F(1, 31) = 0.23$, $p = .64$ (see figure 1). Furthermore, results suggested that women with an onset of depression symptoms prior to first suffering from substance-use problems also presented a more complex clinical case, reporting a greater number of different anxiety disorders than their male counterparts, $F(1, 23) = 7.15$, $p = .01$ (see figure 2). Again, this gender difference did not exist for individuals suffering from depression symptoms following the onset of substance-use problems, $F(1, 11) = 1.06$, $p = .31$ (see figure 2). Similarly, women who experienced depression symptoms even when abstaining from drugs or alcohol reported a greater number of different anxiety disorders than their male counterparts, $F(1, 37) = 9.67$, $p =$

Table 4
Severity of Current SUD Represented by Mean Number of Symptoms Endorsed, as a Function of Depression

		Number of Symptoms Endorsed					
		Women		Men		Total	
		Mean	SD	Mean	SD	Mean	SD
Screen for Depression							
	Positive	6.30	3.23	7.30	2.94	6.77*	3.10
	Negative	5.46	3.80	5.32	4.04	5.38*	3.50
Onset of Depression Symptoms							
	Before SUD	6.94	2.74	5.44	1.67	6.40	2.48
	After SUD	6.29	3.45	6.80	2.39	6.50	2.94
Symptoms of Depression When Abstaining from Substances							
	Yes	6.57**	3.49	5.24	3.80	5.97	3.64
	No	3.40**	2.41	6.71	3.68	5.33	3.52
Total		6.00	3.41	6.33	3.62	6.17	3.50

NOTE: SUP = Substance Use Problem; Means with similar subscripts differ from one another at: *p < .10, **p < .05 (one-tailed test). All comparisons are within-group comparisons.

.004, but again there were no differences between those women and men who did not experience depression symptoms when abstaining, $F(1, 10) = 0.32$, $p = .59$ (see figure 3).

The number of AUD or SUD symptoms endorsed (i.e., indicating alcohol- or drug-use severity) by women and men is presented in table 4 as a function of screening positive for depression and of meeting each of the two criteria for independent versus substance-induced depression. There were no overall differences between men and women in SUD severity, $t(73) = 0.41$, $p = .68$ (see table 4, bottom row). On the other hand, screening positive for comorbid depression was marginally associated with increased substance-use-problem severity, $F(1,71) = 2.96$, $p = .09$ (see table 4, top panel). There was also a marginal interaction between gender and depression symptoms, even when abstaining

Figure 1
Effects of Gender and Presence of Depression on Number of Comorbid Anxiety Disorders

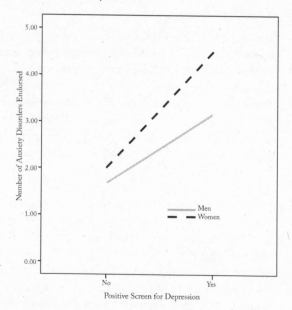

Figure 2
Effects of Gender and Relative Order of Onset of Substance-Use Problems vs. Depression on Number of Comorbid Anxiety Disorders

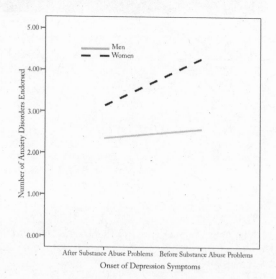

from alcohol and drugs, on severity of substance-use problems, F (1, 46) = 3.83, p = .06. Simple effects revealed that for women, but not for men, experiencing depression symptoms even when abstaining was associated with more severe substance-use problems, t (24) = 1.91, p = .04 (one-tailed) for women, and t (22) = 0.87, p = .20 (one-tailed) for men (see table 4, lower-middle panel). There were neither significant main nor interaction effects for gender or for experiencing symptoms of depression before the onset of SUD symptoms on SUD severity (all p values were > .10) (see table 4, upper-middle panel).

Figure 3

Effects of Gender and Presence of Depression Symptoms Even When Abstaining From Drugs or Alcohol on Number of Comorbid Anxiety Disorders.

Discussion

The overall goal of the present study was to examine whether comorbid depression in women represents a more serious clinical picture than in men. Contrary to expectation, SUD women were not more likely than SUD men to experience independent depression. Although these findings did not support the hypothesis, they are consistent with findings

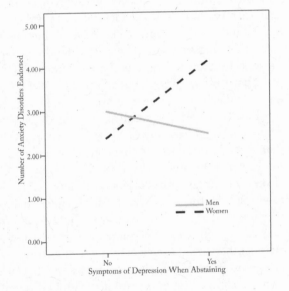

from other studies that did not find gender differences in independent versus substance-induced depression for cocaine dependence specifically (e.g., Herrero, Domingo-Salvany, Torrens, & Brugal, 2008). Because our study did not differentiate between different classes of drugs other than alcohol, it is possible that a large number of participants in the present study were also seeking treatment for cocaine dependence, which might account for the findings in the present study.

However, when examining within-gender differences, findings more consistent with expectations were observed. Specifically, it was revealed that women clients were more likely to experience independent depression than substance-induced depression. This pattern was not found for men clients in the case of depression onset prior to a substance problem, and was stronger in the women clients than in the men clients in the case of symptoms of depression when abstaining. This pattern suggests that for treatment-seeking SUD women, more so than for treatment-seeking SUD men, the depression would be less likely to remit after a period of abstinence from alcohol and drugs (Brown et al., 1997). This pattern is also consistent with the possibility that treatment-seeking SUD women in particular may have a pattern of substance use that involves attempts to self-medicate for depressive symptoms (Brown & Stewart, 2008). In fact, there is documentation of high rates of childhood abuse, physical abuse, and domestic violence experienced by women with SUDs, which may give rise to depressive symptoms and the need to self-medicate more so among SUD women than SUD men (Stewart & Israeli, 2002).

It was also found that women with comorbid depression had a greater number of co-occurring anxiety disorders than did comorbid men. Further analyses revealed that this gender difference was specific to women with comorbid independent depression relative to their male counterparts. This latter finding suggests that women with comorbid independent depression may experience a more severe clinical presentation relative to their male counterparts, particularly given the established links of co-occurring anxiety disorders to difficulties in recovering from an SUD (e.g., Kushner et al., 2005).

Finally, the results partially supported the hypothesis that independent depression would be associated with more severe substance-use problems than substance-induced depression for women, but not for men. That is, for women, experiencing depression symptoms even when abstaining from alcohol and drugs was associated with more severe SUD presentation. This result suggests the possibility that independent depression is directly related to the exacerbation of the severity of SUD symptoms in women (e.g., self-medication ultimately worsening the substance-abuse problem), whereas factors other than independent depression contribute to severity of SUD symptoms in men. This observed association between independent depression and clinical severity for women with SUDs indicates a specific need to address depression symptoms in women clients with comorbid SUD and depression. However, it was surprising that this hypothesis was only supported in analyses of one of the two indices of independent depression (i.e., it was not supported when the index was depression onset prior to onset of substance problems). This discrepancy highlights the need to continue to employ both indices in future investigations of independent versus substance-induced depression until it is established which is the most valid index of independent depression among SUD clients.

There were a number of potential limitations to the present study that should be considered when interpreting the results. First, although the PDSQ has shown excellent psychometric properties, it remains a screening and not a diagnostic tool. Thus, conclusions are limited to probable diagnoses of psychiatric disorders only. Results should thus be replicated using other structured clinical interviews, for example, the Structured Clinical Interview for DSM-IV Axis 1 (First, Spitzer, Gibbon, & Williams, 1988). Second, because individuals with more than one disorder are more likely to seek treatment, clinical samples may in fact inflate comorbidity estimates (Berkson, 1949), thus potentially limiting the generalizability of the current findings to a community population. Third, we relied on retrospective reports of relative order of onset of depression symptoms and SUD symptoms, and retrospective reports can be subject to memory distortions. There may be gender differences in the tendency to attribute one's substance use to self-medication for depression that could effect memories of relative order of onset of symptoms as well as perceptions of having significant mood symptoms independent of substance use. This possibility could be explored through future studies examining gender differences in such attributions, as well as through longitudinal studies examining relative order of onset of depressive symptoms and substance abuse in girls versus boys. Finally, the small sample size (N = 76), coupled with the fact that some participants failed to respond to all measures, might have compromised our ability to uncover some of the expected gender differences in certain subgroups of clients participating in the present study (e.g., frequencies of men and women who experience depression symptoms prior to SUD symptoms).

The present study aimed to further explore how the experiences of women with comorbid depression and SUD differed from those of men in a treatment-seeking sample. Results suggest that individuals with SUD who suffer from comorbid depression present a more complex and severe clinical picture than individuals who do not suffer from comorbid depression. This pattern appears to be even stronger for women than for men, especially for women with independent versus substance-induced depression. Treatment efforts need to recognize the complex relationship between depression and SUD. Only recently has treatment research begun exploring integrated treatments for addictions and psychopathology. Integrated treatments simultaneously incorporate the best treatment for each disorder, and incorporate in their treatment strategy an understanding of the interplay between the clients' addictions and comorbid psychiatric disorder (Sabourin & Stewart, 2007). Thus, integrated depression and SUD treatments may be beneficial for all individuals with comorbid depression and SUD, but especially for comorbid women. This type of treatment approach appears to be the most recommended by "expert opinion"; however, few of the recommendations are supported by randomized controlled trials, or even by quasi-experimental designs. Future research needs to be conducted to develop and evaluate integrated treatments. The present study's exploration of the complex relationship between depression and SUD, with consideration of how this relationship differs for women as compared with men, provided an important step in tailoring treatment programs that are able to deliver the best possible care to both women and men who suffer from SUD and depression—two common and debilitating disorders.

Notes

We would like to thank Mr. Tom Payette, Ms. Jean MacClelland, and the counselors and staff at Community Counseling and Support Services (CCSS), Capital Health Addictions Prevention and Treatment Services, in Halifax, Nova Scotia, for their support in this project, and their assistance in recruiting participants for the present study. We would also like to thank the two project managers, Ms. Dubravka Gavric and Ms. Adrienne Girling for their tireless efforts during both the initial and later stages of this project. Their assistance has been invaluable in ensuring the smooth functioning of the present study.

1. The PDSQ proposes a total symptom count as a rough measure of overall level of psychopathology. It does not, however, mention the use of symptom counts for any specific sub-scale individually. However, the present practice parallels a practice used with another alcohol screening tool (i.e., the Michigan Alcohol Screening Tool) that frequently uses symptom count as a measure of alcohol severity (e.g., Zack, Stewart, Klein, Loba, & Fragopoulous, 2005). Moreover, several other studies use symptom counts as an index of severity of substance-use problems (e.g., Conrod et al., 2000).

References

American Psychiatric Association (1994). *Diagnostic and Statistical Manual of Mental Disorders* (4th Edition). Washington, DC: American Psychiatric Association.

Berkson, J. (1946). Limitations of the application of fourfold tables to hospital data. *Biometrics Bulletin*, 2(3), 47–53.

Brown, C. G., & Stewart, S. H. (2008). Exploring women's use of alcohol as self-medication for depression among women receiving community-based treatment for alcohol problems. *Journal of Prevention and Intervention in the Community, 35*, 33–47.

Brown, S. A., & Schuckit, M. A. (1988). Changes in depression among abstinent alcoholics. *Journal of Studies on Alcohol 49*, 412–417.

Brown, S. A., Inaba, R. K., Christian, G.J., Schuckit, M. A., Stewart, M. A., & Irwin, M. R. (1995). Alcoholism and affective disorder: Clinical course of depressive symptoms. *American Journal of Psychiatry, 152*, 45–52.

Brown, R. A., Evans, D. M., Miller, I. W., Burgess, E. S., & Mueller, T. I. (1997). Cognitive-behavioral treatment for depression in alcoholism. *Journal of Consulting and Clinical Psychology, 65*, 715–726.

Brown, R. A., Monti, P. M., Myers, M. G., Martin, R. A., Rivinus, T., Dubreuil, M. E., et al. (1998). Depression among cocaine abusers in treatment: Relation to cocaine and alcohol use and treatment outcome. *American Journal of Psychiatry, 155*, 220–225.

Brown, T. (2007, October). *The impact of brief motivational interviewing in DUI offenders who fail to comply with sanctions.* Paper presented at the 25th annual meeting of the International Medical Advisory Group, Halifax, NS.

Castel, S., Rush, B., Kennedy, S., Fulton, K., & Toneatto, T. (2007). Screening for mental health problems among patients with substance use disorders: Preliminary findings on the validation of a self-assessment instrument. *Canadian Journal of Psychiatry, 52,* 22–26.

Charney, D. A., Paraherakis, J. C., & Gill, K. J. (2001). Integrated treatments of comorbid depression and substance use disorders. *Journal of Clinical Psychiatry, 62,* 72–677.

Charney, D. A., Paraherakis, J. C., Negrete, J. C., & Gill, K. J. (1998). The impact of depression on the outcome of additions treatment. *Journal of Substance Abuse Treatment, 15,* 123–130.

Conrod, P. J., Stewart, S. H., Pihl, R. O., Côté, S., Fontaine, V., & Dongier, M. (2000). Efficacy of brief coping skills interventions that match different personality profiles of female substance abusers. *Psychology of Addictive Behaviors, 14,* 231–242.

First, M. B., Spitzer, R. L., Gibbon, M., & Williams, J. B. W. (1998). *Structured Clinical Interview for Axis I DSM-IV – Patient Edition (With Psychotic Screen) (SCID-I/P (W/Psychotic Screen) (Version 2.0, 8/98 revision).* New York: New York State Psychiatric Institute.

Grant, B. F., Stinson, F. S., Dawson, D. A., Chou, S. P., Dufour, M. C., Compton, W., et al. (2004). Prevalence and co-occurrence of substance use disorders and independent mood and anxiety disorders. *Archives of General Psychiatry, 61,* 807–816.

Greenfield, S. F., Weiss, R. D., Muenz, L. R., Vagge, L. M., Kelly, J. F., Bello, L. R., et al. (1998). The effect of depression on return to drinking. *Archives of General Psychiatry, 55,* 259–265.

Hasin, D., Liu, X., Nunes, E., McCloud, S., Samet, S., & Endicott, J. (2002). Effects of major depression on remission and relapse of substance dependence. *Archives of General Psychiatry, 59,* 375–380.

Helzer, J. E. & Pryzbeck, T. R. (1987). The co-occurrence of alcoholism with other psychiatric disorders in the general population and its impact on treatment. *Journal of Studies on Alcohol, 49,* 219–224.

Herrero, M. J., Domingo-Salvany, A., Torrens, M., & Brugal, M. T. (2008). Psychiatric comorbidity in young cocaine users: Induced versus independent disorders. *Addiction, 103,* 284–293.

Kessler, R. C., Berglund, P, Demler, O, Jin, R, Merikangas, K. R., & Walter, E. E. (2005). Lifetime prevalence and age-of-onset distributions of DSM-IV disorders in the National Comorbidity Survey Replication, *Archives of General Psychiatry, 62,* 593–602.

Kessler, R. C., Crum, R. M., Warner, L. A., Nelson, C. B., Schulenberg, J., & Anthony, J. C. (1997). Lifetime co-occurrence of DSM-III-R alcohol abuse and dependence with other psychiatric disorders in the National Comorbidity Survey. *Archives of General Psychiatry, 54,* 313–321.

Kessler, R. C., Nelson, C. B., McGonagle, K. A., Edlund, M. J., Frank, R. G., & Leaf, P.J. (1996). The epidemiology of co-occurring addictive and mental disorders. *American Journal of Orthopsychiatry, 66,* 17–31.

Kessler, R. C., Nelson, C. B., McGonagle, K. A., Liu, J., Swartz, M., & Blazer, D. G. (1996). Comorbidity of *DSM–III–R* major depressive disorder in the general population: Results from the U.S. National Comorbidity Survey. *British Journal of Psychiatry, 168*(Suppl. 30), 17–30.

Kushner, M. G., Abrams, K., & Borchardt, C. (2000). The relationship between anxiety disorders and alcohol use disorders: A review of major perspectives and findings. *Clinical Psychology Review, 20,* 149–171.

Kushner, M. G., Abrams, K., Thuras, P., Hanson, K. L., Brekke, M., & Sletten, S. (2005). Follow-up study of anxiety disorder and alcohol dependence in comorbid alcoholism treatment patients. *Alcoholism: Clinical and Experimental Research, 29,* 1432–1443.

Loosen, P. T., Dew, B.W., & Prange, A. J. (1990). Long-term predictors of outcome in abstinent alcoholic men. *American Journal of Psychiatry, 147,* 1662–1666.

Magruder, K. M., Sonne, S. C., Brady, K. T., Quellos, S., & Martin, R. H. (2005). Screening for co-occurring mental disorders in drug treatment populations. *Journal of Drug Issues, 22,* 593–606.

McKay, J. R. (2005). Co-occurring substance dependence and depression: Practical implications and next questions. *Addiction, 100,* 1755–1757.

McKay, J. R., Pettinati, H. M., Gallop, R., Morrison, R., Feeley, M., & Mulvaney, F. D. (2002). Relation of depression diagnoses to 2-year outcomes in cocaine-dependent patients in a randomized continuing care study. *Psychology of Addictive Behaviour, 16,* 225–235.

McKay, J. R., Rutherford, M. J., Cacciola, J. S., Kabasakalian-McKay, R., & Alterman, A. I. (1996). Gender difference in the relapse experience of cocaine patients. *Journal of Nervous and Mental Disease, 184,* 616–622

Miller, N. S., Hoffmann, N. G., Ninonuevo, F., & Astrachan, B. M. (1997). Lifetime diagnosis of major depression as a multivariate predictor of treatment outcome for inpatients with substance use disorders from abstinence-based programs. *Annals of Clinical Psychiatry, 9,* 127–137.

Penick, E. C., Powell, B. J., Liskow, B. I., Jackson, J. O., & Nickel, E. J. (1988). The stability of coexisting psychiatric syndromes in alcoholic men after one year. *Journal of Studies on Alcohol, 49,* 395–405.

Persons, J. B. (1986). The advantage of studying psychological phenomena rather than psychiatric diagnoses. *American Psychologist, 41,* 1252–1260.

Ramsey, S. E., Kahler, C.W., Read, J. P., Stuart, G. L., & Brown, R. A. (2004). Discriminating between substance-induced and independent depressive episodes in alcohol dependent patients. *Journal of Studies on Alcohol, 65,* 672–676.

Regier, D. A., Farmer, M. E., Rae, D. S., Locke, B. Z., Keither, S. J., Judd, L. L. O., et al. (1990). Comorbidity of mental disorders with alcohol and other drug abuse: Results from the Epidemiologic Catchment Area (ECA) study. *Journal of the American Medical Association, 264,* 2511–2518.

Rounsaville, B. J., Dolinsky, Z. S., Babor, T. F., & Meyer, R. E. (1987). Psychopathology as a predictor of treatment outcome in alcoholics. *Archives of General Psychiatry, 44,* 505–513.

Sabourin, B.C., & Stewart, S.H. (2007). Alcohol use and anxiety disorders. In M.J. Zvolensky & J. A. J. Smits (Eds.), *Health Behaviors and Physical Illness in Anxiety and its Disorders: Contemporary Theory and Research* (pp. 29–54). New York: Springer.

Schuckit, M. A., Tipp, J. E., Bergman, M., Reigh, W., Hesselbrock, V. M., & Smith, T. L. (1997). Comparison of induced and independent major depressive disorders in 2,945 alcoholics. *American Journal of Psychiatry, 154,* 948–956.

Schuckit, M. A., & Winokur, G. (1972). A short term follow up of women alcoholics. *Diseases of the Nervous System, 33,* 672–678.

Siqueland, L., Crits-Christoph, P., Gallop, R., Barber, J. P., Griffin, M. L., Thase, M. E., et al. (2002). Retention in psychosocial treatment of cocaine dependence: Predictors and impact on outcome. *American Journal on Addictions, 11,* 24–40.

Sinha, R., & Rounsaville, B. J. (2002). Sex differences in depressed substance abusers. *Journal of Clinical Psychiatry, 16,* 616–627.

Stewart, S. H., & Israeli, A. L. (2002). Substance abuse and co-occurring psychiatric disorders in victims of intimate violence. In C. Wekerle & A. M. Wall (Eds.), *The Violence and Addiction Equation: Theoretical and Clinical Issues in Substance Abuse and Relationship Violence* (pp. 98–122). New York: Brunner-Routledge.

Swendsen, J. D. & Merikangas, K. R. (2000). The comorbidity of depression and substance use disorders. *Clinical Psychology Review, 20,*173–189.

Walitzer, K. S., & Dearing, R. L. (2006). Gender differences in alcohol and substance use relapse. *Clinical Psychology Review, 26,* 128-148.

Zack, M., Stewart, S. H., Klein, R. M., Loba, P., & Fragopoulos, F. (2005). Contingent gambling-drinking patterns and problem-drinking severity moderate implicit gambling-alcohol associations in problem gamblers. *Journal of Gambling Studies, 21,* 325–354.

Zilberman, M. L., Tavares, H., Blume, S. B., & el-Guebaly, N. (2003). Substance use disorders: Sex differences and psychiatric comorbidities. *Canadian Journal of Psychiatry, 48,* 5–13.

Zimmerman, M. (2002). *The Psychiatric Diagnostic Screening Questionnaire.* Los Angeles: Western Psychological Services.

Zimmerman, M., & Mattia, J (2001). The Psychiatric Diagnostic Screening Questionnaire: Development, reliability and validity. *Comprehensive Psychiatry, 42,* 175–189.

Zimmerman, M., Sheeran, T., Chelminski, I., & Young, D. (2004). Screening for psychiatric disorders in outpatients with DSM-IV substance use disorders. *Journal of Substance Abuse Treatment, 26,*181–188.

Zvolensky, M. J., & Schmidt, N. B. (2004). Anxiety and substance use disorders: Introduction to the special series. *Journal of Anxiety Disorders, 18,* 1–6.

S. A. Wiebe and S. W. Sadava

The Impact of Psychosocial Factors on the Health and Well-Being of Women with Fibromyalgia

Fibromyalgia, a condition characterized by widespread musculoskeletal pain and stiffness, is a complex illness that seems to arise from various factors (Bergman, 2005) and often requires an integrative treatment plan, including various therapies such as psychotherapy (Van Koulil et al., 2008), pharmacotherapy, and massage therapy, among others (Clayton & West, 2006). Theories point to a number of factors involved in terms of etiology, including physiological factors such as lower serotonin levels and a hyperactive hypothalamic-pituitary-adrenal (HPA) axis. The HPA axis is a location in the brain responsible for processing stress, the hyperactivity of which signals high levels of stress. This often leads to higher levels of a hormone called cortisol, which is another signal of high stress. Other physiological factors may include physical trauma or infection. Psychological factors such as stress and emotional distress have also been found to play a role in the development of fibromyalgia (Bergman, 2005). A dominant theory in the literature is that fibromyalgia arises from a problem with pain perception. The theory states that physical pain is neurologically processed and perceived in a case where there is no tissue damage, and therefore no pain should be processed (Staud & Domingo, 2001).

Unfortunately, this often leads to stigma surrounding the illness. Women with fibromyalgia often report feelings of stigmatization (Looper & Kirmayer, 2004), and fibromyalgia has been found to hold a low status with physicians (Åsbring & Närvänen, 2002). That physiological, neurological, and psychosocial factors cause physical pain in fibromyalgia also often leads to stigma; however, it is this combination of factors that makes the illness a true example of the so-called biopsychosocial model of health (Åsbring & Närvänen, 2002).

Fibromyalgia most commonly affects women, although the reasons for this are not clear (Staud & Domingo, 2001). Results of a large-scale study done in Ontario reported that 5% of female participants had fibromyalgia, in contrast with 1.6% of the male participants (Okifuji & Turk, 2002). Being a chronic illness, fibromyalgia is usually not "cured" per se, but rather is coped with, and often causes significant difficulties over a long period of time (Okifuji & Turk, 2002). Given this, it seems particularly important to investigate what factors influence well-being for these women even while struggling with the debilitating illness.

Research on health and well-being suggests that interpersonal relationships play a significant role in both physical and mental health for people in general (Diamond & Hicks, 2004). Loneliness is considered a serious health hazard, and has even been linked with mortality and morbidity to the same extent as smoking (House, Landis, & Umberson, 1988). Social-support networks, quality of social support, and quality of close relationships have been found to buffer against ill health and promote optimal healthy functioning (Berkman, 1984); Diamond & Hicks, 2004). Interestingly, as outlined by MacDonald and Leary (2005), social pain and physical pain may share some of the same emotional and physiological components. Clearly, interpersonal relationships play a crucial role in the health and well-being of women. A study by Picardi et al. (2007) suggests that women's immunity is significantly affected by the quality of their attachment relationships. Specifically, the more secure the women were in their attachment relationships, the higher was their natural killer cell cytotoxicity, a sign of stronger immune-system function. Additionally, in a sample of women recently diagnosed with breast cancer, better-quality social support and larger social-support networks was related to lower mortality rates eight years later (Weihs, Enright, & Simmens, 2008).

Turning more specifically to women with fibromyalgia, there is evidence that for these women, quality of social support is significantly linked with better physical and psychological health (Franks, Cronan, & Oliver, 2004). However, there are other aspects of relationships besides peripheral social supports that may influence health and well-being. Often the most important social contacts we have are with those closest to us, our close-attachment relationships, which most often include close family or romantic partners (Johnson, 2004). This may be especially true for women with fibromyalgia, who may be limited by the illness in terms of making social contact.

In a sample of women with fibromyalgia, difficulty in maintaining social networks and participating in social activities was reported, suggesting that their closest relationships may become ever more important and central to their sense of well-being and health (Soderberg & Lundman, 2000).

Adult attachment theory is a very useful framework in the study of close relationships. According to this theory, secure attachment to one or a few main attachment figures is integral to individual well-being. The attachment relationship serves as a safe haven and secure base (Bowlby, 1969)—someone to turn to in times of stress and trouble and someone to provide encouragement to go out into daily life with confidence; therefore, attachment relationships ultimately serve the function of affect and stress regulation. The more secure the sense of attachment, the better it will be in serving these functions. Security of attachment is often measured using two independent dimensions of attachment anxiety and attachment avoidance, where a combination of low attachment anxiety and low attachment avoidance is indicative of greater attachment security (Bartholomew & Shaver, 1998). Attachment anxiety is characterized by high levels of relational distress; worry of rejection; and a hyper-activated drive for closeness versus trust that the person will be there, and low levels of preoccupation with that person's availability. Attachment avoidance is characterized by a hypo-activated drive for closeness and relational strategies of distancing or affective dampening rather than comfort with closeness and emotional intimacy (Searle & Meara, 1999; Mikulincer & Shaver, 2007).

Secure attachment serves the function of affect regulation, promoting positive affect and minimizing negative affect. It has been suggested that it is through the emotion-regulation function of attachment that attachment plays a role in both mental and physical health and in well-being due to the impact that affect has on cognition and physiological systems (Diamond & Hicks, 2004), and the role played by each of these factors directly in determining mental and physical health.

Secure attachment has been found to be linked with lower levels of reported chronic pain in general. A study by Meredith, Ownsworth, and Strong (2008) found a link between lower attachment anxiety and lower intensity of pain; however, different syndromes were not differentiated and the potential cause and nature of the pain was not specified. A literature review by Porter, Davis, and Keefe (2007) reported that attachment anxiety and attachment avoidance appear to be linked with all aspects of pain, from initial pain perception to seeking of healthcare; however, the authors note that more research needs to be done in this area, with larger samples, a greater variety of pain-related variables, and the investigation of possible mediators. Moreover, there seems to be no research to date that has specifically studied the link between attachment and health for women with fibromyalgia.

In this study we measured social support, attachment, and loneliness in relation to measures of health and well-being. We included loneliness as a measure of lack of closeness with others, that is, a psychologically dissatisfied state of emotional separation from others (Rosedale, 2007). Loneliness can be seen as arising from a lack of or problems within attachment relationships or relationships in general (Bowlby, 1979; Rosedale, 2007).

The present study tests a model of psychosocial variables predicting health and subjective well-being, mediated by affect, in a large sample of women with fibromyalgia. The hypothesis was that larger social-support networks, greater satisfaction with social support, more secure attachment (lower attachment anxiety and avoidance), and less loneliness will predict more positive affect, less negative affect, better mental health, better physical health, and greater life satisfaction in a sample of women with fibromyalgia. We proposed that more positive affect and less negative affect would mediate between the psychosocial and well-being variables.

Method

Participants

Participants were 1,671 women with fibromyalgia between the ages of 16 and 106 ($M = 45.89$, $SD = 11.17$). The mean length of illness was 5.75 years ($SD = 3.98$), ranging from less than 1 year to 11 years. This sample seems to capture a wide range of women with fibromyalgia of various ages, and lengths of time with the illness.

The participants were part of a larger sample that was recruited for a study of psychosocial variables and health in individuals with a chronic illness. The original sample included individuals with a variety of chronic illnesses.

Measures

Social Support
The Social Support Questionnaire was used to measure social support (Sarason, Sarason, Shearin, & Pierce, 1987). This measure provides separate scores for size of social-support network and satisfaction with the support received. Participants are asked to indicate how many people are able to support them in each six certain ways, such as to help them feel better when they are feeling down or to help them relax. After each of these questions, participants were asked to indicate on a six-point Likert scale how satisfied they are with the support they receive.

Positive and Negative Affect

The Positive and Negative Affect Scale was used to measure affect (Watson, Clark, & Tellegen, 1988). Participants were asked to report on a five-point Likert scale how much on average they tend to experience various positive and negative emotions, including distressed, upset, inspired, and strong, among others.

Attachment Orientation

The Experiences in Close Relationships Scale Revised (Fraley, Waller and Brennan, 2000)) was used to measure attachment. It uses a seven-point Likert scale in which 1 indicates "strongly disagree" and 7 indicates "strongly agree" in response to each of the 36 items (e.g., "I rarely worry about my partner leaving me"). This measure produces two dimensions, one of attachment anxiety and one of attachment avoidance.

Mental Health

Mental health was measured using the short-form-36 (SF-36) health survey (Ware, Snow, Kosinski, & Gandek, 2000). The survey's mental-health composite consists of four sub-scales pertaining to mental health: vitality, social functioning, role-emotional, and mental health.

The vitality sub-scale consisted of four questions pertaining to how often participants have experienced energy/enthusiasm for life in the past four weeks (e.g., "How often did you feel full of pep?) on a six-point Likert scale, with 1 indicating "none of the time" and 6 indicating "all of the time."

In the social-functioning sub-scale, participants were asked to indicate on a five-point Likert scale the extent to which their physical or emotional health interfered with their normal social activities (1 indicates "not at all," 5 indicates "extremely").

The role-emotional sub-scale consisted of three questions, which asked participants whether in the past four weeks their emotions have interfered with their roles in life (e.g., "Have you cut down the time you spend on work or other activities?"; 1 = yes, 2 = no).

The mental-health scale consisted of questions pertaining to how often participants experienced symptoms of anxiety and depression in the past four weeks on a six-point Likert scale, with 1 indicating "none of the time" and 6 indicating "all of the time."

The composite of these measures was obtained by finding the mean of the z scores for each of these sub-scales.

Physical Health

Physical-health scores were obtained using the SF-36 survey's (Ware, Snow, Kosinski, & Gandek, 2000) four physical-health sub-scales: physical functioning, role-physical, bodily pain, and general health.

The physical-functioning sub-scale was used to ask participants to indicate the extent to which their physical health limited them in performing each of ten daily activities, such as "Lifting or carrying groceries." Responses ranged on a three-point Likert scale ranging from 1 ("yes, limited a lot") to 3 ("no, not limited at all").

On the role-physical sub-scale, participants were asked to indicate if they have experienced problems with work or other regular daily activities as a result of their physical health in the past four weeks with a "yes" or "no" response.

The bodily-pain sub-scale consisted of two questions. The first question was used to indicate on a six-point Likert scale the severity of any bodily pain they may have experienced in the past four weeks (1 = not at all, 6 = very severe). The second question was used to indicate to what extent the bodily pain they may have experienced interfered with their normal work functioning.

The general-health sub-scale consisted of five questions. The first question was used to ask how they perceive their own physical health, ranging from 1 (excellent) to 5 (poor). The other four questions asked how true each of the following statements were (1 = definitely true, 5 = definitely false): "I seem to get sick a little easier than other people," "I am as healthy as anybody I know," "I expect my health to get worse," and "My health is excellent."

Life Satisfaction

Life satisfaction was measured using the Satisfaction with Life Scale, which asked participants to report how much they agree with each of five items on a seven-point Likert scale (e.g., "The conditions of my life are excellent").

Procedure

The participants were recruited in 2007 through three pre-existing websites that provide support and information for people with fibromyalgia and their families, including discussion boards, access to support groups, and information on available treatments and new research. A short description of the research purpose and procedure, along with a link to an online consent form and questionnaire, was posted on each participating website. After reading the consent form, participants had the option to click on a tab indicating that they had read and understood the content of the consent form and agreed to participate. By clicking on this tab, participants were led to the online questionnaire. If participants did not agree to participate, they had the option to click a tab indicating that they did not agree and did not wish to participate, which would then close the web page.

Results

Data Analysis

Means were used in variable computation. Frequencies were obtained for all items measured, and frequency of missing data did not exceed 8.5% on any item. All data was considered normally distributed, as the kurtosis and skewness did not exceed 2.5 on any measure. Means and standard deviations for all variables used can be found in table 1.

Bivariate correlation coefficients were obtained between all measures. Regression analyses were conducted to determine whether each of the psychosocial variables significantly predicts the well-being variables (mental and physical health, affect, and life satisfaction). The Baron and Kenny (1986) method of regression analysis with mediating variables was used to investigate whether each of the psychosocial variables significantly predicts physical health, mediated by affect.

Correlations

Results of a Pearson r (bivariate correlation analysis) indicated that larger social-support networks (r = .11, p < .05), greater social support satisfaction (r = .19, p < .01), and lower attachment anxiety (r = -.21, p < .01) correlated significantly with better mental health. Larger social-support networks (r = .18, p < .01), greater social-support satisfaction (r = .21, p < .01), and lower attachment anxiety (r = -.10, p < .01) also correlated significantly with better physical health. Moreover, these same variables correlated significantly with greater life satisfaction: larger social-support networks (r = .35, p < .01), greater social-support satisfaction (r = .42, p < .01), and lower attachment anxiety (r = -.20, p < .01). More positive affect correlated significantly with larger social-support networks (r = .36, p < .01), greater social-support satisfaction (r = .33, p < .01), and lower attachment anxiety (r = -.15, p <

Table 1 Means and Standard Deviations for All Variables		
Variable	M	SD
Age in Years	45.89	11.17
Social-Support Network	21.06	12.63
Social-Support Satisfaction	25.81	8.77
Attachment Avoidance	3.74	.97
Attachment Anxiety	3.57	.88
Loneliness	6.86	6.75
Life Satisfaction	16.71	7.45
Vitality	50.24	12.64
Social Functioning	48.40	10.33
Role-Emotional	34.94	40.52
Mental-Health Sub-Scale	26.86	1.86
Bodily Pain	24.21	16.90
General Health	28.07	18.38
Role-Physical	8.30	19.55
Physical Functioning	39.48	22.97
Negative Affect	27.67	8.31
Positive Affect	27.70	6.93

.01). Less negative affect also correlated significantly with larger social-support networks ($r = -.36$, $p < .01$), greater social-support satisfaction ($r = -.36$, $p < .01$), and lower attachment anxiety ($r = .32$, $p < .01$). Lower attachment avoidance correlated significantly with better mental health ($r = -.23$, $p < .01$) and greater life satisfaction ($r = -.24$, $p < .01$), more positive affect ($r = -.15$, $p < .01$) and less negative affect ($r = .22$, $p < .01$), but not with physical health. Less loneliness correlated significantly with better physical health ($r = -.08$, $p < .01$), better mental health ($r = -.25$, $p < .01$), greater life satisfaction ($r = -.16$, $p < .01$), and more positive affect ($r = -.12$, $p < .01$), but not with negative affect. Additionally, less negative and more positive affect significantly correlated with better physical health ($r = -.36$, $p < .01$; $r = .35$, $p < .01$), better mental health ($r = -.20$, $p < .01$; $r = .16$, $p < .01$), and greater life satisfaction ($r = -.42$, $p < .01$; $r = .41$, $p < .01$).

HYPOTHESIS 1: Larger social-support networks, greater satisfaction with social support, more secure attachment (lower attachment anxiety and avoidance), and less loneliness will predict better mental health, mediated by affect.

As shown in table 2, results of a regression analysis indicated that lower levels of attachment avoidance and lower levels of loneliness significantly predicted better mental health ($p < .05$). Social-support networks, satisfaction with support, and attachment anxiety were not significant predictors. Results of a regression analysis detected that larger social-support networks, greater social-support satisfaction, and lower attachment anxiety predict lower levels of negative affect ($p < .01$). Attachment avoidance and loneliness were not significant predictors of negative affect. A regression analysis found that larger social-support networks, greater satisfaction with social support, and less loneliness significantly predicted greater positive affect ($p < .01$). Lower attachment anxiety also significantly predicted greater positive affect ($p < .05$).

According to the results of a regression analysis, less negative affect and more positive affect did not predict mental health when all other variables were controlled. Therefore, positive and negative affect were not significant mediators of the relationship between any of the interpersonal relationship variables and mental health.

HYPOTHESIS 2: Larger social-support networks, greater satisfaction with social support, more secure attachment (lower attachment anxiety and avoidance), and less loneliness will predict greater life satisfaction, mediated by affect.

As can be seen in table 2, a regression analysis was carried out indicating that larger social-support networks, greater satisfaction with social support, lower levels of attachment avoidance, and less loneliness significantly pre-

Table 2
Mediation Analyses, Psychosocial Variables Predicting Mental Health, Physical Health and Life Satisfaction

	Mental Health			Physical Health			Life Satisfaction		
	Beta	ΔR^2	F^{**}	Beta	ΔR^2	F^{**}	Beta	ΔR^2	F^{**}
Step 1		.09	6.93		.06	13.57		.21	60.46
Social-support network	-.08			.08*			.15**		
Social-support satisfaction	.05			.16**			.24**		
Attachment anxiety	-.01			-.10**			-.07*		
Attachment avoidance	-.17*			-			-.12**		
Loneliness	-.19**			-.06*			-.16**		
Step 2		.10	5.43		.18	34.85		.30	69.21
Social-support network	-.10			-.02			.06		
Social-support satisfaction	.05			.09*			.18**		
Attachment anxiety	.02			-.01			-.01		
Attachment avoidance	-.16*			-			-.12**		
Loneliness	-.17*			-.01			-.12**		
Negative Affect	.09			-.24**			-.18**		
Positive Affect	-.04			.23**			.22**		

$^*p < .05$ $^{**}p < .01$

dicted greater life satisfaction ($p < .01$). Less attachment anxiety also significantly predicted greater life satisfaction ($p < .05$). A regression analysis indicated that less negative affect and more positive affect both predicted greater life satisfaction when all other variables were controlled for ($p < .001$).

A hierarchical regression analysis was conducted in order to determine whether less negative affect and more positive affect would mediate the relationship between the interpersonal relationship variables (social-support network, social-support satisfaction, attachment anxiety, attachment avoidance, and loneliness) and life satisfaction. Results of the first step show that all of the interpersonal relationship variables significantly predicted life satisfaction. In step 2, negative affect and positive affect were entered as predictors of life satisfaction. Social-support network and attachment anxiety were no longer significant predictors of physical health, while negative and positive affect remained significant ($p < .01$). Negative and positive affect fully mediated between attachment anxiety and social-support network with life satisfaction. In other words, it seems that having a larger social-support network and lower attachment anxiety tended to encourage more positive and less negative affect, which in turn promoted greater life satisfaction.

HYPOTHESIS 3: Larger social-support networks, greater satisfaction with social support, more secure attachment (lower attachment anxiety and avoidance), and less loneliness will predict better physical health, mediated by affect.

As shown in table 2, a regression analysis was carried out indicating that greater social-support satisfaction, and lower levels of attachment anxiety, significantly predicted better physical health ($p < .01$). Larger social-support networks, less attachment avoidance, and less loneliness also significantly predicted better physical health ($p < .05$). According to the results of a regression analysis, less negative affect and more positive affect both predicted better physical health when all other variables were controlled for ($p < .01$).

A hierarchical regression analysis was conducted in order to determine whether less negative affect and more positive affect would mediate the relationship between the interpersonal relationship variables (social-support network, social-support satisfaction, attachment anxiety, attachment avoidance, loneliness) and physical health. Results of the first step show that all of the interpersonal relationship variables significantly predicted physical health. In step 2, negative affect and positive affect were entered as predictors of physical health. In this same step, social-support network, attachment anxiety, and loneliness were no longer significant predictors of physical health, while negative and positive affect remained significant ($p < .01$). Positive and negative affect fully mediated the relationship between social-support network and attachment anxiety with physical health. Positive affect mediated the relationship between loneliness and physical health. Based on these results, it seems that more positive and less negative affect tends to be encouraged by a larger social-support network and less attachment anxiety, which in turn tended to lead to the experience of better physical health.

Discussion

The results of this study provide evidence that psychosocial variables pertaining to women with fibromyalgia, such as social support and close relationships, are significant factors impacting their mental and physical health as well as life satisfaction. The mediation model was supported in some cases, suggesting that the reason for the link between the psychosocial variables and well-being is due in part to negative and positive affect. Specifically, the size of social-support networks and attachment anxiety seem to impact on physical health and life satisfaction through the mediation of affect. The mediation model was not supported for mental health, and was predicted only by attachment avoidance and loneliness.

This study replicated previous research by finding that size of social-support network as well as satisfaction with support both seem to play a role in the health of women with fibromyalgia (Franks et al. 2004). In addition, this study found that social support also played a role in life satisfaction. Moreover, attachment and loneliness were found to play a significant role in the health and well-being for women with fibromyalgia.

It is not surprising that many aspects of health and life satisfaction for women with fibromyalgia seems to be intertwined with psychosocial factors given the large abundance of evidence to the idea that health and well-being in the general population is related to psychosocial factors (Diamond & Hicks, 2004). It is particularly interesting, however, that this illness, known for its combination of psychological and biological etiological factors, seems to depend on psychosocial factors in addition to biological ones in the ongoing coping process.

The question of how interpersonal relationship variables may impact upon physical health and life satisfaction seems to be at least in part due to the role of affect. The promotion of positive affect and diminishment of negative affect encouraged by a large social-support system and secure close attachment relationships seems to be beneficial for the physical health and subjective well-being of women with fibromyalgia. Based on these findings, a larger social network seems to be particularly important for women with fibromyalgia. It is conceivable that the diffusion of social-support responsibilities across a larger network is beneficial for women with fibromyalgia because it increases the probability of social support being available at any given time, places less responsibility on any one support giver, and offers the assurance that there will always be someone that can be counted on when support is needed.

Similarly, lower attachment anxiety is particularly beneficial for women with fibromyalgia because it also offers the assurance that there is one trusted person that can be turned to in times of trouble and relied on as a secure base. Indeed, the affective advantage of these two psychosocial variables seems quite clear. The impact of attachment avoidance and loneliness on the mental health of women with fibromyalgia seemed to exist for reasons other than affect, since affect was not a significant mediator; however, it is possible that the affective-dampening characteristic of attachment avoidance diminished the awareness of affect for participants, and thus the detection of affect as a mediating variable.

The importance of psychosocial variables and affect in relation to the health and well-being of women with fibromyalgia has implications for treatment options. Treatment available for women with fibromyalgia is particularly diverse, which includes, among others, medication, psychotherapy, and massage therapy. The results of this study provide further support for the usefulness of a combined therapy approach that includes psychosocial types of treatment in addition to traditional medical approaches (Clayton & West, 2006). Individual therapy that works with psychosocial variables including relationships and emotion may be particularly useful to promote the best possible health and well-being outcomes for women with fibromyalgia. It is possible that the strengthening of social relationships and the ability to function socially may promote better coping not only in terms of affect and mental health but also in terms of physical health and life satisfaction.

This study had limitations that should be considered, such as the fact that an online questionnaire was used, meaning that participants were not met in person. Instructions were not given face-to-face, which may have led to some misinterpretations (and which may be the case with all question-naires), and there is a somewhat increased risk of repeat participants and false information. A second limitation common to correlation data is that it is not possible to determine causation. Future research may address these limitations by addressing similar research questions using experimental, in-terview, and longitudinal data.

Future research may address similar questions using different methods that may better determine causality, such as longitudinal data and interview methods that could gather a greater amount of detail from each individual. New questions sparked by this study include what the role of therapy could be in terms of promoting the best levels of well-being while coping with fibromyalgia. Does individual therapy help to strengthen social connec-tions for these women, and does that in turn affect their well-being? Would couples therapy that serves to strengthen attachment bonds be helpful in promoting well-being on mental and physical levels? This study supports the role of relationships and emotions in health and well-being for women with fibromyalgia. Approaches such as emotion-focused therapy have been found successful in promoting secure attachment by working with emotions specifically (Johnson, 2004). Other research may focus on how women with fibromyalgia cope with very specific symptoms, and whether relationships play a role in the management of those symptoms.

Note

Our gratitude is extended to Michael Busseri, Nancy De Courville, Sasha Lovegrove, Jeff McLeod, Danielle Molnar and Colin Perrier for their assistance. Preparation of this paper was enabled by a general research grant to the second author by the Social Sciences and Humanities Research Council of Canada.

References

Åsbring, P., & Närvänen, A. (2002). Women's experiences of stigma in relation to Chronic Fatigue Syndrome and Fibromyalgia. *Qualitative Health Research, 12,* 148–160.

Baron, R. M., & Kenny, D. A. (1986). The moderator-mediator variable distinction in social psychological research: Conceptual, strategic, and statistical considerations. *Journal of Personality and Social Psychology, 51*, 1173-1182.

Bartholomew, K., & Shaver, P. (1998). Measures of attachment: Do they converge? In W. S. Roles & J. A. Simpson, *Adult attachment, theory, research and clinical implications* (pp. 25-45). New York: Guildford Press.

Bergman, S. (2005). Psychosocial aspects of chronic widespread pain and fibromyalgia. *Disability and Rehabilitation, 27*, 675–683.

Berkman, L.F. (1984). Assessing the physical health effects of social networks and social support. *Annual Review of Public Health, 5*, 413-432.

Bowlby, J. (1969). *Attachment*. New York: Basic Books.

Bowlby, J. (1979). The making and breaking of affectional bonds. London: Travistock Press.

Clayton, A. H., & West, S. G. (2006). Combination therapy in fibromyalgia. *Current Pharmaceutical Design, 12*, 11–16.

Diamond, L. M., & Hicks, A. M. (2004). Psychobiological perspectives on attachment. In W. S. Roles & J. A. Simpson, *Adult attachment, theory, research and clinical implications* (pp. 240–255). New York: Guilford Press.

Fraley, R. C., Waller, N. G., & Brennan, K. A. (2000). An item-response theory analysis of self-report measures of adult attachment. *Journal of Personality and Social Psycology, 78*, 350-365.

Franks, H. M., Cronan, T. A., & Oliver, K. (2004). Social support in women with fibromyalgia: Is quality more important than quantity? *Journal of Community Psychology, 32*, 425 – 438.

House, J. S., Landis, K. R., & Umberson, D. (1988). Social Relationships and Health. *Science, 241*, 540–545.

Johnson, S. M. (2004). *The practice of emotionally focused couple therapy: Creating connection*. New York: Brunner-Routledge.

Looper, K. J. & Kirmayer, L. J. (2004). Perceived stigma in functional somatic syndromes and comparable medical conditions. *Journal of Psychosomatic Research, 57*, 373–378.

MacDonald, G., & Leary, M. R. (2005). Why does social exclusion hurt? The relationship between social and physical pain. *Psychological Bulletin, 131*, 202–223.

Meredith, P., Ownsworth, T., & Strong, J. (2008) *Clinical Psychology Review, 28*, 407–429.

Mikulincer, M., & Shaver, P. S. (2007). *Attachment in adulthood: Structure, dynamics and change*. New York: Guilford Press.

Okifuji, A., & Turk, D. C. (2002). Stress and psychophysiological dysregulation inpatients with fibromyalgia syndrome. *Applied Psychophysiology and Biofeedback, 27*, 129 – 141.

Picardi, A., Battisti, F., Tarsitani L., Baldassari, M., Copertaro, A., Mocchegiani, E. & Biondi, M. (2007). Attachment security and immunity in healthy women. *Psychosomatic medicine, 69*, 40–46.

Porter, L. S., Davis, D., & Keefe, F. J. (2007). Attachment and pain: Recent findings and future directions. *Pain, 128,* 195–198.

Rosedale, M. (2007). Loneliness: An exploration of meaning. *Journal of American Psychiatric Nurses Association, 13,* 201 – 209.

Sarason, I. G., Sarason, B. R., Shearin, E. N., & Pierce, G. R. (1987). A brief measure of social support: practical and theoretical implications. *Journal of Social and Personal Relationships, 4,* 497–510.

Searle, B., & Meara, N. M. (1999). Affective dimensions of attachment styles: Exploring self-reported attachment style, gender and emotional experience among college students. *Journal of Counseling Psychology, 46,* 147–158.

Soderberg, S., & Lundman, B. (2000). Transitions experienced by women with fibromyalgia. *Health Care for Women International, 22,* 617–631.

Staud, R., Domingo M. (2001). Evidence of abnormal pain processing in fibromyalgia syndrome. *Pain Medicine, 2,* 208-215.

Van Koulil, S., Van Lankveld, W., Kraaimaat, F. W., Van Helmond, T., Vedder, A., Van Hoorn, H., Cats, H., et al. (2008). Tailored cognitive-behavioural therapy for fibromyalgia: Two case studies. *Patient Education and Counseling, 71,* 308–314.

Ware, J.E. (2000). The SF-36 Health Survey Update. *Spine, 25,* 3130–3139.

Watson, D., Clark, L. A., & Tellegen, A. (1988). Development and validation of brief measures of positive and negative affect: The PANAS scales. *Journal of Personality And Social Psychology, 54,* 1063–1070.

Weihs, K. L., Enright, T. M. & Simmens, S. J. (2008). Close relationships and emotionalprocessing predict decreased mortality in women with breast cancer: Preliminary evidence. *Psychosomatic Medicine, 70,* 117–124.

Notes on Contributors

PAULA BARATA is Assistant Professor of Applied Social Psychology at University of Guelph. Her research deals with the psychosocial determinants that influence women's health and wellbeing. Currently, she is working on projects dealing with housing discrimination against battered women and the incorporation of HPV technologies into cervical cancer prevention.

CYNDI BRANNEN is research director in the Centre for Research on Family Health at the IWK Health Centre. A registered psychologist and assistant professor of pediatrics at Dalhousie University, Dr. Brannen is principal investigator on several research studies exploring caregiving and family health through a gender lens. These include stress in rural families, impacts of living with a family member with post-traumatic stress disorder, child health, and family literacy.

Dr. Brannen recently received a CIHR New Investigator award to develop Strong Starts, Healthier Futures Together, an education and support program for parents of infants at high risk for developmental challenges related to premature birth. Dr. Brannen is a recognized expert in community-based participatory health research and family-level statistical analyses. She supervises undergraduate and graduate students in disciplines including health promotion, interdisciplinary studies, and psychology. She has two sons, ages 18 and 4. Her oldest son's chronic health problems inspired her research program.

TOBA BRYANT is an Assistant Professor in the Department of Sociology at York University in Toronto. She has published extensively on housing policy and health policy fields. She is co-editor of Staying Alive: Critical Perspectives on Health, Illness and Health Care, and the author of An Introduction to Health Policy, published by Canadian Scholars' Press.

SOMA CHATTERJEE is a community health educator at Women's Health in Women's Hands Community Health Centre in Toronto. She is interested in health and social policy analysis as it relates to immigrants/refugees/non-status populations. Class, race and gender dominate her analytical frameworks. Soma identifies as South Asian, was born in India and educated in India and Canada. In her spare time, she reads literature and history and teaches a social work practice course at Ryerson University, Toronto.

SUZANNE COOPER SUZANNE COOPER is a PhD candidate at Carleton University. Her research interests include gender issues, with a particular focus on the pychology of women and issues related to violence against women and children. She is currently conducting research on the long-term after-effects in late life of earlier trauma, particularly with regard to disclosure and help-seeking among senior trauma survivors. She has also conducted research on topics such as gender biases in the diagnosis of women trauma survivors, gender dimensions of HIV/AIDS transmission among intravenous drug users and women in the sex trade, and restorative justice in cases of violence against women. Suzanne coordinated the Section on Women and Psychology institute (Canadian Psychological Association) in 2008, from which this collection emanates.

DEONE CURLING holds a master's degree in counselling and has worked in the field for more than ten years. She is presently working at Women's Health in Women's Hands Community Health Centre for black women and women of colour in Toronto. Deone is also a doctorial student at the University of Toronto. Her dissertation aims at investigating depressed Canadian Black women's resilience.

DONNA M. EANSOR, LL.B. (Wayne State), of Osgoode Hall, Barrister-at-Law, teaches Property Law and Wills, Succession and Feminist Legal Theory. A former Associate Dean, Professor Eansor has a longstanding research interest in academic support and access to justice issues with a focus on women, aboriginal Canadians and vulnerable groups. Her current research, funded by the Canadian Bar Association Law for the Future Fund and the University of Windsor is looking at the health of women in the Legal Profession. She is the recipient of the 2004 Teaching Excellence Award from the Student's Law Society as well as the 2006 Alumni Award for Distinguished Contributions to University Teaching. Professor Eansor received the 2007 Leadership in Faculty Teaching award for her ability to motivate and inspire students and was one of six recipients of the prestigious OCUFA teaching award in Ontario in 2008.

JOANNE GALLIVAN, Professor Emeritus of Psychology, recently retired after 28 years of service at Cape Breton University, including terms as Psychology Department Chair, Dean of Research and Dean of Science. She has published research in the areas of language and reading development, gender, and psychology of humor. Her past professional activities include terms as a Director of the Canadian Psychological Association and Coordinator of CPA's Section on Women and Psychology. She currently serves as a Director of the Nova Scotia Health Research Foundation.

LAURA HAMBLETON is a research and assessment assistant at the IWK Health Centre within the Centre for Research in Family Health in Halifax, NS. She completed her Honours degree in Psychology this year at Mount Saint Vincent University. Her future aspirations are to travel and attend graduate school within the field of international human rights psychology.

PETER HORVATH obtained his PhD in clinical and counselling psychology from the University of Ottawa in 1979. Currently he is Full Professor and Graduate Program Coordinator in the Department of Psychology at Acadia University in Wolfville, Nova Scotia, and a Registered Psychologist in the Province of Nova Scotia. In the past few years his research has focused on the personality correlates of depression in women.

JOANNA M. KRAFT has an MA in Applied Social Psychology from the University of Windsor, and is currently a doctoral student in the Applied Social Psychology program at the University of Windsor. Her research interests lie within the area of industrial-organizational psychology, and are specifically in the area of employer-employee relations and psychological contracts.

KATHRYN D. LAFRENIERE has an MA and PhD in Social and Personality Psychology from York University, and is a Professor in the Psychology Department of the University of Windsor. Kathryn currently serves as Undergraduate Program Chair in Psychology and teaches courses in research methods, community psychology, and health psychology. Her research interests are in health and community psychology, and are primarily concentrated in the areas of women's health and prevention issues, stress and coping, perception of health risks, and personality and health.

NOTISHA MASSAQUOI is currently the Executive Director of Women's Health in Women's Hands Community Health Centre. She is also a PhD candidate in Sociology and Equity Studies at Ontario Institute Studioes in Education, University of T. Her most recent publication is the anthology entitled Theorizing Empowerment: Canadian Perspectives on Black Feminist Thought.

JENNIFER J. NICOL is an Associate Professor at the University of Saskatchewan, with further professional credentials as an Accredited Music Therapist and Registered Doctoral Psychologist. Her research focuses on the benefits of music, especially as readily accessed and available for use in everyday life.

BRIGITTE SABOURIN is in her third year of the doctoral training program in clinical psychology at Dalhousie University in Halifax, Nova Scotia. She is funded through a Nova Scotia Health Research Foundation Scholarship, and has recently been awarded a Canada Graduate Scholarship through the Canadian Institute of Health Research. She is conducting her doctoral dissertation research under the supervision of Dr. Sherry Stewart, where she is exploring the role of an interoceptive exposure (i.e., physical exercise) component in explaining the efficacy of a brief cognitive behavioural intervention for anxiety sensitive women. She is also involved in a study that is examining the efficacy of matching gambling treatments to underlying motivations for gambling.

STANLEY SADAVA is a professor at Brock University. His research interests include the social psychology of health, relationship intimacy, attachment orientations and health related behaviours, determinants and outcomes. As co-author of the only Canadian-authored textbook in social psychology, Prof. Sadava also has a general interest in the Canadian context of social psychology.

ELSA SARDINHA has a BA in Political Science and International Relations from the University of British Columbia and an LL.B. from the University of Windsor. She worked as a research assistant at the University of Windsor, a caseworker for Community Legal Aid and was the Chief Articles Editor for the Windsor Review of Legal and Social Issues. She will be clerking at the Ontario Court of Appeal commencing August 2009.

SHERRY H. STEWART holds a Killam Research Professorship in the Departments of Psychiatry and Psychology at Dalhousie University. She is also currently Director of Clinical Training for the Doctoral Program in Clinical Psychology at Dalhousie. She is internationally respected for her research on psychological factors contributing to addictive disorders, and the co-morbidity of mental health and addictive disorders. Dr. Stewart has published several clinical trials of novel approaches for the treatment and prevention of substance abuse and co-occurring mental health problems. She has received more than $10 million to support her addictions and mental health research from granting agencies worldwide.

PAMELA WAMBOLT obtained her Honours degree in psychology from Mount St. Vincent University in 2004 and her Master's degree in clinical psychology from Acadia University in 2007. Pamela is a Psychologist (Candidate Register) in Nova Scotia and is currently employed as an Associate with Dr. S. Gerald Hann Psychological Services in Halifax.

STEPHANIE WIEBE is a PhD candidate in the clinical program at the University of Ottawa. Her primary interests include emotional processing, attachment theory and emotionally focused couples therapy.